Praise for *The Last Lone Inventor*

"A wonderful tale, riveting and bittersweet."   —*The New Yorker*

"A fascinating and important story. . . . Farnsworth and Sarnoff are . . . great characters."   —*New York Times Book Review*

"Compelling. . . . Strong, dramatic prose. . . . Vividly captures America's twentieth-century transformation from an independent, frontier culture to a modern, media-driven society."
     —*Kirkus Reviews*

"Farnsworth is probably the most influential unknown person in the past century, and Evan I. Schwartz tells the fascinating inside story of how this eccentric loner invented television and fought corporate America."   —Walter Isaacson, former chairman, CNN

"Microsoft is hardly the first company to try to leverage its monopoly in one area to gain control over the next generation of technology, as Evan I. Schwartz makes clear in his fascinating tale of the early history of television."   —*Washington Post*

"Decades after the fact, the world is just tuning into the work of TV inventor Philo T. Farnsworth. . . . In Schwartz's view, few lives have been more remarkable."   —*Boston Globe*

"By the time TV really took off in the 1950s, Farnsworth was all but forgotten, and RCA had become a TV powerhouse. . . . This intriguing tale is revealed in *The Last Lone Inventor*."
     —*San Francisco Chronicle*

"Schwartz's cogent and elegant book persuasively argues Farnsworth's case and describes the heartbreak that defined his life."
     —*Publishers Weekly*

"You'll find a fascinating history and a cautionary tale for today in *The Last Lone Inventor*."

—PC magazine

"[Schwartz] has produced a riveting account of a decades-long battle."   *—Worcester Telegram & Gazette* (MA)

"The saga of Philo Farnsworth may have a special resonance in the dot-bust era, as battles rage over intellectual property and corporate turpitude dominates the headlines."   *—Reason* magazine

"Lively and engaging. . . . Schwartz's well-researched biography is sure to appeal to anyone who has ever dreamed of coming up with 'the next big thing.'"   *—Library Journal*

"[David Sarnoff] set out to destroy [Philo Farnsworth] through espionage, propaganda, delaying tactics, and corporate muscle. How well he succeeded is evinced by the fact that today not many people know the inventor's remarkable story, or name."

—Forbes

"[A] gripping and eminently readable saga of the birth of television and the death of the Edisonian myth."   *—Darwin* magazine

"Schwartz gives the reader a precise and exciting chronicle of the moving image's creation and transmission."   *—All Media Guide*

"The book has much to say about large corporations like AT&T, IBM, and GE. The real drama here is the contest between an individual inventor facing a giant megamogul."

—Rocky Mountain News

"*The Last Lone Inventor* . . . provides excellent overviews of the complex personalities and issues behind the development of one of the world's most important inventions."

—*Salt Lake Tribune*

"[A] suspenseful account of the unknown man who influenced the world." —*Booklist*

"One helluva tale of genius, deceit, screw-u, screw-em-all arrogance and brilliance and absolute greed punctuating the birth of television." —*Boston Post-Gazette*

© 2002 by Frank Rapp

About the Author

EVAN I. SCHWARTZ is a journalist and the author of *Digital Darwinism* and *Webonomics*. He is a contributing writer for *Wired* and MIT's *Technology Review*, and a former staff editor at *BusinessWeek*. He lives in Brookline, Massachusetts.

THE LAST LONE
INVENTOR

THE LAST LONE INVENTOR

A TALE OF

GENIUS, DECEIT,

and the Birth of

Television

Evan I. Schwartz

Perennial

An Imprint of HarperCollinsPublishers

A hardcover edition of this book was published in 2002 by HarperCollins Publishers.

First Perennial edition published 2003.

Designed by Lindgren/Fuller Design

The Library of Congress has catalogued the hardcover edition as follows:
Schwartz, Evan I.
    The last lone inventor : a tale of genius, deceit, and the birth of television / by Evan I. Schwartz.
      p. cm.
  ISBN 0-06-621069-0
    1. Farnsworth, Philo Taylor, 1906–1971. 2. Television—Biography. 3. Inventors—United States—Biography. 4. Television—History. I. Title.

TK6635.F3 S38 2002
621.388'0092—dc21
[B]   2001051735

ISBN 0-06-093559-6 (pbk.)

03 04 05 06 07 ❖/RRD 10 9 8 7 6 5 4 3 2 1

To my sister, Jennifer,
who grew up fighting with me over what to watch

CONTENTS

Author's Note | xiii

Prologue: A Miscalculation | 1

1   Fields of Vision | 9

2   Making a Great Man | 29

3   Community Chest | 51

4   Patently Brilliant | 65

5   Going Hollywood | 79

6   Networking | 93

7   Life on Green Street | 111

8   Confrontation | 143

9   End Run | 179

10   Who Owns What? | 199

11   Narrow Escape | 223

12   All's Fair, World's Fair | 259

13   Breakdown, Breakout | 271

14   Post War | 281

Epilogue: Perceptions and Reality | 295

Acknowledgments | 301

Notes | 305

Index | 315

I couldn't have written this book without the help of Elma G. "Pem" Farnsworth, the widow of Philo T. Farnsworth. After reaching her by telephone, I first met her in person at the Farnsworth family's home in Fort Wayne, Indiana, in December 1999. Her recollections were remarkably vivid, especially given the fact that she was close to her ninety-second birthday. She has since shared her story with me in dozens of hours of interviews, many of which were taped. As her husband's closest confidant and companion during his entire career, Pem Farnsworth not only was able to provide firsthand accounts of many events but also enabled me to get inside the head of my main character in a way that would not have been possible otherwise. She also granted me permission to draw quotes from her self-published memoir, and she read my manuscript for accuracy.

The book also benefited greatly from the assistance of Alexander Magoun, director of the David Sarnoff Library in Princeton, New Jersey. This facility, located within the former RCA Laboratories (since renamed Sarnoff Corporation), was designed late in life by Sarnoff, the longtime president of RCA and the founder of its NBC network, as the main repository for his papers, correspondence, awards, photographs, and other corporate and personal possessions. As an employee of the Sarnoff Corporation, Alex Magoun has been loyal to the legacy, but as a historian, he has been forthcoming about providing an accurate rendering of events, hosting me on visits, supplying his own analysis, and opening up the RCA document and photo archives for this project.

"Anything that is truly great or inspiring is created in the mind of one individual laboring in freedom."

—ALBERT EINSTEIN

THE LAST LONE INVENTOR

Philo T. Farnsworth with transmitter, 1928.

A Miscalculation

THERE WAS A TIME WHEN PHILO T. FARNSWORTH WAS CONSIDERED the perfect picture of pure inventive brilliance. On September 3, 1928, a photograph of him appeared on the business page of the *San Francisco Chronicle*, alongside bold type hailing the "young genius" who was "quietly working away in his San Francisco laboratory" on his "revolutionary light machine." Just twenty-two years old, he had recently grown a mustache to mask his youth. His unsmiling expression barely hinted at his inner exhilaration, and his eyes were fixed somewhere beyond the lens of the camera, as if to deflect attention away from himself and toward the two tubes he was holding in his hands. The article described these quart jar–sized devices as the first all-electronic "sending and receiving tubes of his new television set," a system that transmits "twenty pictures per second," each frame containing "8,000 elements, or pinpoints of light, to insure detail."

The night the story was published, Farnsworth was driving down Market Street in an open-air roadster, heading back home from an evening at the movies. His twenty-year-old wife was riding next to him, and another couple sat in the backseat. When the foursome heard a newsboy shouting the headlines from the next morning's paper, Farnsworth pulled up to the curb and took a coin from his pocket. As he unfolded a copy, he was startled by the grainy image of himself. His wife attempted to read the story aloud as he continued driving, but the other two passengers were hooting and hollering, trying to grab the paper out of her hands and get a better look at the picture.

As usual, Farnsworth had trouble falling asleep after he and his wife arrived back at their apartment in a row house on Vallejo Street, itself just a short walk from Farnsworth's laboratory, a creaky loft over a garage on Green Street, at the base of Telegraph Hill, which provided a view of the San Francisco Bay. Overworked, rail thin, and beset with chronic insomnia, the inventor had bright blue eyes that were encircled by shadows of exhaustion. His shock of thick, sandy brown hair was finger-combed straight back atop a large rotunda of a forehead that was out of proportion to his slight build. He lived in a perpetual state of low-level anxiety that made his whole body seem to vibrate.

By now, Farnsworth's youthful determination had grown into a relentless obsession. Even when he did manage to get some rest, he would usually assign himself a technical quandary beforehand, then work it out in a dream state, often arising to scribble down notes in the darkness. He was convinced that television would wipe out ignorance and misunderstanding, and his resolve to get people to watch television was just as great as his will to create it in the first place.

When Farnsworth was a boy, the legends of Edison, Bell, Morse, the Wright Brothers, and other individuals with singularly brilliant ideas burned brightly, and he set out to be a lone inventor who could transform the world just like them. He was fourteen, just a farm boy in Idaho, when he memorized Albert Einstein's Nobel Prize–winning photoelectric theory and perused piles of radio industry magazines, resulting in a growing belief that he would be the one to invent television. He was fifteen when he disclosed a simple but remarkably workable sketch of his idea to his high school science teacher, nineteen when he raised his first seed money to start building his system, twenty when he applied for his two basic patents, one for the electronic television camera and one for a compatible reception set. Now, his secret was finally unleashed, as the *Chronicle* story was picked up by newswires and reprinted in dozens of newspapers around the world.

Among the people most interested in reading the article was David Sarnoff. Sitting at his glass-top desk at RCA headquarters, high up in New York City's towering Woolworth Building, Sarnoff spent much of the day reviewing and responding to press clippings, reports, and memoranda. The founder of the NBC broadcasting network, Sarnoff had recently been named acting president of NBC's parent company, the Radio Corporation of America, as the actual president had taken a leave of absence to work full time on Herbert Hoover's 1928 run for the White House.

Sarnoff used the opportunity to solidify his reputation as the Babe Ruth of broadcasting. Drawing a salary equal to that of the Yankee right fielder, and with a belly to match, Sarnoff wore three-piece suits that were so finely tailored that one didn't notice his girth. He was thirty-seven years old and his dark hair was just beginning to gray and recede. He usually carried with him nothing more than an oak walking stick, while his minions scrambled to summon his chauffeurs, make his reservations, pay his tabs, open his doors, carry his coats, pull out his chairs, hand him his memos, and light his cigars.

To Sarnoff, it must have seemed far-fetched that some kid from California, working independently, would be anywhere near getting so complex an invention to a commercial stage. Still, Sarnoff was worried about the television situation in general, and he was especially concerned that a breakthrough in visual broadcasting would disrupt the market for radio. Under Sarnoff, RCA was the most aggressive corporation in the world when it came to hiring the best scientists and engineers, buying out their patent rights, and controlling the terms of the licensing to the rest of the industry. Legally, no one could build a radio without a license from RCA, and no radio could be sold without a royalty flowing back to the company. Thanks largely to this arrangement, shares in RCA became the single hottest stock in the wildly euphoric market of the late 1920s. RCA's fiercely competitive radio monopoly also drew steady fire from members of Congress and the U.S. Justice Department.

After reading the article about Farnsworth, Sarnoff wasted little time in launching a public relations offensive. He crafted a detailed essay on the state of television, stressing two points: that the new technology is nowhere near ready for the public, and when it is, RCA will be the leader in bringing it to market. The article, entitled "Forging an Electric Eye to Scan the World," was published under Sarnoff's own byline, in the Sunday edition of the *New York Times*, on November 18, 1928, shortly after Hoover's convincing Election Day victory. "It would be easy, and it might be profitable, to cry 'Television is here,' and to provide crude receiving equipment for the will-'o-the wisps of the air," Sarnoff wrote, "but it would not advance the day when sight is added to sound in an adequate service to the home through the medium of radio communication."

A month later, Sarnoff struck again. "Leaders Dispel Television Fears," said a *Times* headline on December 16. Quoting David Sarnoff as the main source, the article assured readers that the latest-model radio sets won't be obsolete any time soon and that they are definitely not threatened by the revolutionary new creation of an unnamed inventor. "Make it a radio Christmas," the story said. "Just think of all the radio entertainment you will miss during 1929 if you keep your house and family out of tune with the ether."

Philo T. Farnsworth didn't fully realize that the process of invention itself was being transformed. Innovation became too important and too lucrative to be left in the hands of unpredictable, independent individuals. The giant corporations that had sprung up around all the new technologies of the past century wanted to control the future and avoid surprises that could topple their empires, and they were growing more and more frustrated over negotiating for patent rights with outside inventors.

They decided to take on the task themselves, and in the first two decades of the new century began launching corporate research laboratories. Enterprises such as General Electric, DuPont, Eastman Kodak and AT&T set up labs employing large groups of scientists and engineers who gave up their independence—and their patent rights—in return for steady salaries. By now, there were hundreds of such labs, and the new RCA Laboratories was about to take its place among the most prestigious. As a result, technological change would become less disruptive and more methodical, so as to give the corporations themselves far greater control over the mass marketing of all the new gadgets and gizmos that would roll out of their laboratories.

By the time Thomas Edison died three years later, the age of the great lone inventor had seemed to come to a halt. Edison had still been working on his own and had continued filing for patents through his final years. When he passed away on October 18, 1931, at age eighty-four, tributes rushed in from the leaders of the world while his body lay in state in his West Orange, New Jersey, laboratory. Edison's obituary in the *New York Times* said the following:

No figure so completely satisfied the popular conception of what an inventor should be. Here was a solitary genius revolutionizing the world and making an invisible force do his bidding—a genius that conquered conservatism, garlanded cities in light, and created wonders that transcended the predictions of Utopian poets ... With him passes perhaps the last of the heroic inventors and the greatest of the line. The future probably belongs to the corporation research laboratory, with trained engineers and chemists directed by a scientific captain. Edison saw the change coming. Yet he must have realized that the electrical forces he had unleashed were too formidable for even a lone Titan to master.

Farnsworth was so certain that Edison would not be the last of the line that he took it upon himself to master the forces of invention that individuals such as Edison let loose. In doing so, he wholly underestimated what he was up against. But just as Farnsworth miscalculated the power of corporate-controlled innovation, David Sarnoff underestimated Farnsworth, who would ultimately consume more of Sarnoff's own time and resources than even the looming government antitrust action against RCA. Whereas Farnsworth viewed Sarnoff as a gigantic but surmountable obstacle, Sarnoff viewed Farnsworth as just one more inventor to be held under his thumb. Buy him out cheap and reap the rewards. He didn't realize that Farnsworth was different from all the other scientists and engineers he controlled, that this inventor was a throwback to an earlier era.

Both men were bursting with such abundant self-confidence that neither could conceive of defeat. They imposed their talents and their wills, their hopes and their fears, and even the quirks of their personalities on this invention. Out of the confrontation between these two mismatched men, the modern television tube would emerge, ingesting images of reality deep inside itself, then spitting out reordered flickers of phosphorescence into living rooms everywhere. By the time the inventor and the mogul would die, in the very same year, the number of homes on Earth with televisions would surpass the number of homes with indoor plumbing. Philo T. Farnsworth and David Sarnoff were fighting over something more than just a box of lights and wires.

Cover of July 1922 issue of Hugo Gernsback's Science and Invention *magazine, illustrating the future possibilities of televisions, which had not been demonstrated by anyone.*

CHAPTER ONE

Fields of Vision

F ROM CLEAR ACROSS THE POTATO FIELD, LEWIS FARNSWORTH COULD
see that his son was in danger. It was an early spring morning
in 1921, and fourteen-year-old Philo was in his usual trance during
one of his many repetitive chores. The kid was sitting on top of a
three-disk plow that engraved three parallel furrows in the soil at
once. The apparatus was being pulled up and down the field by a
team of three horses. Philo was supposed to be holding three sets of
reins, but his mind was somewhere else. He grasped only two, inad-
vertently dropping the third. The sight of the stray leather strap dragging on the ground alarmed the elder Farnsworth.

The plow's rotating metal blades could shred a man to pieces in
a few moments. Lewis Farnsworth had heard that it happened to a
farmer back in their home state of Utah. A startled horse dragged
the sharp edges of the disks into his back, and the man died of his
wounds before any medical help could arrive. Without control of
the harness, Philo might meet the same fate. He wouldn't be able to

halt a rampaging horse, and Lewis Farnsworth knew this particular horse to be especially skittish.

He also knew that he couldn't shout across the field or surprise the horses in any way. With steady strides, he walked toward the end of the row that Philo was finishing. As he stooped to lift the rein, Philo leaped from his seat, shouting, "Papa! Papa! I've got it!"

The horse, irritated by the boy's sudden exclamation, let out a loud neigh. But Lewis Farnsworth was now clutching the third strap, and he reined in the beast just in time.

What on Earth could this boy be yelling about?

"I got the idea that will win the prize money!" Philo exclaimed.

"Philo," he growled back, "You could have been killed!"

His father's anger snapped Philo out of his daze. When he became aware of what had just occurred, he apologized and promised never to let it happen again. Then he started to explain what was preoccupying his mind. He'd been working on an idea.

The Farnsworths lived on a ranch in Idaho's Snake River Valley, where granite-faced mountains peered over pine-green forests. True to its name, the river snaked through the valley, irrigating the fields of potatoes and sugar beets through a network of diversion dams and canals. Hundreds of rural acres separated the homesteads, but the nearby town of Rigby had its own schools and churches, plus a bustling Main Street with a savings and loan, a telegraph office, a newspaper publisher, a general store, a furniture shop, and a bar.

Philo was a good-looking but skinny boy with a serious gaze and a square jaw. He detested the drudgery of farmwork, and he was constantly searching for ideas that could enable the family to escape their dependence on the land. He desperately sought his father's approval of these ideas. He knew his father was upset over what had happened that morning, but he needed to explain himself. After dinner that night, he brought his dad a recent copy of *Science and*

Invention magazine. There was something special inside, and he needed to show him.

The cover of the magazine featured a painting of a bright red monorail bullet train suspended above the bustling streets of Chicago. No train like it actually existed. This particular edition was important because the magazine was now renaming itself. It had previously been known as the *Electrical Experimenter.* Inside, the editor, Hugo Gernsback, explained that the original title had too narrow an appeal given the sudden rush of new technology into the mainstream of society. But he assured readers that the periodical would remain true to its roots as *the* monthly for experimenters and inventors, "that vast horde of intellectual Americans, in whom the physical progress of the country is centered." He said the goal was to build the circulation from the current 200,000 households up to 500,000.

The magazine was chock-full of ads for electrical training institutes: Earn Up to $175 a Week! Be a Certified Electrician! Be an Expert in 3½ Months! Electricity Is the Biggest Force in the World Today! The Very Existence of the World Depends on the Electrician! Get into It as Quick as You Can! Choose Your Future Now!

What had caught Philo's eye was a monthly contest that the magazine was sponsoring, offering a twenty-five-dollar first prize, a fifteen-dollar second prize, and a ten-dollar third prize for the best invention to improve the automobile in any way. The Farnsworths did not own a car, but they knew people in town who did. From watching them sputter up hills and careen down roads, Philo could see that the popular Model-T Fords were rather crude affairs. They could certainly use all the help they could get. Any improvements, so far, seemed as primitive as the cars themselves. The second prize in the previous installment of the contest went to an idea for starting a car in damp weather: simply stuff a handkerchief into the air intake pipe. That idea fetched fifteen dollars.

First prize, meanwhile, went to the idea of attaching a horn beneath the rear fender. If the horn was not first switched off by the owner, a stranger stepping onto the running board would complete an electric circuit, setting off an obnoxious wail that would alert neighbors. It was said to be the first electric "thief alarm" for automobiles. And for that, the magazine revealed, a woman named Edna Purdy would collect twenty-five dollars.

Philo had an idea that would even top Edna Purdy's. Instead of an alarm, why not have a lock on the steering column? All the keys that started the Model-Ts were the same—a piece of flat, straight metal. Thus, pretty much any key could start any Model-T. Philo had a question: why not have it so that no one could operate the vehicle without the right key? An ignition lock.

His dad said that this sounded reasonable enough. But how would he do it?

Philo told him that he was reading about atoms, those tiny building blocks that make up everything in the universe. He was reading that all atoms have magnetic fields that attract or repulse other atoms. Those fields are created by the motion of the atom's electrons. An electron is a negatively charged particle with a tiny mass, and it moves at an incredible speed in orbit around the atom's nucleus, much the same way the earth (by the force of gravity) orbits the sun. The motion and the spin of an electron creates a magnetic field that can exert a force on other charged particles, and the direction of an atom's force, he learned, is something called a magnetic moment.

The elder Farnsworth didn't say much in response, as he tended to take Philo's word on such matters.

What if, Philo asked, someone magnetized the starting mechanism near the Model-T's steering column? He read that many metals can be magnetized by aligning the magnetic moments of their atoms in the same direction, as if they were soldiers facing the same way. This could be done fairly simply: you can magnetize a piece of iron or steel by stroking it in one direction with another magnet. Or it could be done by placing it in a strong magnetic field and hitting it again and again on one end. Or by heating it red-hot and then cooling it in a magnetic field. If the key was also magnetized in one of these ways, it could set off a trigger that would enable the car to start.

The idea that had popped into Philo's head that morning while plowing the potato field was sophisticated by scientific standards back then, and Philo was just fourteen years old when he thought of it.

Naturally, Lewis Farnsworth was skeptical; he had only the faintest idea what his son was even talking about. If it was such a good idea, why hadn't someone else already thought of it? Wouldn't there be lots of competition? The handkerchief concept, if it really worked, must be brilliant. How could a fourteen-year-old go up against such geniuses? Yet he was no longer mad at Philo, and he didn't want to discourage him. Actually, he felt very strongly that it was his God-given duty to encourage Philo in whatever he wanted to do.

Born on August 19, 1906, in a log cabin with no electricity, Philo Taylor Farnsworth was named after his paternal grandfather, an ordained Mormon bishop and a pioneer who was sent from Illinois by Brigham Young to settle the township of Beaver in the promised land on the Utah frontier. According to genealogical records, the original Philo Taylor had two wives. Meanwhile, the maternal grandfather, Jacob Bastian, a man of the sea descended from Danish Vikings, kept four wives while living in Utah. But the practice of polygamy ended with the grandparents. Lewis Farnsworth took Serena Bastian as his wife after his first wife died, and Serena was not much older than Lewis's eldest daughter from his prior marriage.

After Philo, the couple had two more sons and two daughters. Supporting ten people on their small farm was becoming impossible. The soil in their corner of Utah was stingy and growing more so each year. Lewis had heard from relatives about cheap, fertile land over the mountains, and during the spring before the end of the Great War, in 1918, when Philo was eleven years old, they loaded up three covered wagons and headed north. One of Philo's grown half-siblings drove the first wagon, with Lewis and Serena holding the reins in the second. Philo drove the third. He had to be careful, as it contained the family's phonograph, which he enjoyed more than anything, as well as a crate of hens and a basket of piglets. The trip took several weeks because the family stopped to visit relatives along the way.

During the journey, Philo was especially awestruck by all the goings on in Salt Lake City. It was his first visit to the big metropolis, and he drank in the marvels of modern life: the electric street lamps, the bustling automobile traffic, telephone and power lines, as well as the giant pipe organ in the Mormon Tabernacle. Ever since he could talk, he had asked an unusual number of questions about all man-made devices. He was told that such things were created by inventors with names like Samuel Morse and Alexander Graham Bell and Thomas Alva Edison. He decided that inventors must be special people.

Interesting things were also awaiting him over the mountain at his uncle Albert Farnsworth's 240-acre farm near Rigby, Idaho, where the family would live and work until they could afford to buy a farm of their own. The farm had two big white houses, one for Albert's family, and the other for Lewis's family. Both were wired for electricity, powered by a Delco generator that could be heard whirring along in a shed that sat between the homes. In the attic of the house where Philo's family lived were stacks of Sears Roebuck catalogs, musty science journals, and technical magazines left by the former owner of the ranch who had originally installed the generator. Philo claimed this as his bedroom.

To Philo, the magazines were a gift from above, and they became his main contact with the world beyond the farm. The only problem was that he had very little time to read them. He had chores and school, and other responsibilities as the oldest of five. So he would set his alarm each night, usually for 4 A.M., giving him an hour or more to read and think before he had to begin his routine. Trying not to wake anyone, he would rise from his bed, switch on the light, get back under the covers, open a magazine, and allow the stories of inventions and scientists to fire his imagination.

During the day, he sought ways to apply his rapidly growing knowledge. The supreme center of his attention sat inside the shed. Not only did the generator power the lights and the water heater in the house, but it ran the farm's electric hay stacker and grain loader. Neither Lewis nor his brother Albert knew anything about it, so when it broke down, it required an expensive visit from William Tall, the local electrical repairman. Philo's favorite activity was watching Tall fix the generator, asking him question after question after question. Philo needed to know how the generator actually worked, and he would often tinker with it when no one was around. His uncle Albert suspected that Philo would break it on purpose, just to prompt another visit from Tall.

From watching Tall and from his reading, Philo learned that electricity could be made by passing a strong magnet by a wire. Just move a magnetic field through time and space near that wire, and you can produce an electrical field—a force that exerts itself on electrons sitting in the wire. The electrical force is what sets the electrons into motion, and the moving electrons are electricity itself. Each electron acts as a tiny car that can carry a little load of energy into a lightbulb or electrical appliance. Generators are simply machines that move magnets past wires to produce electricity.

All this was startling news to Philo. Magnetism and electricity were not separate phenomena; they were part of the same wonder. Electricity is magnetic, and magnets are electrical. This meant that streams of electrons could be manipulated by magnets. Such amazing knowledge was already decades old, but Philo didn't personally know anyone who cared about it or even understood it. Even William Tall didn't seem all that interested in anything beyond the mechanical workings of the machine.

One day, the generator broke down not long after it had been serviced. Uncle Albert was at his wit's end, as he couldn't keep paying to have it fixed, and the family couldn't afford to replace it. But everyone agreed they couldn't run the ranch without it. Albert was discussing the predicament with his own grown sons, and with his brother Lewis, when Philo, then age twelve, stepped forward and asked if he could try to fix it. His older cousins laughed and tossed a few derisive comments Philo's way.

"Why don't you give him a chance, Albert?" said Lewis. "What do we have to lose?"

Albert agreed, reluctantly.

Philo used kerosene to carefully clean the gunk from the metal pieces and wires. Then he reassembled the machine just as he had watched William Tall do it. The entire extended family was now gathered to see this, including Philo's sisters Agnes and Laura and his brothers Lincoln and Carl. Everyone was watching intently as Philo stood up and confidently pressed the "on" button. The generator sprang into action and started humming more smoothly than ever. Everyone but Philo was surprised.

Uncle Albert thumped Philo on the shoulder and appointed him engineer-in-chief of the farm. His father gave him a hug and said, "Good work, son." Never before had Philo experienced such a proud moment.

The local economy was picking up, the autumn harvest was quite profitable, and Philo's family could now afford a down payment on a farm of their own. In the spring of 1921, they bought a 140-acre ranch just a few miles away from Uncle Albert's farm. At the new place, Philo strung up lights in the barn and set up an even more elaborate laboratory in the attic. He had scavenged an old telegraph set, reels of electrical wire, burned-out motors, and machine tools. At one point, he hooked up a motor to his mother's sewing machine. But Philo's mom, a rugged woman accustomed to hard work, wasn't easily impressed with this so-called laborsaving device. She still had to sit there making and mending clothes. She was accustomed to her own foot power, and she didn't want to change. She told Philo to unhitch the motor, and Philo reluctantly complied with her request.

He met with more success in hooking up a motor and some pulleys to the long wooden lever of the family's manual washing machine. This invention freed his sister Agnes from long hours pushing and pulling the handle back and forth. It was a great success, and Agnes couldn't believe the free time she now had on her hands.

To Lewis Farnsworth, Philo's interest in all things electrical was little more than a hobby. Of what great use was it, careerwise? After all, growing up to be like Mr. Tall wouldn't be that remarkable an achievement. Philo's real gift was musical. The boy had bought himself a violin from the Sears catalog with his own money he had gotten when he sold a brood of baby lambs that he'd raised. Philo's true destiny, his father suspected, was as a concert musician, a master violinist, a member of a famous symphony orchestra.

Philo had been taking lessons at school for the past four years, and his parents made sure he practiced every evening up in the attic—yet another endeavor that ate up Philo's time. But he got so good on the instrument that his music teacher gave him a job with the local four-piece orchestra that played at Friday night dances in the school gymnasium. Philo could play classical pieces as well as big hits such as "Down by the Old Mill Stream," and each week he earned five dollars for these performances.

But there was something he enjoyed even more than performing. He used his performance earnings to buy more books and magazines, including a set of texts about electricity and the twenty-five-cent copy of *Science and Invention*, the issue announcing the contest, which he was now holding in his hands and showing to his father.

"I'm pretty sure this idea will work," Philo said. "Do you know where I can find an ignition to try it out?"

His father didn't, but his older cousin Kent kept tabs on a lot of what was happening in town. Kent knew of someone who had just wrecked his car. So they headed out, on horseback, to a barn a few miles away to see the wreck. The owner said the ignition was his for the taking. After Philo pried it from the car, he brought it back home and up to his attic bedroom, which he was turning into his own little laboratory as well as his musical studio. After a few days of work, Philo was able to magnetize the ignition so that it could be switched on only with his newly magnetized key. The idea actually worked! Philo drew up diagrams and an explanation of the concept and prepared to mail it into the magazine.

He needed to have those documents officially notarized beforehand. The local notary also happened to be the president of the local bank. The following afternoon, Philo road by horseback downtown, hitched the animal up to a street post, went inside the bank, and introduced himself. The bank president was so impressed with Philo's idea that after stamping the documents he called a reporter from the *Rigby Star*, the town newspaper, which had offices just down the street. The newspaper sent over a reporter and photographer right away. The write-up and photo in the next edition turned Philo into a local celebrity of sorts.

As he hoped, Philo indeed won first prize in the *Science and Invention* contest. The description of his entry appeared in the magazine several months later, and when the twenty-five-dollar check arrived, Philo decided to use the money not for more books and magazines, but to order from the Sears catalog his first suit with long pants. He was still playing violin at the weekend dances wearing his childhood knickers. That was becoming far too embarrassing. After all, the girls from school would see him there.

Even with everything he had to do, Philo continued to rise before dawn, giving himself enough time to read and think. How could he not? Radio was now the dominant topic in all the science magazines. Hugo Gernsback's hottest publication, *Radio News*, was for those who assembled their own crystal radio receivers, built their own transmitting devices, and tuned in to the new commercial stations broadcasting from the big cities. The magazine offered program listings as well as a regular stable of stories about the latest equipment and inventions. For a two-dollar annual subscription, the future was neatly summarized and delivered each month to Philo's farmhouse.

The ads in the magazines touted all the radio components that a kid like Farnsworth could desire. For a few dollars, you could order all the parts needed to assemble the best radio in town. The actual radio receiver was a piece of wood wound tightly with insulated copper wire. You also needed crystals, usually a mineral such as galena that detected the radio waves and converted them into sound electricity. Then you attached an earplug or a set of headphones. There was absolutely nothing as magical on the face of the earth as staying up late with the headphones tight to your ears, scanning the radio dial for faraway voices and music. An entire generation of boys grew up mesmerized by the sounds of their crystal radios.

Philo happened across a few articles about the idea of transmitting not just sound but pictures over the airwaves. "Schemes on television are not new," wrote Hugo Gernsback. "Inventors have busied themselves for several generations with it, but so far nothing of note has been produced." This struck Philo as a fantastic opportunity, and he started setting his alarm for 2 A.M. to give himself extra time to read and ponder the problem.

He learned how Paul Nipkow, a Russian inventor working in Germany, had applied in 1884 for a patent on a theoretical system for scanning images. It became known as the Nipkow Disk. Bright light reflecting off a person or object would pass through a spinning black disk that was punctured with small holes. As the wheel spun around, it would mechanically scan the image, turning the patterns of light picked up by the holes into electrical impulses. The impulses would then travel by wire to another disk spinning at the same speed as the first. The receiving disk would transform the impulses back into the original image, projecting it onto an adjacent screen. For decades, the Nipkow disk remained the basis for all television research in the United States, in England, in France, and in Germany, but progress had been painfully slow.

The more Philo thought about it, the more he became convinced that this mechanical setup would never work. How could the disk ever spin fast enough to pick up an image in enough detail? If it transmitted only shadows and flickers, people wouldn't watch it. There had to be a better way, a method of sending images so quickly that it could fool the eye into perceiving pulses of light as sharp, fluid pictures.

He had read about vacuum tubes, thus named because all the air was sucked from them before the glass was sealed. Inside was an environment perfectly suited for transmitting electrons without any interference from air molecules. He was especially intrigued by an article about a special, oversized vacuum tube. In 1897, a German scientist named Karl Braun found a way to shoot an electron beam from one part of a vacuum tube, called the cathode, to a screen on the other end. The inside of the screen could be coated with a fluorescent substance that would light up when struck by the electrons. It was called a cathode ray tube—*cathode rays* simply being another term for electron beams. Philo was amazed.

One early morning in the summer of 1921, when Philo was about to turn fifteen, he once again rose to read and then head out to the fields, again to cultivate potatoes. The birds were chirping, the sun was coming up, and a clear blue sky slowly emerged. The ground was drenched with dew. He climbed into the seat of a single-disk harrow that was pulled by two horses. Philo lapsed into his typical trance, meditating on the problem at hand, brainstorming for an idea.

He already knew that electron beams could be controlled, manipulated, and redirected by magnets. Why wasn't anybody capturing an image electronically, then using an electromagnet to guide the light through the tube and to project the signals onto the surface of the screen?

As Philo turned the horses to cultivate another row parallel to the previous one, he gazed back at what he had already done. He saw row after row of furrows. An inspiration struck him like a jolt of electricity to the heart. It hit with so much force that he froze and nearly fell off his seat. This time he managed to keep hold of the reins. He saw television in that field.

Just as a field needed to be plowed line by line, light had to be captured line by line. Philo knew that light energy could be converted into electrical current. What if patterns of electrons could represent patterns of light? After an image was scanned, the process could be reversed. The electron beams could be shot through a tube and converted back into an image that could be re-created on a screen in evenly painted lines. Electrons moved so fast that an entire image could manifest itself this way in a wink.

He wanted to tell someone about this idea, but when he tried to explain his inspiration to his dad, Lewis Farnsworth was simply unable to enter Philo's subatomic universe. Lewis certainly had faith in his son, but he didn't have enough knowledge to share in the boy's excitement. Instead, he offered a stern command.

"You need to keep this secret," he said. "Do you understand?"

Philo thought it was an excellent suggestion. He was already thinking that he had sold his ignition lock idea way too cheaply. Once he had made his invention public in the newspaper and the magazine, it could no longer be eligible for a patent. To receive a patent, an invention needs to be useful and original. If it's already in the public domain, like his ignition now was, it no longer qualified for a patent. He learned a valuable lesson from that experience and vowed to keep his new idea under wraps.

Patents were the farthest thing from Lewis Farnsworth's mind. "You need to keep this secret," he said, "because everyone already thinks you're a bit odd. This would convince them for sure."

In the fall, Philo T. Farnsworth entered Rigby High School. The building itself was one of the most impressive in town, a symmetrical three-story brick structure with a center staircase flanked by hallways lined with classrooms. Right away, Philo wanted to take chemistry, the senior-level science course, but the teacher, Justin Tolman, turned down his request. Philo appealed to the principal, who also refused to let the freshman skip ahead.

Within a few weeks, he had persuaded his introductory science teacher, a feisty lady named Mrs. McCoy, to give him the entire class load of assignments and tests almost all at once. He aced everything. She was impressed enough to petition herself on Philo's behalf, and once again the principal refused.

Finally, Philo approached Mr. Tolman directly and asked if he could just sit in on his chemistry lectures. He said he needed this knowledge for his "work" but didn't explain. The soft-spoken Mr. Tolman was intrigued. He was completely dedicated to teaching, so how could he refuse? He finally gave in, believing Philo would soon grow bored with the subject just like most of the other students. But after a few days, it became clear from the questions Philo was asking that he already understood atoms and molecules and chemical structures much better than most of the seniors.

Mr. Tolman then met with the principal and proposed an idea: he would spend time after school each day tutoring the student. This way, Philo could be prepared for chemistry. The principal relented.

One day, however, Philo put his victory in jeopardy. He was sitting in the front row of a quiet study hall when a pretty girl next to him whispered a question about an assignment. As Philo began to answer her, one thing led to another, and he gradually began to raise his voice as he noticed others beginning to listen. Until then, he was shy and quiet around the other kids, and his sudden lack of inhibition probably was surprising even to himself, but the question the girl had asked touched on his favorite new topic.

Philo had read and reread Albert Einstein's photoelectric theory of light as well as his shocking and controversial theory of relativity, which many leading scientists thought to be false. One article Philo had read, in *Science and Invention*, amounted to a scathing attack on Einstein and his theory. In the very next issue was a reply under the byline of Albert Einstein himself. The explanation was stated so simply and convincingly that Philo read it over and over until he not only had committed it to memory but thought constantly about what it all meant.

Now, the fifteen-year-old was standing before the study hall, drawing pictures in the air with his hands. The students had been learning the accepted wisdom, about Sir Isaac Newton, his basic laws of motion, and his centuries-old theory of the "clockwork universe," that all actions happened in constant time everywhere. What Philo was telling them about Einstein's theory contradicted their textbooks as well as their teacher. Einstein was revolutionary because he said Newton's laws didn't hold up in special circumstances and therefore weren't universal.

To explain Einstein's theories to the class, Philo needed to come
up with a simple example. For instance, imagine that you are standing up in an open automobile that is being driven toward a person
at twenty miles per hour. That person throws a baseball to you at
thirty miles per hour. When you try to catch it, the ball will hit your
hand at the sum of those two speeds, or fifty miles per hour. Wouldn't
that hurt?

Now imagine you are in that vehicle while it is being driven away
from a person at twenty miles per hour, and he throws the same
baseball to you at thirty miles per hour. The ball will now meet your
hand at the difference between the two speeds, or only ten miles
per hour. When you catch it, it wouldn't hurt a bit, right?

That was simple Newtonian mechanics. Everyone agreed to it
because it was so easy to observe and prove. But while Newton knew
that speed, or velocity, is relative to one's vantage point, he didn't
take this knowledge to the extreme. Einstein did.

Mr. Tolman was walking down the hall. Overhearing a loud voice
in a study hall that was supposed to be silent, he poked his head in
and saw Philo at the front of the room. Mr. Tolman was so captivated that he pulled up a chair in the back row to listen.

Caught up in the excitement of his subject, Philo didn't even
notice that his teacher had slipped inside. Now, Philo continued,
what if you were standing by a stationary train, and that train put on
its headlights? The light, of course, would be moving at the known
speed of about 186,000 miles per second. Now let's say the train
started moving at fifty miles per hour. Wouldn't the speed of the
light beam be increased by fifty miles per hour?

Some of the students nodded their heads yes.

And what if you were on the train itself? Wouldn't the light beam
appear to be traveling fifty miles per hour slower than to people on the

ground? While this made common sense, scientists generally agreed that the speed of light is constant no matter what your vantage point, neither increasing nor decreasing, no matter at what speed the observer is moving or at what speed the source of the light beam is moving. Einstein and others referred to this universal constant by the letter c.

How can this be so? How can the speed of light be constant no matter what your frame of reference was? No one in the class had a clue.

This is the part that had ignited Philo's mind. The speed of anything needs to be measured by a clock, but when you're measuring something moving at superhigh speeds, such as light, it depends on how the clock itself is moving. What if clock A was sitting on a train moving toward the light source, and clock B was sitting on a train moving away from the source of the light? Since the speed of light is constant, it has to be true that the two clocks are not constant with one another. Time, Einstein said, did not move at the same rate everywhere. From the point of view of the light beam itself, each of two otherwise identical clocks would appear to be ticking at a different rate.

Philo posed to the class the same question that Einstein had. Which clock is correct?

No one seemed to know.

The answer, he said, was "both" and "neither."

There isn't one way to measure time. It all depends on where in the universe you are trying to measure it. Only because we are all on the same planet, in the same physical atmosphere, can we agree on a common standard for time, but in the universe at large, time is relative. A minute in outer space is different from a minute on Earth. If a person were to travel in a spaceship approaching the speed of light, time would slow down. The person would actually be getting younger relative to the people standing on Earth. Time, therefore, cannot be universally clocked.

With that, the bell rang, and the students dispersed. Philo was now alone with Mr. Tolman. The teacher told the student that he had never heard or read Einstein's theory explained with such clarity and passion. He also told Philo never to do something like that ever again.

The tutoring with Mr. Tolman lasted through the following spring. Philo would show up early every day for school and stay late. It got to the point that the janitor registered a complaint to the principal about having to put in overtime to lock up the building. Mr. Tolman would meet to discuss the lessons with Philo and assign more readings, and Philo would devour book after book and come back with more questions. During their discussions, Mr. Tolman could see that Philo had something on his mind that he wasn't talking about.

Although he had promised his father that he wouldn't tell anybody about his revelation in the potato field, Philo found it hard to keep it to himself. As he grew to trust Mr. Tolman, he was becoming more and more eager to bounce the idea off him. After all, his teacher was the only person he knew who could possibly judge whether it had any merit at all.

One day after school, Philo walked into the empty study hall and began chalking diagrams and equations on the giant blackboard in the front of the room. His outline took up nearly the entire wall. Mr. Tolman walked in, glanced at the board, and sat down in a chair, watching as Philo completed his drawings. When he finished, he picked up a long wooden pointer. This, he said, with a dramatic flourish, is my new invention.

What does this have to do with the chemistry assignment? Mr. Tolman asked.

Nothing, came the reply. It's just my idea for television. Philo explained that this was what had been absorbing his thoughts for quite a while.

Mr. Tolman listened with interest as Philo explained how this system would work and how it would bring images from a distance into people's homes, just as radio was now transmitting sound. He explained his concept for scanning images and said that pictures needed to be encoded just as a plow traverses a field or the human eye reads a page of print—row by row, line by line. To simplify his explanation, Philo tore out a page from his notebook with a much less complicated sketch of the image scanning device, and he handed it to Tolman. The sketch was of a cylinder with a lens on one end that would focus the incoming optical image onto a photoelectric cell. The patterns of light received by the cell would be converted into an electrical representation of that image which could travel out the back of the cylinder.

Philo explained how the varying current could travel by wire to a nearby transmitter that would project electromagnetic waves from an antenna, just as with radio sound. The final part of the system would be a receiver that sat in people's homes. This box would pick up the waves from the air. Inside, a transformer would convert them into electric current once again. The electron beam would be received in a pear-shaped cathode ray tube. When the beam was projected onto a photoelectric surface that coated the inside of the screen, the electrons would revert back into line after line of light values that represented the original moving picture.

The result would be the illusion of motion, a persistent image coming alive before the eyes of the viewer. Persistence of vision. This was the student's concept. After explaining it, Philo was eager to see what Mr. Tolman thought before the blackboard would be erased.

Mr. Tolman's conclusion was exactly what Philo wanted to hear.

"It just might work," he said.

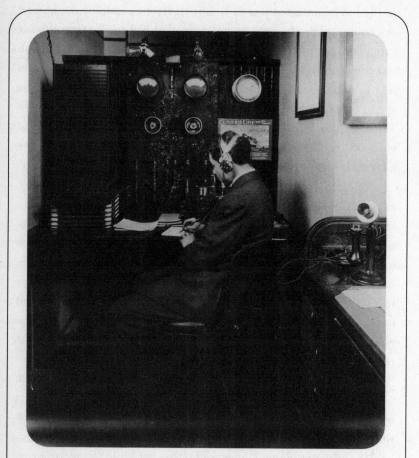

David Sarnoff, twenty-one, in an RCA publicity photo, in which he is purportedly operating a wireless transmitter in contact with the sinking Titanic in April 1912. In this airbrushed image, Sarnoff's head appears on someone else's body. (DAVID SARNOFF LIBRARY)

CHAPTER TWO

Making a Great Man

I N THE SUMMER OF 1921, WHILE THE FIFTEEN-YEAR-OLD PHILO T. Farnsworth was conjuring the idea of electronic television, David Sarnoff was riding the express elevator to his new office at the Radio Corporation of America. The company was headquartered in a suite near the summit of New York City's Woolworth Building, at 233 Broadway, then the tallest skyscraper in the world. Sarnoff had just been granted the rank of general manager, which came with a salary of $15,000 per year. For the first time, he had the power to hire, fire, initiate, and negotiate.

Just thirty years old, Sarnoff had eyes of cold blue steel that he would use to compel important people into important conversations. His hairline was still dark and youthful, but his middle was beginning to expand due to his hearty appetite for bread, meat, and potatoes and the fact that he had hardly engaged in a moment of physical exercise in his life. His soldierlike walk and his inner air pump of self-assurance seemed to lift his five-foot-eight-inch frame to a loftier height.

Sarnoff was a man of obsessions, and his current fixation was on turning radio into an entertainment device. Until then, wireless was known mainly as a hero of the Great War. German U-boats had cut the underseas cables that allowed the Americans and British to communicate by wire with their naval fleets. To the rescue came the new technology of wireless, which enabled Allied commanders to transmit through the air messages encoded into bleeps and blips. When President Woodrow Wilson took to the airwaves to broadcast his peace proposal, the Fourteen Points, people all over the United States and Europe got the message with unprecedented quickness. After the Armistice, wireless continued as America's fastest-growing hobby. Tens of thousands of people each year were assembling primitive crystal radio sets. At first, they were content just to pick up bits of Morse code and the occasional live human voice.

Sarnoff sensed a hunger for something more, and he had a plan to deliver it. There was a boxing match set for Saturday afternoon, the second of July. The venue was known as Boyle's Thirty Acres, an outdoor arena in Jersey City just over the Hudson River across from lower Manhattan. The promoter of the bout, the smooth-talking Tex Rickard, had convinced the press that this was not just a sweaty brawl but a battle of good versus evil. Cast as the role of the villain was legendary heavyweight champion Jack Dempsey. The public loved to hate this man. Known as the Manassa Mauler, he was a scar-faced bruiser, alleged wife beater, and, worst of all, a draft dodger. The valiant challenger was French champ Georges Carpentier, a handsome, graceful ladies' man and a decorated combat pilot.

Several years after the episode, as Sarnoff rose to prominence, he would begin to tell the press the dramatic story of his master plan to manufacture the first big electronic media event. According to Sarnoff's tale, his first order of business was a call to Rickard to ask if he could place a microphone at ringside. The promoter agreed. Then Sarnoff set his sights on a powerful new radio transmitter made by

RCA's corporate parent, General Electric. The instrument was supposed to be delivered by rail to the Navy Department in Washington, D.C., but Sarnoff made a call to a loyal friend of RCA, former assistant navy secretary Franklin D. Roosevelt, and the two arranged to have the transmitter diverted to a secret shed near the sports arena.

Sarnoff then persuaded telephone company technicians to connect the microphone to the transmitter, and he enlisted some of his engineers to attach a makeshift transmission antenna to a nearby railroad crossing tower.

To infuse a noble purpose to the broadcast, Sarnoff came up with the idea of turning it into a charity event. He recruited Anne Morgan, daughter of financial baron J. P. Morgan, to help set up parties and gatherings in town halls, theaters, school auditoriums, Elks Clubs, anywhere that large groups could gather. In the New York area, Marcus Loew agreed to contribute the use of all his movie houses. Anne Morgan, with some assistance from Roosevelt, arranged hundreds of listening events, held throughout the Northeast. As a cover charge, attendees would bring cash donations for her charity, a committee for reconstructing war-torn France, as well as Roosevelt's cause, the Navy Club. According to Sarnoff, all of this was done without the knowledge or consent of RCA's top brass.

There was a small problem. Back then, radio receivers had earpieces or headphones, not speakers, as they were made for semiprivate communication between two people. Sarnoff located 300 of those old tulip-shaped phonograph horns, bought them for thirty cents apiece, and had his engineers go around rigging the horns to hundreds of radios. This way, big groups could listen.

More than 90,000 fans came to Boyle's Thirty Acres by train on that hot July afternoon. It was the biggest crowd that had ever been assembled for a sporting event. Sarnoff sat at ringside next to his handpicked announcer, J. Andrew White, a boxing buff and the editor of RCA's own magazine, *Wireless Age*. White had never done anything like this before—Sarnoff just happened to like his voice. Sitting there, dressed in his typical dark suit, white shirt, and silk tie, puffing on a cigar, Sarnoff didn't exactly mesh with the shouting, hooting working-class crowd. He was perhaps the only person in the arena that night who didn't care a whit for boxing or who won. His only concern was that the broadcast should come off without a hitch.

As usual, Dempsey showed no mercy on his opponent. He clobbered Carpentier to the ground in just eleven minutes on the official clock, with White describing every blow to an unseen audience. It was lucky for Sarnoff that the fight was short. The referee's final count came right before an electrical overload blew out the borrowed equipment.

The broadcast had been received up to 500 miles away, with more than 300,000 people listening, the largest audience that had ever been assembled for anything, and newspaper headlines around the world lauded the event as a watershed for radio. Both Morgan and Roosevelt collected big bounties. Sarnoff's boss, RCA president Edward Nally, who was away on business, sent a telegram from London that said: "You have made history." The blessing from above had major ramifications. Sarnoff was now granted permission by Nally to construct a broadcast studio and transmission center in New York. Suddenly, everyone in the United States seemed to want two things: a radio and an opportunity to be on the radio. The Roaring Twenties were now good to go.

There is only one problem with this story. It's only a story. Yes, Dempsey knocked out Carpentier in the fourth round at Boyle's Thirty Acres in Jersey City. Yes, it was the first major sports broadcast, and yes, the excitement from that event helped set off the sudden explosion of radio. But David Sarnoff wasn't the prime mover. Julius Hopp, a man no one remembers, was the real mastermind behind the broadcast that made history. In 1921, Hopp was the manager for concert events at Madison Square Garden, and the actual account of how this historic broadcast came together was published in vivid detail right after the event, in the August 1921 issue of *Wireless Age*. Sarnoff's own story wouldn't start appearing in the press until five years later.

According to the original account, it was Hopp, not Sarnoff, who presented the idea to Tex Rickard. The idea was sparked during Hopp's attendance of an amateur radio announcers convention in New York several months earlier. He was impressed with the announcers' skills and the equipment he saw on display there. As in the Sarnoff account, Rickard indeed loved the idea right away. After all, he was a boxing promoter. What's not to like about magnifying your audience tenfold, a hundredfold, or more? But Rickard placed the task of acquiring the equipment and personnel in the hands of Hopp, not Sarnoff.

Anne Morgan did in fact handle the charity drive for French reconstruction, although no one ever confirmed how much money was really raised, and the transmitter was obtained with the help of Franklin Roosevelt. Sarnoff may have had a role in enlisting their support, but he didn't conceive or arrange the entire production, as he would later claim.

Scores of people worked along with Hopp to broadcast the fight, so many that the National Amateur Wireless Association issued to each of them a certificate as "a permanent record of invaluable co-operation in making available to the American public a description transmitted by radio telephone of the World's Championship Boxing Contest." The certificate went on to honor "the unprecedented undertaking and scientific triumph of simultaneous transmission of the human voice to 300,000 persons without the aid of wires, including audiences in theatres within an area of 125,000 square miles."

Under an official seal were the signatures of Anne Morgan, Tex Rickard, J. Andrew White, Jack Dempsey, Georges Carpentier, and Franklin D. Roosevelt. Sarnoff's signature was not included. The certificate itself was reproduced in the magazine, along with dramatic photos of the event and the radio equipment, plus a list of all the theaters that held listening parties. The largest gathering, some 1,200 people, was packed into a Loews Theater on Broadway and Forty-fifth Street. There was no mention of David Sarnoff anywhere in this account.

David Sarnoff was indeed at the event. He saw everything and was able to describe it in detail years later. But all evidence points to a much more modest role, perhaps as the supervisor of the ringside equipment, certainly as a middle manager anticipating accolades from his bosses. On the morning after the fight, the *New York Times* noted at the very end of a long series of articles that the telephones at ringside were operated by a "David Saranoff."

The Dempsey broadcast was just one of several episodes that David Sarnoff selectively edited, embellished, positioned, sharpened, back-lighted, and recast with himself in the spotlight. But how did he do it? And more important, why did he do it?

The actual facts of his life story seemed dramatic enough. Like Philo T. Farnsworth, Sarnoff was the eldest child in a poor family of a religious minority. He too was born in a remote, rural area, in the humblest of houses, without any modern conveniences. His birth-place, however, was halfway around the world. The town was but a speck in the vast pale of Russia. Called Uzlian, it was a shtetl in the province of Minsk. For decades, the czars relegated their third-class Jewish subjects to these bleak villages with their long, white winters. Uzlian was one of many ghetto enclaves where Yiddish was spoken and the Talmud was studied. Life in this particular shtetl was so isolated that it wasn't even interrupted by the pogroms, the waves of unwelcome and violent visits from cruel Cossacks or drunken peasants.

David's parents had high hopes for him. They fully expected him to be a rabbi. At age five, he was sent off to live in the village of Korme with his granduncle, a learned rabbinical scholar, to study the Torah and memorize the entire Jewish liturgy. Located more than 100 miles from home, this new place was even more secluded than Uzlian. During his four years there, David was all but completely separated from normal childhood pastimes as basic as playing games and laughing, which probably led to his workaholic discipline. But the more David was forced into rote memorization, the less he was interested. Later, he would completely reject his orthodox background in favor of the reformed, Americanized rendition of the religion.

While David was off studying, his father left for the United States to work odd jobs and save enough money to send for his family. In the year 1900, word arrived that it was time to pack up and go.

At the age of nine, David embarked on a trip not unlike Farnsworth's early journey from Utah to Idaho. On horse-drawn carts laden with bundles of clothing, linen, and kosher foods, he rode with his mother and two brothers to Minsk. It was the first time he had ever seen paved roads and streetcars and buildings higher than one story. David also witnessed Cossacks charging on horseback against a large gathering of demonstrators demanding political freedom. As the cavalry advanced on the crowd, he clung to his mother's skirt and recoiled in horror. "I saw them lashing out with their whips, trampling women and children with their horses' hooves," he later wrote. "It trampled out of me any lingering feeling I might have had for Russia as my homeland."

Like millions of others in the immigrant tide, Sarnoff would board a steamship and pass over the Atlantic not knowing a word of English. At one point at the outset of the long journey, the family's bin of food was mistakenly mixed up with other luggage and tossed down into the cargo hold. Seeing this, David leaped a dangerous distance from the ship deck to snatch it back. Fortunately, he landed on something soft. A crew member, witnessing this, said: "Boy, you're going to do all right in America."

It's quite possible that these little childhood tales are also apoc-
ryphal, as Sarnoff's own accounts are all that survive, but they certainly ring true to Sarnoff's future. He arrived with little more than
a revulsion for Russia and an idealized vision of what was then still
referred to as the New World. Almost as soon as he stepped onto U.S.
soil, he felt newly baptized as an American. He would soon grow
determined to fill the empty void of his past with an entirely new
self, created from scratch.

His family ended up wedged into the most cramped section of
Manhattan's dangerous, filthy, and crowded Lower East Side tene-
ments. In many ways, this was worse than the conditions in Russia.
At least the shtetl didn't rumble around the clock from adjacent
elevated trains. At least the shtetl didn't reek from rotten rubbish
and squalid sewage. Escaping this new ghetto would be like a second immigration.

In America, though, he had the freedom and opportunity to use
the shabby setting as a springboard to success. Sarnoff's assimila-
tion was a dive into the pool of concrete capitalism on the streets of
the city. He mastered English quickly, then peddled penny newspapers to help support the family, usually rising at 4 A.M. to deliver
copies of the *Jewish Daily Forward*. Legend has it that he soon owned
his own newsstand, in Hell's Kitchen on the west side of the city,
before deciding that he wanted something with more of a future.

By the time he was fourteen, it was clear that his father was
dying of tuberculosis. The support of the family fell to the teenager,
so he dropped out of school after eighth grade and went looking for
full-time work. He ended up in the lobby of the *New York Herald*
Building, which jutted to the sky from the square at Thirty-fifth and
Broadway. It was the city's tallest at the time, before the Woolworth
Building would take the title for the next few years. Sarnoff marched
into an office on the ground floor to inquire whether the company
needed a messenger boy. It turned out that the people inside were

indeed in the market for one, but Sarnoff had entered the wrong office. This wasn't the *Herald* but a sister firm called the Commercial Cable Company, which made its money sending, receiving, and delivering communiqués via telegraph.

After just a few months on the job, the manager fired Sarnoff when he refused to work during the Jewish holidays of Rosh Hashanah and Yom Kippur, but by now, he'd been bitten by the telegraph bug and had learned how to send and transcribe messages. Within a few weeks of being fired, he had heard of the potential for a somewhat similar job. He showed up, with telegraph key in hand, at the Wall Street offices of the American Marconi Company, which was engaged in the radically new business of overseas wireless communications.

Not long after Sarnoff joined the firm, Guglielmo Marconi himself paid a visit to the office. What happened next was later corroborated by the famous Italian inventor. Sarnoff went out of his way to shake the hand of Marconi and then managed to strike up a lengthy conversation with him. In place of his real father, a weak man with a hacking cough, a man he hardly knew and didn't especially admire, Sarnoff had secretly idolized Marconi and would come to regard him as a surrogate father. Marconi was already being mentioned as a Nobel Prize candidate for his 1896 discovery of how to transmit information signals through the ether to an aerial. He was a dogged self-promoter, and the press fawned over him as "the sorcerer of the airwaves."

The young Sarnoff was struck by the elegant way the trim Marconi dressed, held his cigarette, and moved around with a gold-plated walking stick, graciously greeting all the employees. He identified with the fact that Marconi had only a grade-school education. He would come to believe the popular myth that Marconi invented radio. It wasn't quite true. Marconi invented the wireless telegraph, the precursor to what became radio. Yet millions of people believed that Marconi did it all, and Sarnoff later would help perpetrate that legend.

On the spot, Sarnoff offered to act as Marconi's personal messenger. As luck would have it, his hero happened to need one at the time. The assignment was more interesting than Sarnoff even imagined. Marconi was by then an international sex symbol and was in high demand among the young ladies of New York's upper crust. The Italian could not resist playing the part, and so Sarnoff found himself busily bicycling boxes of chocolates and bouquets of roses to plush apartments all over town. On subsequent visits to New York, Marconi began treating Sarnoff not just as a messenger but as a protégé of sorts, answering Sarnoff's many technical questions and offering the teenager access to company files and papers. Sarnoff thus became the sorcerer's apprentice.

From his indelible exposure to Marconi and from reading in his American grade school about Lincoln, whom he also came to identify with, Sarnoff began to believe more and more strongly in what was known as the Great Man Theory of History. "The history of the world is but the biography of great men," wrote the Victorian philosopher Thomas Carlyle. "In all epochs of the world's history, we shall find the great man to have been the indispensable savior of his epoch." Opponents of this theory, most notably Lev Tolstoy, argued that history was the result of much broader social and economic forces, with prominent individuals acting merely as instruments of those changes. But Sarnoff was squarely in Carlyle's camp on this one.

Sarnoff began to infuse his own life with a sense of destiny, as if every move he made was a step toward his final goal, and that goal was greatness. He began to see the birth of broadcasting as not just a once-in-a-lifetime event but a transformation that would only come along once in human history. He became determined to be the great leader of the most important company in the world's most

dynamic industry. Not just a businessman, but a Great World Figure
and a prophet of the electronic age.

Sarnoff's first big step on his march to greatness supposedly
came after he was promoted at American Marconi, to the position
of wireless telegraph operator, for the wage of $7.50 per week. He
was stationed on top of the Wanamaker department store, at the
corner of Ninth and Broadway. It acted as a sister station to a larger
installation on top of the store's main building in Philadelphia.
Mainly, this New York operation served as a publicity showcase both
for American Marconi and for the purpose of attracting more customers to the store. Visitors would take the elevator up to the top
floor to peer into the future of communication.

The job was relatively easy. The twenty-year-old operator would
explain the wonders of wireless to semicurious shoppers and chat
with amateur ham operators in and around the city. The regular
business hours of the job enabled him to take an intensive evening
course in electrical engineering at Pratt Institute. Out of a class of
sixty students, Sarnoff later claimed, he was only one of eleven to
complete the program, and the other ten all had high school or college degrees. However, neither Pratt nor Sarnoff were ever able to
produce evidence of his graduation.

The tale of the Pratt degree was hardly tall compared to the other
one he told from that time. At 10:25 P.M. on Sunday night, April 14,
1912, Sarnoff was said to be operating the apparatus atop the Wanamaker. "Leaning forward suddenly," an RCA publicity release
stated years later, "he pressed the earphones more closely to his
head. Through the sputtering and static . . . he was hearing a message: *S.S. Titanic ran into iceberg. Sinking fast.* For the next seventy-
two hours, Sarnoff sat at his post, straining to catch every signal
that might come through the air. That demanded a good operator
in those days of undeveloped radio. By order of the President of the
United States, every other wireless station in the country was closed

to stop interference. Not until he had given the world the name of the last survivor, three days and three nights after that first message, did Sarnoff call his job done."

The original distress signal came from the *RMS Olympic*, a sister ship more than 1,000 miles away from the *Titanic*. The two ships were in touch via each of their on-board wireless stations. How fantastic this must have been for Sarnoff, to be the one and only person to pick up this urgent piece of news. If it really happened.

RCA's corporate version was culled from Sarnoff's own account, as told fourteen years after the tragedy to a reporter at the *Saturday Evening Post*:

I have often been asked what were my emotions at that moment. I doubt if I felt [anything] at all during the seventy-two hours after the news came. I gave the information to the press associations and newspapers at once, and it was as if bedlam had been let loose. Telephones were whirring, extras were being cried, crowds were gathering around newspaper bulletin boards. Everybody was trying to get and send messages. Some who owned sets had relatives or friends aboard the *Titanic*, and they made frantic efforts to learn something definite. Finally, President Taft ordered all stations in the vicinity except ours closed down so that we might have no interference in the reception of official news. . . . Word spread swiftly that a list of survivors were being received at Wanamakers, and the station was quickly stormed by the grief-stricken and curious. Eventually, a police guard was called out and the curious held back, but some of those most interested in the fate of the doomed ship were allowed in the wireless room. Vincent Astor, whose father John Jacob Astor was drowned, was among those who looked over my shoulder as I copied the list of survivors. . . . Much of the time I sat with the earphones on my head and nothing coming in. It seemed as if the whole anxious world was attached to those phones during the seventy-two hours I crouched tense in that station. I felt my responsibility keenly, and weary though I was, could not have slept. At the end of my first long tryst with the sea, I was whisked in a taxicab to the old Astor House on lower Broadway and given a Turkish rub. Then I was rushed in another taxicab to Sea Gate [at the southern tip of Brooklyn], where communication was being kept up with the *Carpathia*, the vessel which brought in the survivors of the ill-fated *Titanic*. . . . Here again I sat for hours—listening. Now we began to get the names of some of those who were known to have gone down. This was worse than the other list had been—heartbreaking in its finality—a death knell to hope. I passed the information on to a sorrowing world, and when messages ceased to come in, fell down like a log at my place and slept the clock around.

Sarnoff told and retold the story—how he was the sole link between the sinking ship and the rest of the world—to illustrate how radio first came to prominence in the public mind. Of course, he also aimed to show that his own destiny was intertwined with the fate of broadcasting itself. "The *Titanic* disaster brought radio to the front," he would say, "and also me."

Like a game of telephone, the account would grow more and more embellished, distorted, and heroic as it was retold. When it was printed in *Fortune* magazine in 1932, the tale was repeated as if factual, with no mention that Sarnoff was the source, and by the time the fable had made its way into official biographies, it became officially true. The story wouldn't be refuted during Sarnoff's lifetime.

At best, Sarnoff was one of many useful wireless operators scrambling as well as he could amid the crisis. He was not the solitary hero he made himself out to be. And common sense tells us that other facts may have been embellished, if not completely fabricated.

The Wanamaker store in New York kept business hours, so the wireless station would almost certainly have been closed so late on a Sunday night, when the *Olympic*'s relay signal was sent. And if the event brought David Sarnoff to fame at this young age, as his official biographer would later note, there would have been some evidence of this in the media at the time. But the *New York Times* and several other newspapers that covered the tragedy extensively did not mention Sarnoff or the Wanamaker store. Many wireless stations were indeed told to shut down to reduce interference, but contrary to Sarnoff's account, the Wanamaker station in New York was actually one of those that *did* shut down for a time soon after the ship went down, as verified by a notice in the *Boston American*.

This was also the only newspaper known to have mentioned David Sarnoff during the entire episode. The *American* was a Hearst publication, which already had an exclusive agreement with Wanamaker to publish whatever news its Marconi stations gathered. The April 16 edition of the paper did indeed report, in just a few paragraphs on an inside page, on the activity at the Wanamaker station, but it in no way singled out Sarnoff. The story made it clear that Sarnoff was only one of three skilled operators on the job at the station; the other two were Jack Binns and J. H. Hughes. "Faint signals were heard from the *Olympic*," the paper said, "but owing to the terrific confusion and disruption of static conditions, Mr. Hughes was unable to pick up the strands of direct communication."

What's more, there's no evidence that President Taft was involved in the episode in the way that Sarnoff later claimed. In fact, Taft claimed bitterly that officials at American Marconi were actually ordering operators aboard the *Carpathia* to *hold back* information about the hundreds of survivors in order to string the story out, bring more attention to the role of wireless, and perhaps auction off the complete account later. Marconi himself, who happened to be holding a ticket for the *Titanic*'s now-canceled return trip to England, later admitted that this was indeed true.

The *Herald* covered this story on April 21, under the headline: "Keep Your Mouth Shut; Big Money for You,' Was Message to Hide News."

> While the world was waiting three days for information concerning the fate of the *Titanic*, for part of the time at least, details concerning the disaster were being withheld by the wireless operator of the steamship *Carpathia* under specific orders from T. W. Sammis, chief engineer of the Marconi Wireless Company of America, who had arranged the sale of the story. This was admitted yesterday by Mr. Sammis, who defended his action. He said he was justified for getting for the wireless operators the largest amount he could for the details of the sinking of the ship, the rescue of the passengers and the other information the world had waited for.

This little revelation produced only a small scandal and was of course totally overshadowed by the *Titanic* tragedy itself. Instead of being punished, Marconi and his company were richly rewarded. The role of wireless in ship-to-shore safety and in the transmission of important notices was now brought into sharp relief, and orders to install and upgrade equipment flooded the company. In the months after the *Titanic* went down, American Marconi's stock skyrocketed. Yes, 1,517 people were dead. But the electronic news business was on its way.

David Sarnoff's own account of this episode started to surface ten years later. The *Titanic* tale, along with the Dempsey broadcast and other exaggerated episodes of his early career, were planted in the press for a very good reason. Beginning in 1922, Sarnoff was suddenly thrust into a very high-profile and unpopular role as the patent policeman for RCA. His mythology was intended to counterbalance negative portrayals, and he needed these yarns to impress upon the public that he was first and foremost a great visionary, not the hard-nosed businessman he was becoming.

The company's sudden patent dilemma was rooted in the formation of RCA itself. The corporation was born in 1919 not as an entrepreneurial venture but as a government proclamation. With its success during the war, wireless was deemed too important to be left to a foreign power, even a friendly one. The Marconi Wireless Telegraph Company pioneered the proliferation of wireless, but the company was headquartered in Great Britain. The U.S. Navy and later the U.S. Congress decided that all the patents of its American subsidiary must be controlled by Americans.

Due to its leadership building the most powerful radio transmitters, General Electric was granted that opportunity. By congressional mandate, GE engulfed the assets, including the entire staff, of American Marconi and pooled the Marconi patents with its own. GE's respected general counsel, Owen Young, was named chairman of the new firm. Edward Nally, a top American Marconi executive, was appointed president, and Nally's assistant, David Sarnoff, was named RCA's commercial manager, a title he held for less than two years before his next promotion.

RCA was thus born as a monopoly, but Sarnoff thought it wasn't the right kind of monopoly. It was Sarnoff who convinced Young that the biggest opportunity for radio would be not as an overseas communications tool but as a domestic entertainment medium. In January of 1920, he had sent a twenty-eight-page memo to Young proposing the creation of what he called a Radio Music Box, an idea that he said he had been honing for the past five years. Hugo Gernsback's magazines had been filled with predictions of radio as an entertainment device for at least that long, but Sarnoff was now

in a unique position to make it all happen. In his memo, he forecasted that RCA could sell a million such radios within three years—
but only if the company were to move quickly.

As a first order of business, RCA's patent portfolio needed to
be expanded. In particular, it did not own the rights to the "audion"
tube, a cornerstone invention that enabled modern radios to receive
signals from great distances. The audion had been invented by Lee
De Forest, a minister's son from Alabama. Hugo Gernsback, among
others, often referred to De Forest as the real "father of radio broadcasting," because his achievement was more important than Marconi's when it came to building tube radios for households, but De
Forest, strapped for cash, had since sold his patent to AT&T, and
Sarnoff knew that RCA couldn't dominate radio without it. Sarnoff
urged Owen Young, the chairman of RCA, to obtain the rights to the
audion and many other key patents from AT&T in return for 10 percent of RCA stock. The deal was done.

A similar agreement was struck with Westinghouse, which was
rapidly expanding into broadcasting. The household appliance maker
set up the world's first regular broadcasting station, KDKA of Pittsburgh, and built several other radio stations on the top of its manufacturing plants. By 1920, KDKA made history by broadcasting live
returns of a presidential election, telling listeners that Republican
Warren Harding had defeated Democrat James Cox and his running
mate, Franklin Roosevelt.

What's more, Westinghouse owned several crucial transmission
circuit patents that it had purchased from Edwin Howard Armstrong, who ranked with De Forest as another key inventor of modern radio. The son of a middle-class New York family, Armstrong
was already growing wealthy from the proceeds his inventions yielded.
Most important, Armstrong invented "regeneration," a circuit that
greatly amplified signal strength and made long-range transmission
possible. For exclusive rights to its patent portfolio, Westinghouse

received about 20 percent of RCA stock. In return for an additional
4 percent of RCA, Sarnoff obtained key antenna patents from United
Fruit, which had developed valuable antennae to communicate with
its Latin American banana boats. After the stock-for-patent swaps,
GE still retained the largest block of RCA shares, about 30 percent.
The remaining 36 percent was distributed to executives and brokerage houses.

RCA now controlled everything on the board, from Baltic Avenue
to Boardwalk, creating a true radio monopoly, and Sarnoff was the
man who had instigated RCA's position in this fledgling industry.
RCA thus became more than just a corporation. It was built like a
trust, in the old-style tradition of the Rockefellers, the Carnegies,
and the Vanderbilts. Critics called it a "combine." It was a capitalist
machine that controlled more than 2,000 patents and had no competition anywhere in sight.

Everything was neatly planned, with RCA acting as the coordinating body and sales agent for radio receivers, transmitters, and
other gear. AT&T, GE, and Westinghouse would share in the manufacturing. Bureaucratic by design, the radio combine came complete with coordinating committees and governing boards.

In the months following the Dempsey fight in 1921, demand for
radio sets materialized with an unexpected ferocity. It took decades
for the electric light, the telephone, and the automobile to reach
millions of households, but with radio, there was no need for new
infrastructure, such as roads or wires to people's homes. It seemed
to catch on at the speed of sound.

Even with their methodical planning and negotiating, Sarnoff
and RCA were caught off guard in 1922. It took months to ramp up
production of RCA's new Radiola sets and get them to dealers. Meanwhile, new vacuum tube sets with speakers were introduced by RCA
rivals, and they began flying off the shelves at department stores
and electronics dealers. More than 200 set makers and 5,000 parts

distributors sprung up practically overnight. Suddenly, there were new radio brands, the most notable of which were from the Philadelphia Storage Battery Company, or Philco, and a Chicago electronics firm named Zenith. Technically, none of these companies were operating legally, since RCA held all the patents. But what could it do in the face of such chaos?

Radio wasn't just a business; it was a craze. Getting into broadcasting seemed too cheap and easy for one corporation to control it. Transmitters were too affordable to buy, and operating them was too simple. A cover of Hugo Gernsback's *Radio News* magazine captured it perfectly, when it depicted a cartoon monkey wearing headphones, operating a giant transmitter. The U.S. Department of Commerce had approved licenses for dozens of new stations. Audiences in New York City, Schenectady, Pittsburgh, Springfield (Massachusetts), Boston, Chicago, and Los Angeles were exploding. Program schedules were appearing in local newspapers across the country.

Pretty soon there were hundreds of applicants for new radio licenses, plus hundreds more that operated without a license on pirated wavelengths, often leading to airwave wars and legal battles. The government and the courts were backlogged. Anyone who could sing a few notes, play a few tunes, or read aloud formed lines out the doors of studios, often spilling into the streets. The airwaves were supposedly owned by the public, and in Chicago, mobs formed demanding airtime. Everyone except mimes wanted in on the action.

Someone had to bring order to the industry. Someone had to subdue the mob that was running away with the radio business. Someone had to enforce the patents. Sarnoff, already the head of RCA's patent committee, was the logical choice to assume the role, and he jumped at the chance. In the spirit of the most wildly unpopular law of the day, Sarnoff would institute a prohibition in the radio industry.

By this time, Sarnoff was married, and his mother had been the matchmaker. At her neighborhood synagogue, she met the mother of a French immigrant family, and the two schemed to bring together their son and their daughter. Lizette Hermant was blonde, slim, and fair-skinned, and when they met for a blind date, David was instantly attracted to her French accent, her quick wit, and her relaxed temperament. She knew nothing about radio, and he knew no French. "So what else could we do?" Sarnoff later said. They were married on the Fourth of July in a Bronx synagogue and moved into a house in leafy Mount Vernon, just north of the city. Shortly after receiving his promotion, Sarnoff rolled into their driveway behind the wheel of their first car, a Lincoln.

The suburban lifestyle was not for him. In his new, more intense role at RCA, Sarnoff was spending almost all of his waking hours, including most weekends, at the office. He came to begrudge the time wasted commuting by train back and forth. Besides, he didn't particularly enjoy the outdoors or the peace and quiet, so selling the house made perfect sense. The couple moved back to Manhattan into a spacious apartment on the Upper East Side.

At the office, Sarnoff orchestrated his patent clampdown. He couldn't sue everyone at once. Besides, most radio companies were fly-by-night operations that wouldn't be around to pay up even if they lost. He had to pick his targets carefully. In a federal court, he launched a lawsuit against A. H. Grebe, one of the biggest radio brands at the time. He also put a squeeze on distributors and dealers. RCA would now refuse to sell tubes and parts to dealers that didn't carry RCA's entire line of radios, and anyone who wanted a replacement tube had to return the used, burned-out tube for credit. It was a way of trying to shutter the black market for parts to build infringing sets.

The judge took one look at the RCA lawsuit against Grebe, and he immediately slapped an injunction on the smaller company. The case was clear. RCA had the patents, and Grebe didn't. The injunction made it impossible for Grebe to continue, and the company almost went out of business. The bosses at RCA liked what they saw. Sarnoff had committed his first public execution.

Immediately, a group of independent radio makers formed an association to fight back in the press and to lobby Washington to take action against the RCA patent pool. The president of Zenith, Eugene McDonald, spearheaded the effort. His criticism of RCA as a monopolist and a predator often veered to personal attacks on Sarnoff that were tinged with anti-Semitic euphemisms of the era, such as his references to Sarnoff's "Russian tricks." The attacks stung and created a huge public relations crisis. The RCA radio combine, according to the *New York Times*, served "to intimidate the trade and to make the evasion of anti-trust laws possible."

This is when Sarnoff began spending more and more time cultivating his image. To head off the emerging caricature as the repressive bully of broadcasting, he began granting interviews and speaking at important functions. He told everyone who would listen about his immigrant background, about his heroic role in the *Titanic* episode, and about how he engineered the Dempsey broadcast. He especially delighted in dusting off a copy of a memo that he claimed he wrote in 1915, but the original document was never found. In that memo, he predicted all the things about radio that were now coming true. He said the only thing he got wrong was that the radio was catching on even faster than he had forecasted.

The message to Sarnoff's enemies and potential rivals couldn't be clearer. Here was a man who could foresee and then mold the future according to his will. At the same time, he could rewrite the past to the way he wanted it to be remembered. He became the personification of the radio combine itself. If you got on the wrong side of Sarnoff, he could steamroll right over you and see to it that no one looked back on your remains.

Philo T. Farnsworth, age twenty-two, at his Green Street Lab in San Francisco in 1928, flanked by his original financial backers, Leslie Gorrell (left) and George Everson (right).

CHAPTER THREE

Community Chest

PHILO T. FARNSWORTH'S FATHER DIED IN THE BITTER WINTER OF 1924. After selling the ranch in Rigby, Idaho, and moving the family back to Utah to be closer to relatives, Lewis Farnsworth caught pneumonia while driving an open wagon through a blinding blizzard, and he never recovered. His wife, Serena, sank into a depression so deep she couldn't get out of bed for three months. Their eldest son was crushed. More than anything, Philo had wanted to prove to his father that he wasn't odd, that he could accomplish great things.

After a period of mourning, Philo remained determined to go to college. The only way he could think of to pay for it was to join the navy and have it foot the bill. On his entrance application, he entered his name as Phil Farnsworth. When he was a kid, bullies used to poke fun at him, often calling him Fido. Philo never thought this was very amusing. So he dropped the *o*, semi-officially. Being mocked for his name was the last thing he wanted in the military.

From then on, he was Phil. At navy boot camp in San Diego, Phil grew muscular and tan from doing drills in the summer sun.

But he quit the navy when he found out that if you develop a new idea while working for the military, you have to give up ownership rights. In other words, if he invented something as a navy officer, the U.S. government would hold the patent. He felt he had no choice but to obtain an honorable discharge. With the help of the navy chaplain, he cited his mother's claim of widow's hardship and got himself released from service, enrolling instead at Brigham Young University, the Provo, Utah, college administered by the Mormon Church.

Thanks to student loans and a janitor job he found on campus, Farnsworth was able to manage paying the balance of the tuition for his freshman year in college, during which he took not only math and physics but drama and public speaking too. After trying out for the university's chamber music orchestra, he was assigned to be the first violin. He also confided in a pair of math and science professors, telling them about his idea for electronic television. They offered encouragement and help with his research into the state of the art in electromagnetics and other topics, but nothing practical was happening. He wouldn't be able to move ahead on the idea without money, and none of the odd jobs he held were yielding enough funds to support himself, let alone his family or his invention.

Finding work was especially urgent now that his father was gone. By the spring of 1926, Farnsworth was at a low point. The busy student often lacked enough money to eat, and the muscular physique that he gained in the navy was giving way to a gaunt form. Everything was falling apart financially, and it was clear that the nineteen-year-old could no longer afford to stay in school. He could think of nothing else to do but to drop out to work full-time. That's what he did, registering at a local job placement office.

At the job placement agency, Farnsworth was assigned to work in Salt Lake City, at the regional headquarters of a national charitable organization. It had nothing to do with television and the assignment was only temporary, but at least the pay was acceptable. In fact, it turned out to be such a pleasant place to work that he helped his sister Agnes and her high school friend Pem Gardner, plus Pem's brother Cliff Gardner, get jobs there too. Thus, at the beginning of May 1926, while David Sarnoff was collecting all the properties required to complete a fierce industrial monopoly, Philo T. Farnsworth was working for something called the Community Chest.

By chance, the job proved to be an important step toward his future. After a long day at work preparing a fund-raising mailing to local businesses, Farnsworth was sitting around a large table with Cliff Gardner, as well as the two men who ran the Community Chest project. George Everson was a dapper dresser with a stylish mustache, and Leslie Gorrell was a fair-haired man with a charming personality who spent his weekends golfing. Everson was in his forties, Gorrell in his thirties, and both were well connected, due to their fund-raising campaigns targeted to businesses all over the West.

Everyone was having a relaxed conversation, just getting to know one another a little bit, when Everson asked Farnsworth whether he planned on finishing school.

"No," said Farnsworth, "I can't afford it. Actually, I've been trying to find a way to finance an invention of mine, but it's pretty tough. In fact, I'm so discouraged that I think I'll write up my idea for *Science and Invention* magazine. I imagine I could get a hundred dollars for it." This, of course, would be tantamount to giving up his hopes, as a disclosure in such a prominent magazine would mean the idea would no longer be eligible for a patent.

"Well, what's your idea?" Gorrell asked.

"It's a television system," came the reply.

"A television system?" said Everson.

"It's a way of sending pictures through the air the same way as we do sound."

"Where'd you get that idea?"

Farnsworth launched into his story, and by the end of his tale, it was getting late. Everyone was tired, and neither Gorrell nor Everson asked about the technical details. The two men regarded the whole thing as little more than "the interesting daydream of an ambitious youngster," as Everson later wrote. At Farnsworth's insistence, they promised to keep the idea under their hats.

Everson probably would have dropped the whole matter, but Gorrell had taken some college courses in engineering, and the more he thought about it, the more curious he became. A few days later, he asked Farnsworth for a more technical explanation. Afterward, he approached Everson. "This television scheme of Phil's has merit," Gorrell said. "You ought to talk to him about it."

The two men asked Farnsworth out to dinner. Everson would later state that his casual interest in the concept led to "one of the most interesting evenings I ever spent." To Everson, the most remarkable aspect of it all was watching the personality of this quiet, under-nourished nineteen-year-old change right before his eyes. Farnsworth's speech went from "halting" to "fluent" to "eloquent." His eyes suddenly "began burning with eagerness and conviction." Everson saw this kid burst out of his cocoon and take on the colors of "a supersalesman," as he put it.

The next line of questioning was an obvious one: if it's such a great idea, aren't other people working on it? On this score, Farnsworth knew everything there was to know, at least everything that was in the public record at the time. He told the men that he had spent hours at the BYU library reading all the technical journals and magazines. He explained that there were four men leading the development of television at the time. Two of them, Herbert Ives at

Bell Laboratories and Ernst Alexanderson at General Electric, were respected scientists at giant corporations. The other two, John Logie Baird of London and Charles Francis Jenkins of Baltimore, were independent inventors.

"They are all barking up the wrong tree," Farnsworth declared. He explained that they were all trying to develop mechanical television, using a spinning disk to scan images. This will never work, he said. Television must be entirely electronic. Scanning, transmitting, and re-creating a sharp moving picture on a screen requires speeds that are so fantastic that this can be done only by manipulating electrons in vacuum tubes.

Farnsworth then described his darkest fear, that someone else would beat him to it, that at any moment he would pick up a magazine to read about how someone else patented the invention of electronic television. Neither Gorrell nor Everson knew anything about the patent process, but they asked how much it might cost to develop the idea so that a patent could be obtained.

"It's hard to say," Farnsworth replied, "but I should think five thousand dollars would be enough." He had never mentioned such a large sum before. That kind of money could buy a big house.

This was an era of wild speculation on Wall Street, and Everson revealed that he had dreams of making a killing. "I have about six thousand dollars in a special account in San Francisco," he said. "This is about as wild a gamble as I can imagine. I'll put the money up. If I win, great. But if I lose it all, I won't squawk."

And so the three men drew up a partnership agreement around the big table at the Community Chest office. Everson threw his $6,000 into the pot. Farnsworth agreed to work full-time on developing his idea to the point that qualified people could evaluate it, all the while receiving living expenses of $200 per month, which was more money than he had ever made. Gorrell, in recognition of his role in recognizing this as a worthy idea, would be along for the ride. If all the money was lost, Gorrell would simply reimburse Everson for fronting his share.

The new partnership, named alphabetically, was called Everson, Farnsworth & Gorrell. The young inventor would own 50 percent of the venture, with the other half being divided up equally between the two investors. After an attorney checked it out, the deal was done.

Pem Gardner was the first person Farnsworth told about the new partnership. Not only was she Agnes's best friend, but she had also become Phil's girlfriend. Agnes had first introduced the two a year and a half earlier, when Phil was about to enter BYU. Five-foot-two with a slim figure, Pem had short brown hair and a devastating smile, with high cheekbones and a hint of mischief. Her real name was Elma, but nobody except her mother called her that. Her nickname seemed to suit her much better.

While he was in college, Phil didn't see much of Pem. During Christmas vacation, however, Phil threw what was known as a "radio party" at the family's house. Now working for a short stint at a local department store, Phil had the job of delivering radios to and rigging elaborate antennae onto customers' homes. Big antennae were needed because the nearest commercial stations were broadcasting from Cincinnati and Los Angeles. For the party, Phil borrowed the most expensive tube radio from the store and invited a bunch of his classmates. Agnes urged her brother to invite Pem, and he agreed.

For much of the evening, the guests sat on chairs and sofas, drinking punch and staring at the radio, which stood nearly two feet high and was housed in a dark wooden cabinet, oval at the top and with two tuning knobs at the bottom.

Phil made a remark that seemed to amuse Pem. Isn't it funny, he said, that people watch the radio, as if there were something to

see. The guests nodded and shrugged their shoulders. It was actually very common then to watch the radio, and Phil's classmates saw
nothing unusual in doing so.

At one point in the evening, the voice from the Los Angeles station announced that the next three songs would be played for Phil
Farnsworth and his party in Provo, Utah. The group burst into ani-
mated chitchat and huddled close to the radio to listen and watch
more intently. Afterward, Phil tuned the dial to the Cincinnati station, and the announcer there dedicated another set of tunes to Phil
Farnsworth and friends. Phil explained how he had written to the
stations with his requested songs and airtimes. His friends seemed
enormously impressed, but none more so than Pem. Yet Phil could
hardly think of anything to say to her directly.

The entire winter went by, and Phil still hadn't invited Pem out
on a date. One day, Pem's older sister Verona told her that she was
going off with her boyfriend, Bill, on a picnic outing next Saturday
to a hot springs resort area in a canyon outside town. Bill had a car,
and Verona suggested to Pem that she should come along for the
ride, and that she should ask Phil to join her.

Pem shook her head. "I've never asked a man out on a date
before," she protested, "and I'm not going to start now."

Instead, Pem and her sister worked up a little ploy. Pem would
ask her friend Agnes to go as well, and Pem would offer to bring her
older brother Cliff to keep Agnes company. Agnes, of course, would
ask her brother Phil if he wanted to go too.

When Bill, Verona, Cliff, and Pem came rolling by to pick up
Agnes and Phil that Saturday, the sky was a clear blue, and the first
hint of spring was in the air. Phil had his hair combed straight
back, and he wore a light suit with a bright yellow tie. Pem was
dressed in homemade clothes, a tan tweed skirt that ended with a
flare at the knees, along with a matching jacket. She had teased a
curl of her hair in the shape of a cute little hook on her forehead.

The two new passengers squeezed into the roadster, and Bill drove everyone off.

When they arrived at the picnic area, they came upon an empty dance hall. They all got out of the car to check it out. The door had been left unlocked, and no one was inside. At the far end of the shiny wooden floor was a nickelodeon jukebox. Bill went over, took a nickel from his pocket, dropped it into the machine, and pushed some buttons. The jukebox had been stocked with all the latest music, and the syncopated ragtime jazz of the new James P. Johnson hit, "The Charleston," blared from the speakers. Bill and Verona already knew the steps to the dance of the same name, and they taught everyone else how to do it. They kicked their heels back and out, bent their knees up and down, and raised their elbows and palms high. Phil and Pem took to it immediately. And pretty soon, all six of them were dancing wildly, song after song after song.

The lyrics they were hearing that day were overflowing with optimism. "Though April showers may come your way, they bring the flowers that bloom in May." Troubles were only temporary in these songs, and good times were always around the corner. The songs weren't just lively; they expressed a revolt against everything traditional, against the stiff, patriotic, and corny tunes of the previous decade, against the very morals of their parents' generation. "What's the use of Prohibition?" asked one song. "You produce the same condition." A popular rebellion was in the air, based on the right to party.

It was "the era of wonderful nonsense," according to one journalist. And it was best expressed in absurd songs such as Eddie Cantor's rendition of "Yes! We Have No Bananas!" The love songs they were dancing to were often about a previously taboo subject, finally out in the open. "If you knew Susie, like I know Susie, Oh what a girl," came the voice of Al Jolson from the jukebox, "There's none so classy, as this fair lassie, Oh, Oh! Holy Moses, what a chassis!" Then came a song called "Paddlin' Madelin' Home," about a boy and girl who sneak off together at night in a canoe. Compared to the past, the songs were so uninhibited and free that they were practically obscene.

One razzmatazz number began with crazy lyrics, a jaunty ukulele rhythm, and a bouncy beat designed to whip dancers into a frenzy. "I just saw a maniac, maniac, maniac, wild! Jumping like a jumping jack, jumping jack, jumping jack, child!" And the chorus seemed perfect, as if it were written for the moment, for it fit the description of Phil's date to a T. "Five foot two, eyes of blue, But oh, what those five foot could do. Has anybody seen my girl?" This girl was bringing out a new Phil Farnsworth. He was always musical, but he never let loose quite like this. He seemed to be having more fun in this single afternoon than he had had in all the days of his life put together.

On the way home, everyone in the car kept right on singing. Pem mentioned to Phil that she played piano, and Cliff said that he played trombone. So Phil invited himself and his violin over to their house for the following Saturday "to jam it up," as he put it, and they all agreed that it was a great idea. Phil was finally thinking about something other than his growing obsession with electronic television. He took to calling her Pemmie, but he kept his ideas about television secret from this new girl so as not to scare her away.

The jam sessions continued at the Gardner house Saturday morning after Saturday morning during Phil's freshman year in college. Phil and Cliff became close friends, and at one point, Phil asked Cliff to go into business with him building and selling radio sets, working in cramped quarters in a radio service shop in Salt Lake City. After a while, Pem began to consider Phil more Cliff's friend than hers. Phil and Pem began going to dances on Friday nights at

BYU, but usually as part of a group, and Phil didn't dance with Pem exclusively.

On Christmas Eve, they were once again out with the whole gang, riding through a light snowfall in the backseat of Bill's roadster, when Phil put his arm around Pem and whispered into her ear. "Pem," he confessed, "I think we were meant for each other." She remarked that she didn't think he was serious about her, but he assured her that he couldn't be more so. Only later that night, when he was walking her back to her door, did Phil and Pem have their first kiss.

One Saturday morning, instead of showing up at Pem's house with his violin, Phil appeared on horseback, leading a second horse. He invited her to mount up for a surprise outing. Phil had a picnic lunch in his saddle bag, and they rode out through Provo Canyon near the mountains of what later became Sundance to an idyllic little nook called Bridal Veil Falls, named after the water falling from the rocks in a white misty veil. They took in the beauty of the green valley, the crashing waterfall, and the majestic Wasatch Mountains. Phil hitched the horses and told Pem he wanted to have a talk.

They sat down on a big flat rock, and he told her that he had something important to say, then he got up and started pacing. He explained that he had been dreaming about a way to send pictures through the air. He told her the whole story—the science magazines in the attic, his revelation in the potato field, his meeting with Mr. Tolman in high school, and his further research at BYU.

This disclosure naturally led to the question of exactly *how* Phil would go about inventing television. And that answer involved an explanation of particle physics and the bizarre properties of something called the electron that must have seemed foreign to Pem.

At one point, Phil pointed to the big rock that she was sitting on. "That rock, you see, it's not really solid."

"It's not?" Pem asked, unsure she even wanted to know anything more.

"No, it's made up of trillions of tiny moving particles."

With that, Pem seemed to get dizzy, almost falling right off.

Now, along with the news of his partnership with Everson and Gorrell, Phil had another surprise for his girlfriend. "Pemmie," Phil said in a telephone call to her home in Provo, "are you be ready to be married in three days?"

"Phil Farnsworth! You've got to be kidding! Of course I can't be married in three days!" She reminded Phil that her mother had died only four months earlier, and she needed to help her father take care of her four younger siblings. Besides, she was only eighteen years old. "I can't," she said. "I just can't."

He said that he would explain everything to everyone tomorrow at her house in Provo, and he told her to arrange for his mother and her father to meet them there at six o'clock the following evening.

At the gathering, Phil came up against a stone wall of skepticism. Undaunted, he picked through it using a plan packed with more surprises. He told the parents about the new partnership, and how the money would be able to support the couple—for a while at least. Eventually, he would make enough so that neither family would have to worry about money ever again. The wedding, he said, would happen on Thursday, the day after tomorrow. The morning after the ceremony, they would take a train to Los Angeles. Phil wanted to be near the California Institute of Technology, which not only had a great technical library but was the center of innovation for the motion picture industry, the perfect place to try to build his electronic television.

Their parents sat in stunned silence. To them, Los Angeles was the city of sin and temptation, and they were worried about the young couple's commitment to their faith. To the chagrin of their parents, neither Phil nor Pem went to church anymore; Pem found the place cold and unfriendly, while Phil was irked when some leaders of the Mormon Church joined other religious groups in taking a stand against Einstein's theory of relativity, on the faulty basis that it seemed to promote moral relativism too. Although they were not active churchgoers, Phil and Pem said they would continue to keep their faith. They wanted to be married by a local church official at the Farnsworth home. This assurance coupled with Phil's intensity eventually wore away the initial opposition. In the end, each of their surviving parents gave the couple their blessing.

The morning of May 27, 1926, was bright, sunny, and filled with flowers. Friends and relatives streamed into the house for the hastily planned ceremony. Cliff was best man, and Agnes was maid of honor. Pem walked slowly down the stairs wearing a gown of peach crepe and accordion pleats. After a short reception, the newlyweds were off, driving away in an open-air Chandler roadster that George Everson loaned to Phil for the occasion. They motored their way to Salt Lake City and checked into a modest hotel near the train station. Phil carried Pem over the threshold, but as soon as he put her down, he explained that he had to return Everson's car because the train to their future was set to leave at 6:30 A.M. the next morning.

When Phil arrived at Everson's place, the man with the money was nervous, and he engaged Phil in a lengthy, detailed discussion of the invention, the business plan, and other courses of action large and small. Their conversation went on for hours, all while Pem was waiting on her wedding bed in her gown. By the time Phil arrived back at the room, all disheveled and windblown, Pem was visibly racked with worry and self-pity at the thought of having her wedding night ruined.

To top it off, Phil opened his explanation of where he was with an attempted joke. "Pemmie," he said, embracing her and staring deeply into her eyes, "I have to tell you something." Pause. "There is another woman in my life."

Before his new bride had a chance to faint from distress and disbelief, Phil added, "And her name is Television!"

It was Phil's way of asking Pem whether she'd be willing to work with him, side by side in the laboratory, developing his idea. "This will be the only way we'll have time together," he said. "How about it?"

David Sarnoff (left) with Italian inventor Guglielmo Marconi, at
RCA's transmission center on Long Island, in 1933. Marconi's U.S.
patents were the cornerstone of RCA's monopoly over radio manufacturing in
the 1920s and '30s. (DAVID SARNOFF LIBRARY)

CHAPTER FOUR

Patently Brilliant

As Philo T. Farnsworth was fixing to set up his first television laboratory, David Sarnoff was searching for a way to lasso all the excitement surrounding radio. Stores all over the United States were now selling factory-made receivers, a sharp improvement from the mail-order radio kits that had to be assembled in basements, attics, and kitchens. Manufacturers had produced 100,000 radios in 1922, and the figure jumped to 500,000 in 1923 and more than 2 *million* by 1926. Prices for basic sets now dipped below twenty-five dollars, making radio affordable to the middle-class masses who weren't inclined to construct their own.

In the mad scramble to reach this new audience, everyone was starting stations. The *Chicago Tribune* launched WGN (for World's Greatest Newspaper), Sears started WLS (for World's Largest Store), and a preacher in Richmond began broadcasting over WLSV (Will the Lord Save Virginia?). Hospitals and colleges took to the airwaves, as did cities, towns, and states (KFKB stood for Kansas Folk Know

Best). Clothing retailers and pharmacies, banks and insurance firms, poultry farms and ice cream parlors, electronics stores and radio dealers—all had their own stations. Companies saw radio as an efficient new way to communicate with their customers, and so they began hiring announcers and technicians by the thousands.

The most popular singers and musicians were flocking to the new medium. "Bring a symphony orchestra into your home without leaving your seat," said one advertisement. One ad for radio tubes pictured a drawing of Al Jolson in black face and white lips. "Funny?" the ad exclaimed. "He's a Riot, a Laugh Factory, A Fifth Alarm! The whole nation knows his name and fame. Listen-in when next he's on the air. Radio leaps the Barriers of Time and Distance!" Over the lower-fidelity shortwave band, listeners almost everywhere were able to tune in broadcasts from as far away as London, Paris, Prague, Berlin, Rio de Janeiro, and Tokyo. Pittsburgh, Schenectady, and Springfield, Massachusetts, became virtual mega-cities because of their powerful Westinghouse and GE stations.

At the Radio Corporation of America, David Sarnoff wanted to show the world that one company towered above it all. He approved a new logo for the company, featuring a line drawing of planet Earth. In the top half of the globe was the distinct shape of North America, and the bottom half was emblazoned with the words World Wide Wireless. The logo was plastered on RCA buildings, tacked onto transmission towers, and propagated in magazine and newspaper advertisements. Sometimes abbreviated as *WWW*, it became the motto that went to the heart of David Sarnoff's vision of RCA as the leader of a global revolutionary movement.

Sarnoff's speeches became more frequent, and they were rich with authority and prophesy. "I regard radio broadcasting as a sort of cleansing instrument for the mind, just as the bathtub is for the body," he told one audience, with a straight face. "The broadcasting station makes possible, for the first time in the history of civilization, communication with hundreds and thousands, and perhaps, millions of people, simultaneously."

Just because corporations and the public fell in love with radio didn't mean they understood exactly what it was. Many people developed irrational fears over electromagnetic shock syndrome. At least one farmer complained to his local radio station that there was a dead bird on his property, and that it must have been struck down by a radio wave. "What if the wave had struck me?" he cried. Others greatly exaggerated radio's powers. The former navy secretary during the Great War made what turned out to be one of the most off-base predictions in military history. "Nobody now fears that the Japanese could deal an unexpected blow on our Pacific possessions," he said. "Radio makes such a surprise impossible."

Despite all the hoopla, despite the incredible growth, despite Sarnoff's high-minded leadership, RCA was still public enemy number one as far as the rest of the industry was concerned. The charges of monopoly escalated. The Federal Trade Commission began investigating the complaints, and it found merit to them. "The Radio Corporation [of America] apparently has the power to stifle competition in the manufacture and sale of receiving sets," noted the FTC in its 1923 report to Congress. The press kept comparing Big Radio to the reviled trusts in oil, railroads, and steel.

In the middle of all this, RCA's chairman, Owen Young, decided the company needed a new president, a new public face to ward off the attacks. Current president Edward Nally was planning to retire, and the person who would replace him had to have a stature beyond reproach. Certainly, the aggressive, brash David Sarnoff was completely wrong for the role, and he was too young besides. Not only did the company choose an outsider, but in a ploy to wrap RCA in the American flag, they chose a war hero. General James G. Harbord, now working in Washington for the U.S. War Department, was a soldier's soldier. He served as one of Teddy Roosevelt's original Rough Riders, and he described war as "a permanent factor in human life and a very noble one." The press and the Congress wouldn't dare attack RCA under the rule of this man.

Harbord knew absolutely nothing about radio when he arrived at the Woolworth Building on January 1, 1923, to command the corporation, but he met up with a willing teacher right away. Sarnoff not only taught Harbord about the technology, but also tutored him on the history of the organization, a history that Sarnoff himself was engineering. He handed Harbord memos that served as evidence of Sarnoff's visionary status. "Some of my predictions have come true," he wrote to his new boss, "and others I think will come true in time." Harbord was an excellent pupil, and he came to rely on Sarnoff without question.

To Sarnoff, the new president represented no threat to his own long-range goal. The general was thirty years his senior, and Sarnoff saw him as only a temporary guardian of the company. Of course, Sarnoff would never express his expansive dream in public, or even within RCA, as the audacity of it could only lead to trouble. Sarnoff spoke of this dream only at home, to his wife, Lizette. RCA will become an industrial empire on a par with none other, he would tell her. Someday, RCA will stand on its own, free of its corporate parent. It will be a beacon of leadership for America. And I will be the supreme leader of it all. Fiercely loyal to her husband, Lizette would just let him ramble on and on. "I never interrupt him," she would tell others.

Sarnoff's first big chance to consolidate power would come soon enough. The appointment of Harbord accomplished very little in terms of deflecting criticism of RCA's position and its business tactics. Within a few weeks, Congress moved against its own creation, empowering the FTC to file formal charges against not only RCA but the entire radio combine, which also included GE, AT&T, Westinghouse, and United Fruit. The government had taken the first step toward the decision that the radio cartel was in violation of antitrust laws.

Sarnoff needed a way out of what he saw as an absurd situation. On one hand, RCA was being lambasted for its far-reaching powers. On the other hand, its stifling bureaucracy rendered it unable to compete. Start-ups were able to get newer, better designed, and cheaper radios to market before the committees of the radio combine were even able to circulate the minutes of their meetings. RCA was being charged with being a monopoly over radio at the same time that 75 percent of the radio market was being captured by other companies.

One late night at the office, David Sarnoff was struck with an idea that he felt should have been obvious to him all along. Instead of trying to put the other radio makers out of business through expensive litigation that would only inflict tremendous damage on RCA's already fragile image, why not just license RCA's patents to anyone who wants them? The new business model was simple, and to Sarnoff's mind, quite fair: RCA would provide its entire pool of patents in return for a percentage of sales. He came up with the figure of 7.5 percent. If a radio retailed for $100, a fee of $7.50 would flow to the coffers of RCA no matter who made or sold the radio.

The plan was brilliant; it had the potential to turn RCA's biggest foes into friendly customers. Young and Harbord blessed the idea, and soon after announcing it to the industry, Sarnoff signed licensing agreements with most of RCA's biggest rivals, including Philco and Zenith. Within a short time, 90 percent of existing radio makers were under license to RCA. The plan worked so well—bringing in so much money, widening RCA's influence and stature, and diffusing, at least temporarily, the harsh image of RCA—that Sarnoff later reduced the rate to 5 percent in order to spur the sales of even more officially licensed radios.

One unintended beneficiary of RCA's new licensing plan was Hugo Gernsback. Until now, all the other radio and parts makers had been operating illegally, as they were technically in violation of RCA's patents. That thousands of manufacturers and distributors were now legit and aboveboard meant something very special to Gernsback: now, they could all advertise! And advertise they did. Within a few months, *Radio News* ballooned from a thin periodical to a phone-book-size monthly catalog of the latest and greatest gear. Gernsback's firm, the Experimenter Publishing Company, moved from its gritty offices on Fulton Street, to more elegant headquarters on Park Place, and later into swanky new digs on Fifth Avenue.

Radio was suddenly no longer just a craze but a burgeoning industry, and Sarnoff's patent-licensing scheme made RCA fabulously profitable, much more so than it could ever have been selling radios alone. After all, now its chief business wasn't merely selling boxes of tubes and wires, but rather selling intellectual property. Not even selling it. Licensing it. It could license the same idea hundreds of times, then sell it again and again. The only drawback was that patents lasted for a limited period of time, seventeen years from the date of issuance. Although RCA now controlled more than 4,000 patents, Sarnoff needed a way to keep replenishing the pool that was originally formed with the patents of Guglielmo Marconi. Under Sarnoff's plan, the patent pool would become RCA's ocean of gold.

The new economic order in the radio industry led to greater respect for inventors as well as new policies for manipulating them. To that end, Sarnoff established RCA's first research department. He hired the best engineers out of the best universities to work there. He paid them competitive salaries, provided them with ample research budgets, and offered them the chance to join his crusade to change the world, working in the most dynamic industry the world had ever seen. Scores of active young minds joined the cause.

Sarnoff issued keys to the kingdom in exchange for patent ownership. Extending the policy that was already in place at General Electric, engineers would be paid their salary, and when their work led to a patent, the corporation would seize it. After all, producing patents was the engineer's job. The scientists' names would be on the filing, but only along with the name of the real owner, RCA. To make sure this agreement was understood and enforced, the corporation would issue a check for each patent filing in the amount of one dollar, payable to the engineer. When the engineer endorsed the check and cashed it, the contract was in force.

The one-dollar-per-patent policy applied to even the brightest scientists in the lab. At GE's main research center in Schenectady, Ernst Alexanderson had become a towering figure. He was the inventor of the Alexanderson Alternator, the powerful transmitter that could broadcast signals over oceans, the very invention that had convinced the federal government to give GE the radio monopoly in the first place, leading to the birth of RCA. Yet GE simply paid Alexanderson a generous salary, plus a bonus of one dollar per patent. He never collected any royalties from his fantastic invention now in use the world over.

One RCA engineer by the name of Bill Eddy thought the one-dollar checks were an absurdity. To him, the honor of receiving the check was worth far more than the dollar itself. Each time he was issued a check, he would paste it on the wall of his working space. Like many RCA engineers, he was quite prolific in filing patent applications. Pretty soon, he proudly covered an entire wall with these checks.

Meanwhile, the comptroller in the RCA accounting department was wondering why he couldn't balance the books. After asking around, Sarnoff's finance chief found out about Eddy's wall. A team of accountants descended on Eddy's cubicle, but they couldn't pry the checks off the wall without ripping them. They tried wetting them down, but the paper still wouldn't come off the wall. Finally, they called some maintenance workers to hack down the whole section of plasterboard. They carried the wall away from the premises, dissolved the plaster in a special solution, removed the checks, waited for them to dry, took Eddy to the bank, got him to endorse the checks, gave him his small pile of bills, and balanced the books of RCA.

Under the direction of Sarnoff, RCA brought such policies to a whole new level, systematizing the process of invention as never before. Overall, the system worked quite well. With the profits from the patent pool, Sarnoff funded wide-ranging research activities, which invariably led to more innovations and patents. This process of innovation became the central focus of what Sarnoff envisioned as his future legacy: RCA must always be the leader, never a follower, perpetually at the forefront of science and engineering. If anything new and exciting happened in broadcasting, it was to be invented at RCA and brought to you personally by David Sarnoff.

For Sarnoff, the biggest challenge to his plan for a greater RCA wouldn't come from other corporations. After all, virtually everyone else in the business was already paying royalties to RCA, money that Sarnoff earmarked to fund future radio developments. By making these payments, rival radio makers were essentially relying on RCA for innovation, and they had less of an incentive to invest in their own research and development. Rather, the greatest test of RCA's complete control of the business was bound to come from outside the establishment. What if some individual came up with an important patent that threatened the RCA monopoly in some way? Sarnoff employed researchers to scan patent filings and press reports to try to nip any potential challengers in the bud.

Occasionally, of course, the lone cry of eureka still occurred. One particular challenge sprang from a source already familiar to RCA: Edwin Howard Armstrong, the independent inventor who was already well-off from the so-called regeneration patents he sold to Westinghouse and which became part of the RCA pool. While the story of the dealings between Sarnoff and Armstrong occurred over a period of many years, the roots of their ultimate clash were planted much earlier, when Sarnoff first cultivated the RCA policies dealing with patents and outside inventors.

Working at his lab at Columbia University in the early 1920s, Armstrong came up with something he called "super-regeneration," a new set of tubes that could amplify a radio signal five times greater than had been possible. When Armstrong began demonstrating it publicly, the press covered it, and Sarnoff was getting nervous. He decided to engage Armstrong directly in negotiations, with no lawyers or other middlemen present. After all, the two men had considered each other friends for years. Their friendship dated back to 1913, when the two young men spent a long, cold January night holed up in a Marconi radio shack on the New Jersey shore, testing new wireless gear and successfully receiving signals from across the Atlantic. Now, Sarnoff dispatched an invitation, and when Armstrong arrived, the two men smoked cigars in Sarnoff's office and chatted about the world they were together creating.

For Armstrong, the negotiation couldn't have gone any better. Fearful that someone else would obtain the patent and undermine the RCA monopoly, Sarnoff felt forced to make a staggering offer: $200,000 in cash, plus 60,000 shares of RCA stock. It was an offer Armstrong couldn't refuse, and in the stroke of a pen, he became the single largest individual holder of RCA stock, owning more than anyone in management, including Sarnoff himself. By the time the two men actually signed the pact in June 1922, RCA's stock doubled in price, and the shares were now worth more than the cash.

Armstrong was so exultant that he climbed up RCA's 400-foot broadcasting tower, which pointed to the sky from the top of Aeolian Hall, across from the New York Public Library. The new prince of broadcasting wiggled his way past RCA's World Wide Wireless logo to a terrifying height, pumping his fists in the air and yelling "Yahoo!" Newspaper photographers captured the moment in black and white, and the pictures were in circulation the next day.

This brazen behavior greatly disturbed Sarnoff, who viewed it as a cry for recognition. As far as he was concerned, Armstrong could have all the money in the world, but all the credit should be reserved for David Sarnoff. These pictures in the papers undermined his authority. He wrote a note warning Armstrong in the harshest of terms. "Keep away from the Aeolian Hall towers or any other property of the Radio Corporation," the letter said. "Don't take this letter as a joke because I am perfectly serious about it."

During the negotiations, Armstrong had flirted constantly with Sarnoff's beautiful, young, blonde secretary, Marion MacInnis. After one session, he whispered to her a bit of news: I'm going to celebrate my new fortune by vacationing in Europe, but when I get back I'm going to drive by in the world's most expensive car and take you for a ride. A few months later, he did just that. Armstrong arrived at RCA headquarters driving a Parisian touring car that he had purchased in France for $11,000 and had shipped back home. He parked out front, took the elevator up to Sarnoff's office, and stole the secretary right from under the nose of the boss. A few months later, Armstrong married Marion and drove her all the way to Palm Beach, Florida, for a honeymoon.

Armstrong was happy, rich, and successful, and he seemed for the moment to be a symbol of the new status of the inventor. While super-regeneration never turned out to be the big breakthrough that Armstrong promoted it to be, the deal kept RCA's monopoly intact. As it turned out, the most important part of the pact was

Armstrong's agreement to offer RCA the first option to buy all of his future inventions. Armstrong didn't know it yet, but he would pay a high price for selling out to Sarnoff so completely.

A few years later, Armstrong hit upon his greatest discovery yet. In an attempt to eliminate the ever-present static from radio broadcasts, Armstrong brainstormed a new way to modulate the airborne, electromagnetic signal known as the carrier wave. Radio worked by converting the modulations of sound into electronic impulses, which in turn modulated the height, or the amplitude, of each successive carrier wave, but engineers couldn't find a way to filter out extraneous noise from this process of amplitude modulation, or AM. In his new approach, Armstrong developed circuits to modulate the rate, or the frequency, of the carrier waves. Frequency modulation, or FM, not only eliminated static but transmitted a much wider range of sounds with high fidelity.

When Armstrong was issued five patents on his invention of FM in December of 1933, he decided it was time to demonstrate it for his old friend. Sarnoff reacted cautiously at first but later proclaimed that he instantly recognized this "revolution." Since he owned the first right of refusal on Armstrong's patents, Sarnoff chose to wait while his staff engineers conducted "tests." He didn't want to disrupt the market for AM-only radios and didn't believe customers would pay extra for better sound, and so his initial delays on FM stretched into years.

Meanwhile, RCA's own engineers were trying to re-create Armstrong's invention in their own laboratory. By now, RCA's "first right" provision had expired, so Armstrong was able to license FM to Zenith and other radio makers. He did so, but FM wasn't going to catch on without the supreme industry leader behind it. Sarnoff's staff spent years attempting to engineer a way around Armstrong's patents, but by 1940 the corporation decided that it needed a license after all, and so Sarnoff offered Armstrong $1 million for it.

Armstrong had become so furious over RCA's delays and what he saw as a lowball sum of money that he flatly refused Sarnoff's terms.

When RCA proceeded to market FM without a license from its inventor, Armstrong filed a patent-infringement suit against RCA. Sarnoff did everything in his power to prolong and delay the case, and it took five years to get Sarnoff to give a pretrial deposition, in which he stated that "RCA had done more to develop FM than anybody in this country, including Armstrong." At that deposition, wrote author Tom Lewis, "those watching Armstrong noted that his look was one of unmitigated hatred for the man who was twisting the truth as never before."

By then, Armstrong's patents were expiring, and the cost of the delays and litigation had depleted almost all of his millions of dollars in personal wealth built up over an entire career. Armstrong's lawyers pleaded with him to settle the case, and they came up with a figure of $3.4 million as the amount RCA should have already paid to Armstrong in FM royalties thus far. Weary of the legal battle, Armstrong agreed that he would settle for something close to that amount. When the lawyers approached Sarnoff with a proposal, however, Sarnoff offered to pay Armstrong just $200,000, a stunningly low bid. With the unanimous consent of his lawyers, Armstrong rejected the settlement.

A few weeks later, at his apartment in the River House on East Fifty-second Street, Armstrong wrote a note in pencil on a yellow legal pad:

Dearest Marion: I am heartbroken because I cannot see you once again. . . . I would give my life to turn back to the time when we were so happy and free. My estate is solvent, especially if RCA comes through. Also, the Telephone Company should pay something, for they have been using my inventions. God keep you and may the Lord have mercy on my soul.

Then Edwin Howard Armstrong put on his overcoat, scarf, and gloves, walked straight out his bedroom window, and plunged thirteen stories to his death. A doorman spotted the mangled body the next morning on the roof of the River Club down below.

Sarnoff was shaken by Armstrong's suicide, and he immediately moved to deny any culpability. "I did not kill Armstrong!" Sarnoff exclaimed to Carl Dreher, a common acquaintance. Of course, it would be unfair to place the blame squarely on Sarnoff's shoulders, as he did not push Armstrong out the window, but there was no doubt that Armstrong suffered through a prolonged period of injustice at the hands of Sarnoff. After the suicide, an arbitrator ordered RCA to pay Marion Armstrong the sum of $1.5 million, and she later collected millions more in back royalties from RCA and others on her late husband's patents.

While Armstrong's death didn't occur until 1954, it was already becoming apparent by the mid-1920s that lone inventors would be waging a nearly unwinnable war if they tried to challenge David Sarnoff and the new system of corporate-controlled innovation. This was something Philo T. Farnsworth would soon learn the hard way.

*Philo T. Farnsworth, nineteen, with his wife, Pem, eighteen, in front of
a train mock-up near Los Angeles shortly after their wedding in May 1926.*
(FARNSWORTH FAMILY ARCHIVES)

CHAPTER FIVE

Going Hollywood

To Mr. and Mrs. Philo T. Farnsworth, everything about their train ride to Los Angeles seemed romantic and exotic. Never before had they tasted food so rich or enjoyed service so prompt. Everything was taken care of by Negro stewards in white coats, among the first black people that either of them had ever seen. After dinner, Phil and Pem retired to their sleeping quarters, where they lost their virginity on a rumbling bed inside a clanking compartment aboard the mighty Southern Pacific Railroad. In the morning, Phil opened the curtains and nudged Pem awake to show her how the scenery outside had changed. The august mountains that they'd known all their lives had given way to palm trees and orange groves.

Back in the spring of 1926, Al Jolson's original hit "California Here I Come" was all over the radio, and this young couple was experiencing the actual feeling expressed in the song. California was a place where anything was possible, a cerebral state of golden dreams, "where bowers of flowers bloom in the sun," as the song goes. Phil and Pem could hardly wait to get their new lives started.

Upon their arrival in the sprawling city, they quickly found a furnished apartment on North New Hampshire Street in Hollywood for fifty dollars per month, including utilities, on the ground floor of a four-unit apartment house. Being in the middle of movie country was exciting for Farnsworth, but not because of the stars. Hollywood, at this particular moment, was on the cusp of perhaps its biggest technological transformation. That summer, Warner Brothers staged a public demonstration of film that coordinated sound with motion, based on technology licensed from Western Electric, a subsidiary of AT&T. Within a few days, Warner's stock leaped from eight to sixty-five dollars per share, only to settle back down when it was discovered that these new projector-fused-to-a-phonograph contraptions didn't always work so well. But as the kinks were being ironed out, Warner Brothers went about signing Al Jolson to act and sing in a screen adaptation of the Broadway hit *The Jazz Singer*. Released a year later, the film bulldozed the business of silent pictures and marked the start of the sound era. The hopes of learning the science behind such breakthroughs was the stuff that had drawn the aspiring inventor here in the first place.

He spent his first few days in the Los Angeles Library, immersed in books about electronics and the motion picture sciences. He had to learn about the workings of the human eye, as he had to figure out how many frames per second needed to flash before the eye in order to fool it into seeing fluid motion. Movie projectors back then typically operated at twenty-four frames per second, and so Farnsworth supposed that television receivers would have to flash imagery at least that fast. That was a tall order; it was one thing to flick frames of film past a lens but quite another to capture sound and motion, transmit it, reassemble it, and represent it on a screen miles away.

After his stint of reading and thinking, Farnsworth went about gathering materials and supplies, scattering whatever he could find on the dining room table of their Hollywood flat, which now would double as a makeshift research laboratory. He brought home lamps, crystals, prisms, lenses, different types of wires, a barrel of shellac, alcohol-based varnish thinner, a hand-cranked coil winder, an electric generator, and all sorts of tools. Before long, equipment was coming out of closets and overflowing into the backyard.

Everson and Gorrell soon arrived in town, and when they came over to the apartment, they not only seemed impressed by all the activity but were perfectly willing to help in any way they could. They went around the city securing tubes and hoses and other equipment that typically was used by those who made moonshine in their basements. They also went with Farnsworth to visit a blower of scientific glass instruments. Farnsworth drew up a sketch of a custom-made tube that was to have a closed, flat, bulb shape on one end and a round, open mouth on the other.

Back at the apartment, Everson volunteered for the task of winding the coils and fastening them in position with gobs of gooey, pungent shellac. The coils would later be attached near the open mouth of the custom-built tube. Everson was winding away out in the backyard, making a mess of his suit, while everyone else was working in the dinning room, under hot lamps, with the curtains drawn, when the front doorbell rang.

Pem answered it, only to be startled by two burly officers from the Los Angeles Police Department flashing his badge in her face and launching into an accusation. "We've had a report that someone is operating a *still* around here," he shouted.

As Phil invited him in to take a look around, Everson spied the cop and decided he wanted no part of this. His hands were dripping with stinky, sticky, orange-colored goo, so he put them up in the air and fled, attempting to escape out the back door when he was nabbed on the spot by two more policemen. One of them chided, "Oh, no you don't, buddy!"

That cop escorted Everson back inside and joined with his partner to search through all the equipment. Basically, the officers ransacked the place. Farnsworth started explaining to one of the officers that he wasn't making booze but doing something completely different. He was trying to build an electronic television. The cop looked at him as if he were nuts. Finally, when these examples of L.A.'s finest became convinced that there wasn't any drinking alcohol there, they shook their heads. "They're doing some kooky thing called electric vision, or something," mumbled one of them. "They ain't got no still in here."

The coils that Everson was working with would serve to guide and focus the electron beam through the vacuum tube. When the proper signal was applied to these coils, they would develop a magnetic field that would deflect the beam to an anode, a positively charged metallic finger. In time, junior high school kids would learn to create electromagnets such as this one by attaching one end of a wire to a dry cell battery and wrapping the other end to a big steel nail. When the circuit was completed, the nail would be able to pick up paper clips.

Farnsworth was using an electromagnet in a far more complex way. What he was planning could be understood by comparing it to the workings of a somewhat similar invention developed years later. The laser, according to the letters that form its name, works through "light amplification by stimulated emission of radiation." A tube is filled with a mixture of gas, typically the elements argon and krypton. When a stream of electricity is shot into this compound, the molecules vibrate and bump into one another in such a way that they incite a highly concentrated beam of electromagnetic radiation. Farnsworth wanted to shoot electricity not into a mixture of gas but into a vacuum, into the absence of any gas at all. And whereas laser beams are typically guided by mirrors, Phil would rely on the electromagnet that Everson helped put together to manipulate his electron beams, or cathode rays. It would do to these rays what a person does with a nozzle on a hose to a stream of water as they play it back and forth across their lawn, except in a far more detailed way.

No one really expected any of this to work on the first attempt, and so no one was too surprised when a summer of trial and error flew by. Everson and Gorrell had left L.A. for business in other cities, and Phil and Pem were having the time of their lives in the meantime. They had full use of Everson's car when he was away. Dining out in a restaurant, they once spotted the actor Boris Karloff at the next table, and he looked even spookier in person. One day, Pem was out for a walk when a terrified woman being chased by a knife-wielding thug suddenly flashed by her. When she looked around in a panic for help, she was relieved to spot a camera crew filming the scene.

One night, at Grauman's Chinese Theater, the couple attended the premier of a movie called *The Sheik*, an event that came complete with a parade of stars in limousines and crisscrossing searchlights shining to the sky. When the film was over, its star, Rudolf Valentino, appeared on stage to thunderous applause. As he took a bow, he knocked into a huge Chinese vase, and in trying to keep it from toppling, he lost his balance and fell straight down into the orchestra pit, ending up trapped in a bass drum.

As the Farnsworths were enjoying the L.A. lifestyle, the funds fueling the partnership were dwindling. Farnsworth placed much of his hopes in the special tube that the glassblower had been working on for more than two months. He hoped it would become the basis of what Farnsworth called his Image Dissector. Essentially, it would be the first all-electronic television camera. It was to work exactly as he drew it on the blackboard and in his notebook for Mr. Tolman back at Rigby High School, capturing an image through a lens and converting the light into electromagnetic impulses.

When the tube was finished, he brought it home. Inside was an anode and a cathode, forming what he hoped would be the first complete electronic television system, including a camera, transmitter, and a smaller reception tube that would accept the signal. If it would only project but a single ray of light, Farnsworth would be overjoyed beyond belief. He invited Everson and Gorrell over to the apartment to witness the results of an entire summer's work. When everyone was assembled, and everything was connected, Farnsworth switched on the electrical generator.

First, everyone heard a loud bang. That was followed by a few pops, then a slow hissing and a sizzle. Pungent smoke rose from the assortment of devices. By the time Farnsworth could shut the power off, it was too late. He had blown up the entire contraption, including his prized Image Dissector.

Farnsworth was stricken. He was hugely disappointed—and worse—he dreaded the reaction from his two investors. Pointing to the pile of smoky junk, he said, "That's all I have to show you for your investment."

As Everson looked over the mess, Gorrell deflected his attention away from it. "It's not the end of the world," he said. "We still have Phil's ideas. Let's sit down and decide what we can do about it."

The partners cleared away the remains of the experiment, transferring the burned tubes and gnarled wires into boxes. Then they sat down at the table to assess their situation.

There was just enough money left to hire a patent attorney. If they drew up a set of schematic diagrams and a detailed explanation of the invention, perhaps the attorney could tell them how they should proceed next. Phil and Pem and Les Gorrell went to work immediately on more polished drawings, while Everson called around for recommendations. Luckily, they were in the right city. Because of all the litigation and conflict surrounding the inventions at the center of the motion picture industry, Los Angeles had several law firms with the right kind of experience. The firm that came most highly recommended was Lyon & Lyon, run by two brothers named Leonard and Richard.

When Everson went to meet with Leonard Lyon in August 1926, he told a condensed version of the Philo T. Farnsworth story and described the basic idea behind the invention. After considering all this information, Lyon appeared quite intrigued. "If you have what you think you have," the attorney said, "you've got the world by the tail. But if you don't have what you think you have, the sooner you find this out the better." He recommended bringing Farnsworth in for a meeting. He also invited his brother, Richard, the firm's technical brain, as well as an electrical engineering expert from Cal Tech, to help in the evaluation.

The meeting lasted an entire afternoon, and once again Farnsworth rose to the occasion. He put on the most passionate performance of his idea yet, explaining it all with a brilliant clarity and answering every question with confidence and precision. The two technical experts agreed that they needed to conduct a patent search to be absolutely certain, but they were reasonably sure that there had never been a patent filing like this.

The questions soon turned to the applications and the potential uses for this invention. The more Richard Lyon heard Farnsworth talk about the possibilities for television—the instant news, the constant entertainment, the immediate transmission of human events— the more engrossed he became, until the attorney was visibly agitated. "This idea, this idea, this idea . . ." He kept repeating it, pacing back and forth, flailing his hands about in the air. He stopped to look Farnsworth squarely in the eye, not only with an expression of excitement, but also with a tinge of horror, as if Farnsworth were some kind of Frankenstein. The attorney seemed to place on the inventor's shoulders a new burden of responsibility that the inventor may not have fully considered. "This idea," he said, "it's . . . monstrous . . . absolutely monstrous!"

Back at his apartment in Hollywood, Philo T. Farnsworth and his two investors were in an urgent meeting around the dining room table. With the last of the original money from the partnership now in the hands of the patent attorneys, they had to raise more cash in a hurry. George Everson said he had anticipated all along the need to seek backing from bankers. What he wanted was a dollar amount. How much would it cost to develop a working electronic television system?

As usual, Farnsworth was optimistic. He figured to have his television up and running within six months and then would require another six months to fine-tune it. "I need a thousand dollars per month for twelve months," Farnsworth said. To a twenty-year-old in 1926, that was plenty of time and a ton of money.

"Phil!" said Everson. "Be realistic! We've been spending money at twice that rate this summer."

Leslie Gorrell was stunned by the kid's self-assurance. "With that kind of confidence," he said, "how can we lose?"

Everson and Gorrell estimated they would need at least double what Farnsworth was asking for, and they told him they would go out looking for $25,000 in fresh capital first thing in the morning. With that, they each shook hands with their young genius and left.

Phil went into the kitchen to tell Pem the latest development. Living with the constant fear that the entire project could close down at any moment, they were reassured by the faith of Farnsworth's business partners. To celebrate, Phil took out his violin, Pem sat down at the piano, and they played music well into the night.

Weeks went by with no luck. Everson and Gorrell went from one bank to the next, but no one in the Los Angeles financial community was enticed enough by the idea to put any money into it, and anyone involved with motion picture money didn't want to fund something that smelled like competition. Everyone kept referring them to someone else, until they ended up in the plush Santa Barbara office of Max Fleischmann, the famous yeast magnate, who seemed interested but didn't understand a word of Everson's explanation. "We have made a success of yeast," Fleischmann declared. "Bacteria I know, but electronics—I wouldn't know an electron if I met one on the street! I'm tempted, but my judgment says I'd better stick to bacteria."

After striking out so badly, Everson had to break the bad news to Farnsworth. "I've raised a lot of money in my day, Phil," he said, "but it's a lot easier to raise money for social welfare than it is to find backing for speculation." Yet every time Everson and Gorrell made up their minds that it was impossible to continue, Farnsworth somehow persuaded them not to give up.

With no one left in L.A. to solicit, Everson took the train to San Francisco to ask the advice of an old colleague named Jesse McCargar, a vice president of the Crocker First National Bank. He arrived at the bank only to discover that McCargar was away on vacation for two weeks. Despondent, he was headed for the door when he passed by a wrinkled, elderly man whose name and title were emblazoned on his raised desk. J. J. Fagan, an executive vice president at the bank, was chewing tobacco and expectorating into a golden spittoon.

Everson knew of Fagan's reputation. This was the most conservative banker in the business, a man who had seen everything and was fooled by nothing. At the beginning of his career, Fagan made a mint wheeling and dealing with the desperate and disappointed who had originally come west for the Gold Rush. Later, he cashed in on the Great Earthquake of 1906, lending money to those rebuilding the city. Fagan could sniff out a con job before it walked in the door, yet he had enormous patience for those he trusted.

"What can I do for you, young fellow?" the old man asked, peering out over his spectacles.

Everson was reluctant to engage this venerable banker in a conversation about a scheme as speculative as television. When Fagan insisted, Everson warned him. "This is just wildcatting," he said, "very wildcatting."

Fagan seemed intrigued. He sat Everson down and made him spill out the whole story. After listening to every word, Fagan leaned back and launched a magnificent brownish globule into the corner of the room. "Well," he said, "that's a *damn fool* idea."

Everson shrugged his shoulders. It was the reaction he was expecting.

"Somebody ought to put some money into it," Fagan continued. "Someone who can afford to lose it."

Everson perked up. He seemed to be catching Fagan in a strange mood. By the next day, Fagan was requesting that Everson summon his inventor to San Francisco for a luncheon meeting with Roy Bishop, an engineer who had become a savvy prospector for promising technology ventures.

Two days later, Farnsworth arrived in town by train looking exactly like what he was: a struggling, haggard inventor with no money. Everson took one look at him and marched him directly to the Knox Shop, perhaps the city's finest haberdashery. When Farnsworth protested, Everson insisted that he wasn't springing for a pricey suit out of sheer generosity, but for the good of their cause. After being fitted for an elegant set of clothes and a smart new hat, Farnsworth found himself being led to the barbershop.

The next day, the involved parties converged on the oldest and best hotel in town, the Palace, for the scheduled lunch meeting in one of the executive suites. The stakes were higher than ever, but Farnsworth again became consumed with conviction as he unfolded his vision while pointing to his new set of detailed drawings. Bishop and another electrical engineering expert brought in for the evaluation listened intently and fired back with a round of astute questions. At the end of the meeting, Bishop was unquestionably won over by the idea itself but remained unconvinced that a lone inventor could beat major corporations to market. "I doubt your ability to work it out commercially," Bishop concluded.

Perhaps because he was so finely dressed, Farnsworth had the good sense not to beg. Instead, he rose from his seat, gathered up his papers, grabbed his hat, motioned to a nerve-racked Everson, and laid down a defiant declaration.

"I am sorry, Mr. Bishop, that you don't see the possibilities for this invention that I do, or that you doubt my ability to make it happen," Farnsworth said. "Thank you for your time and the very nice lunch." With that, Farnsworth led Everson toward the door, opened it, and began walking out.

"Wait a minute," Bishop called out. They stopped in their tracks as Bishop held up a finger and whispered with his associate. At the end of this brief consultation, Bishop offered up one more possibility. Perhaps Farnsworth could run the concept by a third engineer, one with more experience with early-stage inventions, and see what he says. Within thirty minutes, they were pitching their plan to Harlan Honn, who understood the significance of electronic television more quickly than anyone Farnsworth had ever met. "Of course this will work," Honn said. "I'm sure of it."

By the end of a very long day, the team of engineers said they needed to write up a report for the rest of the investment group; they also said any decision would have to wait until Jesse McCargar, Everson's original contact, returned from vacation. Everson and Farnsworth were tense but happy to have their hopes kept alive.

When Farnsworth and Everson were called back to the bank one morning in September 1926, the decision had been all but formalized. McCargar greeted Everson by putting his arm around him. "I think we're going to back you boys," he said, then invited his guests into the mahogany-lined boardroom. Inside were a group of executives and board members with the finest financial pedigrees, including J. J. Fagan, plus a vice president of Standard Oil as well as the bank's president, William H. Crocker, and his son, William W. Crocker. In financial circles, the name Crocker was as good as gold. The Crocker family was among the backers of a little project that became known as the transcontinental railroad, joining Leland Stanford in financing the cross-country construction. The family built its reputation on taking big but calculated risks.

From the way these men spoke, it was clear that the terms that they proposed were not negotiable. They would put up $25,000 in return for a 60 percent ownership stake in this new venture, and the whole deal was based on Farnsworth's promise that he would achieve a television transmission within a year. This would resize the pie of the original partnership. Everson and Gorrell would now own 10 percent apiece, with Farnsworth holding the remaining 20 percent. The meaning of this arrangement was obvious to Farnsworth: No longer would he have control over his own fate. He would be working for the bankers.

Bishop turned to Everson and made it clear that the offer was a generous one. "This is the first time anyone has gotten money from this bunch without putting something on the table," he said. "All we have are the ideas in this young man's head. We're going to treat him like a prized racehorse."

There was a minor glitch, discovered when it came time to sign the papers. Still only twenty, Farnsworth was not yet old enough to enter into an official California contract. Everson had to assume the responsibility as the boy's legal guardian. It made for an embarrassing moment, but Farnsworth was over it completely when he heard the next bit of good news. As part of the deal, the backers had agreed to make available, for a modest monthly rental fee, laboratory space that another one of its ventures had recently vacated. The lab for the Farnsworth's company would be located at 202 Green Street, on the base of Telegraph Hill, which overlooked San Francisco Bay.

David Sarnoff (left) arm in arm with Boston financier and friend Joseph P. Kennedy (middle), and an unidentified RCA executive. In 1928, the two men formed a joint venture, RKO Pictures, a movie studio and cinema chain. (DAVID SARNOFF LIBRARY)

CHAPTER SIX

Networking

On Wall Street, traders and brokers referred to RCA simply as Radio, as in "How much Radio did you buy today?" When pronounced out loud, that five-letter word became a magic mantra. Anything associated with it turned to gold. A product called the Radio Flyer didn't have a radio and didn't fly. It was actually a hand-pulled red wagon and just so happened to be named after the two most exciting new technologies of the day. People loved it, and it became a huge seller.

Curiously, David Sarnoff never cared to own much Radio. He considered stocks too risky. Granting options to management was not yet a common practice, and so what little RCA shares he owned, he had to buy on the open market. He remembered quite well the poverty of his childhood, and he wasn't inclined to gamble his money away. Besides, he made a more-than-comfortable salary, and he was able to indulge in anything he wanted through his unlimited expense account. At the snap of his fingers, the grandest limousine would take RCA's general manager, its most important vice president, to the fanciest restaurant in town. Most often, he chose Delmonico's, a hot spot for business bosses since the Gilded Age. Holding court at his regular booth, Sarnoff would negotiate and bond with associates. "I'm not a millionaire," he would say, "but I live like one."

Sarnoff's financial conservatism caused him to miss out on quite a ride. RCA's stock was on a trajectory never before seen, rising more than 10,000 percent in the five-year period from its debut on the New York Stock Exchange in 1924 to the peak of the market, when it would split five for one. An investment of $10,000 could morph into $1 million in a flash. Owning shares in Radio was an absolute must, or you risked appearing the fool in cocktail party conversation. The biggest party thrower of them all, F. Scott Fitzgerald, sunk the royalties from his novels *This Side of Paradise* and *The Great Gatsby* into Radio, and for a time parlayed those proceeds into yachts, vacation homes in Europe, and the best food and drink for his friends at all-night wingdings. It didn't seem to matter that the price of Radio was being manipulated by a new class of hypesters and con artists who could be heard jabbering on radio itself to spread misinformation that would goose the price. In the words of a popular dance song, Radio was "hotter than hot, newer than new, meaner than mean, bluer than blue. Gets as much applause as waving the flag!"

All this posed a problem for the government. How can you go about investigating a company that makes so many people so rich and happy? As the stock took off, neither the FTC nor Congress could seem to remember why they were probing RCA's business tactics in the first place. No one but RCA was really making any profits in the radio business, but everyone who had anything to do with radio kept issuing stock that only went up, up, and away. By one count, more people were investing in radio stocks than actually owned radios. During this preposterous period of speculation, the harsh complaints about the radio combine subsided to a dull roar. Unceremoniously, all the charges against the cartel were dropped, at least for now.

Amid the frenzy, Sarnoff developed a relentless work routine. He labored harder and longer than anyone else at the company, and he led by example. Any employee who failed to show this kind of dedication and loyalty was not welcome to work at RCA for very long. His staff knew that only one piece of paper was to cross his desk at a time. He would render a decision on the matter at hand, make some notes, and then methodically move on to the next order of business.

Once, when an employee stepped out of line, Sarnoff issued a written reprimand. "This is not the way RCA functions. It is a company of clean desks, orderly files, and prompt return of telephone calls, particularly those of the general manager." He was forming a cult of personality, and it was working very well.

In addition to his management duties, Sarnoff continued to brainstorm about the future. One of his favorite subjects—the future of radio programming—began as a series of internal memos dating back to 1922. The novelty of radio was wearing off, Sarnoff wrote, and programming needed to improve greatly because "the broadcasting station will ultimately be required to entertain a nation." Not only would this endeavor be expensive, but it would call for specialists in talent and public taste. The engineers, managers, and technicians at RCA were not qualified to do the job well.

"Let us organize a separate and distinct company," he wrote, "to be known as the Public Service Broadcasting Company or the National Broadcasting Company or American Radio Broadcasting Company, or some similar name."

As Sarnoff envisioned it, the business model of the company had to be one of a nonprofit organization. To defray the cost of producing news and entertainment shows, he suggested that RCA, GE, Westing-house, and all of their licensees contribute 2 percent of their radio revenue to the venture. Better programming, after all, could only lead to sales of more radios. Perhaps it could even be run like a university, with an endowment. He didn't favor the idea of taxing the public to support programming, an idea that was being put into practice for the government-owned stations in England and other European countries, but from his memos, Sarnoff clearly viewed broadcasting as a public service of the highest order. Since the public owned the airwaves, radio was a national resource not to be compromised, akin to a great public library or a museum.

Apparently, one of these memos found its way to an AT&T executive named Walter Gifford, then the company's vice president of finance and a member of RCA's board of directors. Although AT&T was originally one of the pillars of the combine, the corporation was starting to behave in strange ways. For instance, in 1924, AT&T suddenly decided to sell all of its RCA stock, and Gifford resigned from the RCA board without offering a plausible explanation for this action. Sarnoff suspected that the telephone colossus was moving to compete with RCA.

What happened next was one of the most fascinating and consequential power struggles in the history of business. Yet because it took place behind the scenes, in offices and boardrooms, the press failed to report a single shred of it, and so the public was unaware that this bitter clash between two monopolies was even going on. When the battle was over, the American broadcasting business emerged, taking on the overall shape it would maintain for the rest of the century, during which time it would rise to become perhaps the single most influential industry of its day.

The entire episode was centered on a very personal fight between Sarnoff and Gifford, who was promoted to the presidency of AT&T in 1925. AT&T was already the world's largest public utility, an industrial behemoth with 350,000 employees and an uninterrupted record of paying dividends to its shareholders for more than two decades. Ma Bell was also a domain of discreet anti-Semitism. The company certainly didn't permit blacks, women, and most ethnic immigrants to join its executive ranks, but it seemed especially wary of Jews.

As far as Sarnoff knew, he was the only Jewish executive in the entire communications industry, and so he was always particularly sensitive to anti-Semitism. Jews at this time simply didn't enter mainstream corporations in tradition-bound industries. Instead, they were mostly found working in marginal businesses like garment shops or running outright disreputable ventures such as motion picture studios. The only way that they could become legitimate was to create their own power from scratch and use it as a blunt instrument against the establishment.

In one dramatic story of this type, Harry Warner of Warner Brothers was outraged over a dispute with a Bell System executive stemming from the licensing agreement for talking-pictures technology used in *The Jazz Singer*. Suspecting the clash was rooted in anti-Semitism, Warner stormed into the office of a top Bell executive.

"Give me the name of one Jew who works for your company," Warner demanded.

Looking horrified, the executive replied, "What do you think— it's the policy of our company to be anti-Semitic?"

"No. Just give me the name of one Jew working for your company."

"Realistically, I don't think I can produce one."

"If it's a policy of your company not to employ Jews," Warner said, "it's a policy of my company not to do business with you." With that, he marched out of the room.

The executive was so embarrassed by the confrontation that he directed his attorneys to settle the contract dispute right away. The discriminatory hiring practices, of course, didn't change any time soon.

Sarnoff, too, knew that he would be trampled if he didn't fight force with force. Just six years older than Sarnoff, Gifford was a New England native, with all-American Protestant roots that reached back for generations. He was a graduate of Harvard, he dressed in pinstripes, spoke with an upper-class tone, and certainly didn't appreciate this brash businessman—a high school dropout, no less—muscling in on what he felt was rightfully his. Gifford revealed his plan in internal AT&T memos: Ma Bell would not only enter the broadcasting business but dominate it, adding broadcasting as its second monopoly. One corporation alone would control wired communication in America as well as wireless communication.

Gifford's first move was to start WEAF (for Wind, Earth, Air & Fire), a high-watt radio station in New York. His business model was simple: any company could rent airtime at fifty dollars per ten minutes. When you called someone on the telephone, you paid for the time you used; why not with radio? Gifford called it "toll broadcasting." Come down to the station, say whatever you want into the microphone, and pay by the minute. Lots of companies took him up on the offer, among them a real estate company hawking co-op apartments, the department stores Macy's, Gimble's, and Wanamaker's, as well as American Express. These were the first paid commercials ever broadcast. To fill in the small gaps of time between the ads, Gifford would have people sing, play piano, and give lectures, but nothing too fancy.

Sarnoff was outraged. Radio was to be a public service, not a forum for crass commercialism. At a high-profile radio conference in Washington, D.C, organized by commerce secretary Herbert Hoover, Sarnoff denounced AT&T's actions and urged everyone to join him in his indignation. As it turned out, Hoover himself was Sarnoff's staunchest ally. "If a speech by the President is to be used as the meat between the sandwich of two advertisements," Hoover proclaimed at the conference, "there will be no radio left! How can we allow so great a possibility for public service, for news, for entertainment, for education, to be drowned in advertising chatter?" And so it was settled, and a resolution was drafted: advertising on radio was to be prohibited.

There was only one problem. Neither this conference nor the Commerce Department really had the authority to prohibit commercial speech. In fact, the Supreme Court soon ruled that the Commerce Department as it existed had no authority over radio whatsoever, a ruling which led to the formation of the separately chartered Federal Radio Commission.

In the meantime, AT&T not only went on with its new business but also strung together twelve other stations to join WEAF in what became the first broadcast network. Until then, broadcasting had mainly been a local affair, and programming among different stations was never synchronized. Since the technology of relaying programs through the airwaves from one station to another was still on the drawing boards, AT&T simply sent the programming and the commercials over its phone lines, where sister stations would pick up the signals and broadcast them from radio towers to their local audiences.

Sarnoff thought this was essentially his idea, and now Gifford was perverting it. To add insult to injury, AT&T delivered a handsome new cabinet radio to President Coolidge, signaling that it would soon enter radio sales as well.

Sarnoff bad-mouthed Gifford and AT&T at every turn, but not in the press, only privately to other executives in the radio combine. His remarks quickly made their way to Gifford's ears. Gifford realized that RCA had objections to what he was doing, but he believed that they could be worked out amicably. He called a meeting with RCA chairman Owen Young and said there would not be a settlement in this matter until RCA fired its "Jewish" general manager.

As luck would have it, Sarnoff was working under two executives, Young and General Harbord, who never displayed even a hint of prejudice. They were livid over Gifford's suggestion. They would go to the mat for their rising young star and fight AT&T to the death if it were necessary, rather than give in to such outrageous pressure. There was one catch: Young and Harbord left it up to Sarnoff to come up with a way out of this mess.

To Sarnoff, it was the chance of a lifetime. Here he was, David, fighting a real-life Goliath. He was pretty sure that what AT&T was doing—using one monopoly to gain another—was illegal under antitrust laws. But he saw only two options: One, he could launch a lawsuit in court against AT&T, which would bring this unseemly brawl into the public spotlight and lead to appeals that could last for years. Or two, he could submit the case to binding arbitration. The original 1921 patent-sharing agreement between AT&T and RCA contained a provision for arbitrating any disputes privately, in total secret, before an impartial referee, usually a retired judge, but there would be no appeals. If RCA lost, it would lose its very future, and the decision would be final.

It was a terrific gamble, yet Sarnoff was eager to take it, and Young and Harbord backed him up. When it was proposed to AT&T, Gifford agreed to go the binding arbitration route as well. He certainly didn't want laundry this dirty aired out in public either. The hearings went on for several months, and when they were over, the arbitrator ruled against AT&T on all counts. Everyone involved was stunned. RCA's victory was so total that Harbord and Young actually felt bad for Gifford. Sarnoff, of course, was triumphant. It was his biggest achievement yet. Now AT&T was forced to come to the negotiating table and settle the whole affair within the provisions of the ruling.

When the RCA executives went to shake Gifford's hand, however, and start the attempt to get over hard feelings, Gifford presented them with a legal hand grenade. He had secretly hired the services of John Davis, the losing presidential candidate from the 1924 race and the main author of the Clayton Antitrust Act. Under Gifford's guidance, Davis drafted a memo arguing that RCA itself was an illegal operation, that all the agreements that led to the creation of the radio combine amounted to restraint of trade. And if RCA shouldn't really have existed in the first place, how could this binding arbitration be held as valid?

This was an act of corporate terrorism of the first degree. Gifford's actions were so low-down and dirty that the Young-Harbord-Sarnoff triumvirate at RCA viewed them as an attempt to give AT&T a little edge in the settlement talks. How could one monopoly call another monopoly illegal? It made no sense. The only logical conclusion to this twaddle would be to break up AT&T as well, and who would ever consider something quite that absurd? Was Gifford trying to blow apart two industrial empires at once? Certainly, no one who went to Harvard could be that reckless.

The RCA team was correct. It really was just a shameful bargaining ploy. Still, Sarnoff and company were rightfully terrified that Gifford would feed the Davis memo to the clueless press. In the end, what everyone wanted was for the settlement talks to be over as soon as possible. Even Gifford himself was growing tired of the whole matter, and he sent an underling to the negotiating table. RCA, of course, sent Sarnoff.

The final settlement turned out to be a rich dessert for RCA; a piece of chocolate cake with whipped cream and a bright red cherry on top. AT&T sold RCA its flagship station WEAF for $1 million, granted RCA rights to transmit on its phone lines for a modest licensing fee paid to AT&T, then signed an agreement to exit broadcasting altogether. The *New York Times* treated this historic turning point as a ho-hum announcement, summarizing it in seven paragraphs, without even a hint of the strife that preceded it.

Shortly after the deal was done, RCA's new broadcasting network became known as the National Broadcasting Company. Initially, NBC consisted of the former AT&T chain of stations. That became known as NBC Red after a second network was put together soon after, using the newer and more versatile wireless relay technology. Originally formed from RCA's flagship stations in New York and Washington, GE's state-of-the-art broadcasting center in Schenectady, plus the Westinghouse stations in Pittsburgh, Chicago, Boston, and Springfield, Massachusetts, the wireless network became known as NBC Blue. The color choices came from the red and blue grease pencils RCA used to mark up giant maps around the office. On July 22, 1926, the formation of the company was duly ratified, with GE and Westinghouse as minority shareholders. RCA was in control, and the official charter carried the signature of David Sarnoff.

After that time of struggle and hard work, there was no way that NBC was going to be a nonprofit public service, as Sarnoff had originally envisioned. The new company, without debate, would generate its own revenue, lots of it, from selling advertising time. Sarnoff would no longer even utter a peep about his high-minded principles. And by now, Hoover was busy organizing his presidential campaign, and so he too seemed to forget his original indignation over the airwaves being filled with "advertising chatter."

Sarnoff had found his true calling. He never did become the electrical engineer he hoped to be as a teenager. Although he certainly could be called a visionary, his record of predicting the future was rather spotty, just like everyone else's. But no one was better at figuring out what motivates people, and his instincts for using that knowledge to get exactly what he wanted were unsurpassed. Sarnoff was a businessman in the truest sense. As his reward for almost single-handedly founding NBC, Sarnoff was promoted to executive vice president and given a raise, to $60,000 per year.

For David Sarnoff, born in the shtetl and obsessed with work every day since, the time to celebrate had arrived at last. A party was scheduled for November 15, 1926, at the old Waldorf-Astoria Hotel, on Thirty-fourth Street and Fifth Avenue, then spelled with a double hyphen to signify the 300-foot corridor that linked the original properties of cousins John Jacob Astor and William Waldorf Astor. That corridor became known as Peacock Alley because every evening thousands of people dressed up just to strut back and forth between the two properties. A magnificent Victorian structure with turreted corners and sweeping penthouse views, the hotel would soon be demolished to make way for the Empire State Building. On this chilly night in 1926, the Waldorf's Grand Ballroom, with its huge crystal chandelier, sparkled with tables set in silver. The chefs prepared the trademark Waldorf Salad for 1,000 guests.

NBC's black-tie coming-out party brought together the entire spectrum of society's movers and shakers, from the new jazzy cultural elite to the old fossils of the upper crust. The blue-blooded Wall Street financiers, the New York press barons, the Washington power class—all were in attendance. Arriving in his private limousine, gallantly stepping out into the searchlights in his new tuxedo, was David Sarnoff. On his arm was Lizette Sarnoff, looking stunning with her hair upswept, diamond earrings sparkling along with her eyes, dressed in a floor-length gown designed especially by a Fifth Avenue couturier.

The affair began in decidedly stuffy fashion, as the four-hour entertainment program reflected Sarnoff's highbrow vision for what broadcasting should become. After a short speech by newly appointed NBC president Merlin Aylesworth, the 100-piece New York Symphony Orchestra, conducted by Walter Damrouch, played pieces by Wagner, Liszt, and Schumann. Titta Ruffo, considered the world's the most powerful baritone, led the Metropolitan Opera Company in a rendition of the "Drinking Song" from *Hamlet.* No alcohol was served, however, this being the height of Prohibition.

The festivities at the Waldorf were broadcast live to the audiences of twenty-five radio stations, including those of the new NBC Red and NBC Blue networks, plus outlets in Buffalo, Detroit, Cleveland, Cincinnati, Minneapolis, St. Louis, Kansas City, and Portland, Maine. At scheduled breaks in the New York program, some of the affiliates chimed in with their own entertainment for the ballroom guests and the entire radio network. From Chicago, soprano Mary Garden sang classic arias. From Independence, Kansas, Will Rogers was on hand to do his impersonation of Silent Cal, the taciturn, drawling president. Back in New York, the vaudeville team of Weber and Fields offered up some more humor, but only for ten minutes, as Sarnoff thought that comedy was a frivolous waste of important airtime.

Later in the evening, the music turned lighter, with some bits from Gilbert and Sullivan's *Pinafore*, followed by Sousa's "Stars and Stripes." Finally, shortly after midnight, Vincent Lopez and his orchestra broke out into some swing, broadcast direct from his Casa Lopez nightclub.

For Sarnoff, the only damper on the evening was that very few people dancing at the Waldorf and probably no one tuning in over the airwaves knew of his role in creating NBC, but the way this man was smiling and eating and dancing and rubbing elbows with the rich and famous, it was certain that it wouldn't be long before the secret was out. "Radio," said the *Washington Post* the next day, "has put aside its swaddling clothes and has become a potential giant." The new medium of network broadcasting stood alone in the spotlight.

In the summer of 1928, with RCA's dominance over radio apparently secure, General Harbord took a temporary leave of absence to campaign for his friend Herbert Hoover, whose presidential run was in full swing. In Harbord's absence, Sarnoff was named acting RCA president, signaling that his succession to the top spot wasn't far off. Now Sarnoff would be able to wield the full power of the radio monopoly to initiate deals with anyone he saw fit. During this time, he initiated three transactions, completed in rapid order, that transformed RCA into the wider media kingdom of Sarnoff's self-imagined manifest destiny.

The most straightforward deal was with the General Motors Corporation. To Sarnoff, the idea of becoming the exclusive provider of radio technology for the mammoth automaker was irresistible, in large part because he so loved the analogy that RCA was to radio what GM was to cars. Shuttling back and forth between Detroit and New York, he negotiated the formation of a new company, the General Motors Radio Corporation, owned 51 percent by GM and 49 percent by RCA. Under the plan, GM's factory in Dayton, Ohio, would manufacture new dashboard sets, under patent license from RCA.

A much more complex deal involved the phonograph. For more than a decade, there had been a raging debate over which invention, the radio or the record player, was the superior way of listening to music. The radio was quickly gaining on its far older rival, but the phonograph was improving too. In 1926, the inventor of sound recording, Thomas Edison, unveiled his latest creation, a phonograph record that held an unprecedented forty minutes of music. "The phonograph is reclaiming its own," declared Edison, by now a cantankerous old man. "The radio is a commercial failure and its popularity with the public is waning. No dealers have made any money at it. It is too complicated. As for its music, it's just plain awful!"

Sarnoff wanted to settle this dispute once and for all. The best way to do that, he surmised, would be to unify both technologies under one corporate roof and in one home entertainment cabinet. By the late 1920s, the Victor Talking Machines Company held one of the most valuable, recognizable, and best-loved brands in the world. There was a real fear inside RCA that if the Victor Company were to start making its own radios, it would quickly zoom to number one. More than anything, the public adored Victor's trademarked dog, a white terrier named Nipper, who sat listening with a raised ear to an old-style phonograph speaker. The public would buy anything with that dog on it.

Sarnoff proposed a high-stakes financial gambit. He would offer a big block of RCA's stock to Victor shareholders, confident that no investor could resist ownership in the soaring shares of Radio. The transaction involved months of tangling with the various interests of thousands of shareholders of both companies, but it was finally completed by the spring of 1929.

The acquisition came with an extra special benefit. In addition to owning Victor's technology and its recording label, which came complete with a roster of stars, and, of course, Nipper, who would be put to immediate work under the new RCA Victor brand, the company took possession of Victor's manufacturing plant in Camden, New Jersey. Situated on the Delaware River, across from Philadelphia, the redbrick building with the tall clock-tower was, in Sarnoff's view, the ideal spot not only to manufacture combined radio-phonograph systems but also to build a world-class research and development laboratory that could churn out patents for all sorts of new communications technologies. Soon all of RCA's scientists and engineers would be based at the complex in Camden.

With the General Motors and Victor deals in progress, the next transaction was by far the most intriguing of the three, as it had the biggest effect on Sarnoff personally. With the era of talking motion pictures now beginning, Sarnoff wanted RCA sound systems installed in theaters nationwide. He initiated a search for a movie company with which he could form an alliance. One of his colleagues introduced him to a fast-rising financial whiz named Joseph P. Kennedy, who in recent years had gained control of a minor film production and distribution company called Film Booking Office, or FBO. The two men were about the same age, and in meetings at restaurants and in telephone conversations, they discovered they had a lot in common.

Sarnoff told Kennedy about his impoverished, immigrant background and his self-propelled rise to power. Kennedy related his own similar story about how his family had escaped the Irish potato famine, although he himself was a second-generation American, born into an already wealthy Boston political family. Among his cronies, Kennedy was known to make the occasional anti-Semitic remark, but Sarnoff didn't know that or the details of Kennedy's earlier success using inside information and collusion to manipulate stocks, a practice that was unethical but not yet illegal. "It's so easy to make money in the market," Kennedy told one of his colleagues, "we'd better get in before they pass a law against it."

Kennedy had a magnetic personality, showing a broad smile that telegraphed how much he enjoyed being with you. By the way he confided in you, he seemed to be a man you could trust. Kennedy knew all the tricks for keeping negative information about himself out of the press and getting positive information in. During Prohibition, the newspapers didn't report how Kennedy operated a liquor importing business from his home office in Brookline, Massachusetts. When his wife, Rose, expressed shock at a newspaper story that simply revealed that they were millionaires, he told her it was news to him as well. Kennedy appeared to be the very model of what Sarnoff himself wanted to be—and was in fact becoming—someone who could rise above his humble background to take his place as a great leader.

In October of 1928, Joe Kennedy took the train to New York to plot the deal with David Sarnoff. They met for dinner at the Oyster Bar in Grand Central Station. Over drinks and steaks, they outlined how RCA would invest $400,000 to finance FBO's expansion into producing feature films. Kennedy, in return, would merge FBO with

Keith-Albee-Orpheum, a company that was converting its chain of vaudeville theaters into movie houses that would be equipped with RCA sound systems. The new company, with David Sarnoff as chairman of the board, would be called Radio-Keith-Orpheum, or RKO. For arranging the merger, Kennedy received a fee of $150,000 plus stock in the new company, which he then turned around and sold at the height of the market for an estimated $8 million. The deal transformed Kennedy from a successful scoundrel into one of the richest men in America, a status that came with unqualified respect.

Sarnoff's new association with Kennedy did wonders for his social life. He and Lizette were invited to join Joe and Rose at their vacation villa in tony Palm Beach, Florida, a haven of the rich and famous. The Sarnoffs were impressed by the family life of their new friends. Rose and her domestic staff were raising Joe Jr., Jack, Rosemary, Kathleen, Eunice, Patricia, Bobby, and soon Jean and Teddy. The Sarnoffs had three sons of their own, Robert, Edward, and Thomas, so commitment to family became one of the favorite topics of discussion among the two couples.

In New York, where Kennedy established a residence away from his family back in Boston, Sarnoff was amazed at how Joe always seemed to have a beautiful young woman on his arm. It was one reason Kennedy was attracted to the movie business in the first place. His torrid tryst with box-office beauty Gloria Swanson was hardly a secret, although his long-running affair with his personal secretary was much better hidden. Here was a man who was able to compartmentalize his life to an extraordinary degree. "Kennedy imparted to Sarnoff a philosophy of living that he never forgot," wrote RCA executive Kenneth Bilby. "More important than the substance of the individual, according to Kennedy's doctrine, was the appearance that the individual projected."

Sarnoff was certainly no stranger to the practice of inventing one's own myth, of manipulating public opinion, of justifying any means necessary by pointing to the noble result at the end, but he never before saw this prophetic message—perception *is* reality—expressed so eloquently through words and deeds. "History could be frozen in a heroic configuration," added Bilby. "Long before the words *image making* had entered the lexicon, Sarnoff had learned their meaning, and their importance, from his Boston friend."

Taking the cue from Kennedy, Sarnoff also experimented with extramarital relations. Unlike Kennedy, however, he was caught and confronted, not by the press, of course, but by Lizette. "He wounded her deeply because of the philanderings that accompanied his march to fame and power," Bilby wrote, but David and Lizette were committed to staying together, and "the marriage proved to be the bedrock of his life." Fooling around simply didn't suit who Sarnoff was.

His ego was best gratified by the glory of building RCA into the first electronic media conglomerate, and the next order of business was something that was now beginning to get considerable press attention, a technological leap that had been looming on his horizon for years, and he now turned to focus on it almost exclusively. Sarnoff needed a plan for controlling the new art of television, which he envisioned supplanting radio and becoming, as one of his early memos put it, "the ultimate and greatest step in mass communications."

Farnsworth, age twenty-three, demonstrating his first electronic television console set, in his Green Street laboratory in January 1930.

CHAPTER SEVEN

Life on Green Street

O N THE WAY BACK HOME TO LOS ANGELES TO TELL HIS WIFE THE
news of the $25,000 investment from the Crocker Bank asso-
ciates, Philo T. Farnsworth stopped off at the telegraph office to
dispatch a message to his brother-in-law, Cliff Gardner, who was
now living in Oregon, summoning him to San Francisco.

HAVE BACKING FROM SAN FRANCISCO BANKERS—STOP—
JOB FOR YOU—STOP—MEET US AT CORNER CALIFORNIA
AND POWELL STREETS NOON EACH DAY STARTING SEPT 19
[1926] UNTIL WE GET THERE—STOP—PHIL

The next day, at the break of dawn, the couple packed all they
owned into the Chandler they had borrowed from George Everson.
Then they were off. The sun climbed higher and higher, reflecting
off the fragrant rose blossoms lining the roadway. As they drove the
open-air roadster up the California coast, the future looked so

bright that Pem burst out singing "Looking at the World through Rose-Colored Glasses, Everything Is Rosy Now," with Phil joining her in a tenor voice. They kept singing until their throats hurt, songs such as "I Want to Be Happy But I Can't Be Happy Till I've Made You Happy Too" and "I'm Sitting on the Top of the World, Just Rolling Along." They finished with a ballad that they considered "our song," Irving Berlin's "Always," with the lyrics "Dreams will all come true, growing old with you, and time will fly."

Later in the ride, Phil began laying out his vision for what television could become. Above all else, he told Pem, television would become the world's greatest teaching tool. Illiteracy would be wiped out. The immediacy of television was the key. As news happened, viewers would watch it unfold live; no longer would we have to rely on people interpreting and distorting the news for us. We would be watching sporting events and symphony orchestras. Instead of going to the movies, the movies would come to us. Television would also bring about world peace. If we were able to see people in other countries and learn about our differences, why would there be any misunderstandings? War would be a thing of the past.

Pem asked how this could be accomplished, as she recalled Phil saying that broadcast signals could only be sent in a straight line. How could he transmit television over an entire ocean? Phil was already working out this problem in his mind. Television stations, he said, would point their signals at objects suspended above the sea. "We'll find a way," he said, "even if we have to relay it using captive balloons."

They stayed the night at an inn in Paso Robles, then got up early and continued their drive along the high coastal cliffs. By early afternoon, they motored into the city of steep hills and street trolleys, passing the Presidio on their left and the pastel row houses on their right. As they approached Powell Street, they spotted good old, skinny, droopy-eyed Cliff sitting on the curb with his head in his palms, clutching the crumpled telegram. Cliff had quit his mill job as soon as he received the wire, kissed his girlfriend, Lola, good-bye, boarded a train south, and checked into the cheapest rooming house in the neighborhood. When Phil and Pem saw themselves in his eyes, the vision of his little sister and his best friend rolling his way, they watched Cliff break out in an ear-to-ear grin, then start jumping up and down and waving his arms in the air.

When the trio drove over to inspect their new digs on Green Street, at the corner of Sansome, they quickly discovered that *laboratory* was a kind word for this second-story loft space over garage converted into a carpentry shop. This gray stucco building wasn't, as they imagined, on top of Telegraph Hill, where it would be free from power lines and other interference, but rather near the bottom, in the middle of all that clutter. The rear windows faced the foot of the hill, which was full of giant rocks in such precarious positions that it seemed as if a rainstorm would send them crashing through the glass.

They climbed the stairs to their working area, which was through a door to their left. On the right was a lab where Harlan Honn was working on a refrigeration invention. "Welcome to the Crocker Laboratory," said the man who had helped Farnsworth bag his seed money. "If we can be of any help as you get settled, let us know."

What they found in their new space was 600 square feet of nothingness—save for shafts of sunlight and a high raftered ceiling. Yet there were a few pluses, including lots of natural light and magnificent views—of the bay to the east and the San Francisco skyline to the south. The building was also hooked up with plenty of electrical power to support their work, and the rent was cheap, just $75 per month, payable out of the company's $1,000-per-month budget.

They started planning how they were going to spruce up the space, when one of them checked the time. It was getting late, and they had no place to stay. They had heard apartments were cheaper on the east side of the bay, so they decided to check into a hotel there and go searching for a place in the morning. They drove up Market Street to the ferry building and rolled the Chandler onto the big boat. Once on board, they watched the sun setting behind the San Francisco skyline as the bow approached the Berkeley Hills. After dinner at a café, they secured a pair of hotel rooms. Phil and Pem went up to bed while Cliff stayed in the lobby, where a big crowd had formed to listen to the radio broadcast of a boxing bout. Cliff was a huge sports fan, and Gene Tunney was challenging Jack Dempsey, in one of the most famous nights in sports history. There was a knock-down, then a long count, and then a miracle: the underdog was the new champion of the world. If Tunney could do it, why not Farnsworth? Cliff was still jazzed up the next morning, throwing punches at an imaginary foe, as they went apartment hunting.

Phil's personal salary had been set at $200 per month, out of which they figured they could afford no more than $50 for rent. Nothing in the classified ads turned into anything promising, but as Phil drove by the university football stadium onto Derby Street, Pem spotted a "For Rent" sign on a brown-shingled house with white shutters. A little old lady greeted them at the door and told them she needed to leave at once to be with her sick sister in Los Angeles. For $62.50 per month, she said, they could have a completely fur-nished apartment beginning that evening. With Cliff chipping in a part of his salary and sleeping in the second bedroom, this arrange-ment would work well.

Each day, Phil and Cliff commuted to the lab, a trip that took an hour by ferry each way. Setting up the laboratory space, they ham-mered together some workbenches and a sturdy six-by-ten-foot wooden table in the middle of the floor. After a few days of bore-dom by herself, Pem decided that she would try working along with them as an all-around handywoman. Phil had expected Pem to come around to this idea, so the lab staff soon had its third full-time employee, at the wage of $10 per month.

When the time came to begin conducting experiments, Phil told
Cliff that the biggest stumbling block would be creating the appropriate glass tubes. Tremendous time would be wasted if they had to
keep going back to a glassblower to make numerous refinements and
repairs.

"I'll do it," said Cliff.

Farnsworth certainly believed that his brother-in-law would be
perfectly willing to do just about anything. That's why he had hired
him. Cliff was completely dedicated and totally loyal, but Farnsworth seriously doubted that Cliff would be able to craft glass tubes,
especially with the precision required for building the Image Dissector camera. For his part, Farnsworth had no experience running
a laboratory. In fact, he had never even seen the inside of a research
lab or a manufacturing plant. He had little idea how difficult it was
to accomplish what he wanted. Instead, he would rely on instinct and
old-fashioned trial and error. "He attacked the whole assignment
with no engineering experience, but to compensate he had courage
and genius," Everson later wrote. "The courage was not the foolhardy
type born of ignorance. His was the courage of the pioneer who knows
the goal but has little knowledge of the intervening terrain."

He and Cliff quickly bought some equipment at local industrial
supply shops, including clamps, a vacuum pump, and blowtorches,
and went to work making tubes. But when their first ones were lumpy
and cracked too easily, they decided to get some professional help.
They were directed to Bill Cummings, a tall, patient, middle-aged
man who headed the glassblowing lab at the University of California, Berkeley. Cummings was greatly intrigued by Farnsworth's idea
and Cliff's enthusiasm. He agreed to work on creating a tube according to Farnsworth's specification, and a few days later he brought
the finished product over to Green Street and began teaching the
boys how to do it. Pretty soon, Cliff picked up the technique. With
his sleeves rolled up, wearing asbestos gloves, clenching an oxygen

hose in his teeth, wielding a torch of fire, Cliff Gardner was becoming practiced in the fine art of blowing glass.

The small staff fastened their first Green Street tube to their new electronic vacuum pump, a clunky machine that extracted all the air from inside. The pump provided a "thwunk-thwunk-thwunk" sound that became the lab's constant background noise, as it typically took many hours to rid a tube of nearly all the gas molecules in it.

They were now ready for their first trial, labeled Experiment Number One, which would be described in detail in Farnsworth's lab journal. Sitting at a desk in the corner, Pem learned how to type, and pecking away on a used Royal typewriter, she copied her husband's handwritten notes. She also learned how to use a professional drafting set to create complex and precise line drawings. These lab reports would be dated, signed, and witnessed, then bound in leather.

Their first Image Dissector tube was less than a foot long and barely four inches in diameter, but it had taken weeks to get to build it. Inside the tube was a cathode—a circular wire mesh screen energized by an external battery and connected to a small metal rod. When light was shined into one end of the tube, the cathode would turn the light energy into electrical impulses, which would shoot through empty space onto a potassium-coated plate, serving as the anode, at the other end. The tube itself was hooked to an electrical meter, which would record the impulses received by the potassium-coated plate. The potassium had a positive charge, and they were hoping it would receive a negative charge caused by the light shining at the other end. But their first try at this was a failure; the needle on the meter measuring the transfer failed to budge. Farnsworth supposed that they needed a thicker layer of potassium, a new way to construct the cathode, and a more sensitive meter, but a new meter was beyond the lab's budget.

The next morning, Farnsworth was called into Roy Bishop's office to explain his progress so that the bank could keep tabs on its investment. As Farnsworth described his predicament, Bishop took a deep breath. "I lost a son not long ago," he began. "He was about your age, and in some ways you remind me of him. He was also interested in radio and electrical things. He had some ideas he wanted to work out, so I bought him three meters he needed. I'd like you to have them." The meters turned out to be a set of expensive, precision electrical gauges.

Farnsworth couldn't believe his luck. He thanked Bishop dozens of times in the span of a few minutes, utterly grateful for this turn of events.

"Well, I'll be," Cliff said, when Farnsworth showed him the meters. "That man must be psychic!"

What Farnsworth was attempting—converting patterns of light into patterns of electrical energy and back into light again—could only have been inspired by the man he admired even more than great lone inventors such as Bell and Edison. That man was Albert Einstein.

Farnsworth had a few things in common with Einstein. As young boys, both learned to play the violin, each showing an abnormal sensitivity to music, appreciating it so deeply that they saw in music a wondrous mathematical structure. Both developed an early interest in physics through books that mentors gave to them, and quickly developed original thoughts that surpassed anything their teachers knew. Both began the quest that would define their lives in their early teens, when they became obsessed with electricity and magnetism. Farnsworth's interest was specific—harnessing the mysterious properties of the electron—while Einstein was moving toward a much broader understanding of the universe, but both lived much of the time in a state of abstraction, dedicated to concepts and ideals. Each had the opportunity to become electrical engineers but shunned a practical profession in favor of a life of thought and discovery. Both Einstein and Farnsworth gave up the formalized observance of their religions, but each remained committed to their faith and stayed spiritual all their lives. Later in life, they each viewed the relationship between religion and science not as opposed to each other but rather as opposite sides of the same coin

Farnsworth was inspired by Einstein, just as Einstein built on and challenged the work of Sir Isaac Newton and the other scientists, inventors, and creators who came before him. Indeed, Newton was the one who best expressed this process of scientific discovery. "If I have seen further," he said, "it is by standing on the shoulders of giants."

In the beginning, as the story goes, God created the universe, and He said, "Let there be light." In 1905, Albert Einstein singled himself out as the first member of the human species to demonstrate a true understanding of what that "light" was and is. In a miraculous masterstroke, he published four articles simultaneously, describing both the beginnings of his theory of relativity and a "viewpoint concerning the production and transformation of light." It was this viewpoint, not relativity, that would "bring Einstein the Nobel Prize for physics sixteen years later," wrote Einstein's biographer, Ronald W. Clark, "and it was to play a key part in the development of modern technology, since the photoelectric effect whose law the viewpoint propounded was to become a cornerstone of television."

The photoelectric effect is a rather simple experiment that broached a great scientific imbroglio. In the 1600s, Newton's theory was that light was made up of tiny particles—corpuscles, he called them—that traveled through space, much like powder blowing in a breeze. In the 1860s, however, James Clerk Maxwell developed the theory that all electromagnetic impulses traveled in oceanlike *waves* moving at the speed of light (abbreviated as the universal constant c), which could be expressed by the equation $c = f\lambda$, with f being the frequency, or the number of waves that propagate per second, and λ being the length of the waveform. As the frequency increases, the wavelength decreases, and vice versa. Light, Maxwell said, consisted of electromagnetic impulses with a very short (high-frequency) wavelength.

Twenty years later, Heinrich Hertz first demonstrated electromagnetic waves by oscillating the current in an electrical wire, which created disturbances in the air that could be detected, or "received," by other circuits that were vibrating at the same rate. The frequency, or the number of waveforms traveling per second, later became measured in units called *hertz*. His experiment verified Maxwell's theory and laid the groundwork for Marconi's invention of the wireless telegraph, a device which vibrates circuits for the purpose of sending patterns of electromagnetic waves to an antenna that can radiate the waveforms in all directions. Those airborne patterns became known as radio waves.

The striking inconsistency in Maxwell's wave theory arose when Hertz and others found that light shining on a conductive surface could *dislodge* electrons into open space, akin to what happens when tennis balls are thrown at a dusty blanket. If the wave theory of light explained everything, the energy of the electrons that are emitted from a metal plate would increase as the light shining on that surface grew brighter. The electrons, after all, should be able to absorb a greater number of light waves, thus increasing the frequency by which they escape from the surface. The experiment, however, showed that the brightness of the light didn't affect the frequency of the emission at all.

This photoelectric experiment identified a serious flaw in the wave theory of light. In 1900, Max Planck revived the Newtonian idea that light traveled in particles, pointing out the fact that different colors—such as red, white, and blue—appear when certain light-bulb filaments or other substances are heated to higher and higher temperatures. Colors, he knew, are simply waves of light traveling at slightly different wavelengths. Red light, for instance, has a longer wavelength (and lower frequency) than that of blue light. This is the reason that the daytime sky appears blue, because the higher frequencies from the wide spectrum of the sun's light ricochet their way much more easily through layers of atmosphere. This also explains why shorter (higher frequency) radio waves can reach around the earth. High-pitched sound travels farther than low pitches for the same reason.

If heat could change the color of light, Planck surmised, there must be some form of matter in the light to absorb the heat. That *something* had to be a particle! Maxwell's wave theory could not explain why the frequency of the light waves, not the brightness of the beam, seemed to control the energy level of each electron emitted from the metal surface.

Einstein stepped in to resolve this conundrum. Light, he said, behaved as particles in some cases and as waves in others. Einstein explained this wave-particle duality by theorizing that light was made up of packets of particles that traveled in waves. Light particles, later to be known as photons, had no mass or electric charge but exhibited a constant velocity. In the photoelectric effect, when a photon hits a metallic plate and dislodges an electron from the surface, the *frequency* of the *photon* determines the energy level of the resulting electronic discharge. The emitted energy, E, equals the tiny mass of the electrons multiplied by the speed of light squared ($E = mc^2$). As the frequency of the photons would change, it would alter the energy patterns of the electrons excited from the metal plate. The photons, according to Einstein, simply transfer their energy to the electrons and then cease to exist.

When the young Einstein published this theory and his other new concepts of time, space, matter, energy, and light, he set off "blazing rockets which, in the dark of the night, suddenly cast a brief but powerful illumination over an immense unknown region," remarked Nobel laureate Louis de Broglie.

These intellectual rockets were what inspired Farnsworth as a boy in Idaho. When light reflects off an image, Farnsworth knew from reading Einstein, the patterns we see are really just waves of photons that are changing in frequency. This knowledge led to Farnsworth's revelation in the potato field: If those frequency changes could be channeled to a metal plate, acting as a cathode, those photons could excite patterns of electrons, or cathode rays, that would represent the original image. The rays could then be transmitted to a fluorescent surface—the television screen—on which the visual image could be reconstructed line by line by line in a tiny fraction of a second.

Albert Einstein, born in 1879, and Philo T. Farnsworth, born in 1906, both believed that new ideas about the nature of the universe had to be divine. How else could one explain the miracle behind the photoelectric effect? The two men would not have the occasion to speak directly to each other until much later in their lives, but their intellects formed a lasting bond much earlier. Perhaps that bond was formed, as Einstein put it, by "the God who reveals himself in the harmony of all that exists."

Farnsworth knew that all his theorizing and experimentation wouldn't be worth a thin dime if he didn't have a patent. He and his backers at the bank were growing nervous that someone else would beat them to the Patent Office. There had been some legendary stories of such cases. In 1876, Alexander Graham Bell, working in Boston, filed his application for the telephone with the Patent Office just two hours before another inventor, Elisha Gray, filed an application stating that he intended to design the very same thing. According to this legend, if Bell had been held up just 120 minutes, it was quite possible that the vast new telephone industry would have been owned and operated by the Gray System.

In early December of 1926, Farnsworth took a train down to Los Angeles and returned to the law offices of Lyon & Lyon. Under the guidance of the Lyon brothers, he formatted his drawings, descriptions, and claims into a formal patent disclosure. He brought the documents back to San Francisco, signed them in the presence of a notary a few days before Christmas, put the papers in the mail, and soon received confirmation. The official filing date was January 7, 1927. The patent application for Farnsworth's "Television System" began:

> This invention relates to a television apparatus and process for the instantaneous transmission of a scene or moving image of an object located at a distance in which the transmission is by electricity. . . . The time during which the human eye will retain a picture is of such short duration that the conversion of the light shades of the original image to electricity and the reconversion of said electricity to light must be performed at a very tremendous speed. All prior attempts at television have attempted to employ some mechanically moving part for dissecting the image. . . . None of these prior attempts have proven successful.

Later in the year, after an initial review by a patent examiner in Washington, D.C., Farnsworth was notified that there appeared to be too many claims in this one application. The notice suggested dividing the application into several smaller ones, although the memo assured Farnsworth that the original filing date would be noted on each. By then, Farnsworth had retained a patent law firm close to his new home, a small San Francisco office headed by a man named Charles Evans. An associate at that firm, Donald Lippincott, an engineer who had worked in the legal department at the Magnavox Corporation, would later form his own private practice and become Farnsworth's personal patent attorney and lifelong friend.

Under the counsel of Evans and Lippincott, Farnsworth extracted three separate applications from the original one, which now focused solely on the television scanning system, or Image Dissector, later known as the television camera. He claimed that his camera would scan a moving image by breaking it down into 500 horizontal lines, and it would do this five times per second. Joining it as co-pending applications were an "Electric Oscillator System," a special tube used to display the images, a "Light Valve," for modulating a beam of light in accordance with the strength of an electric current, and a "Television Receiving System," which was on a par with the Image Dissector in terms of its importance, as it claimed to be a description of the first electronic television set.

My invention relates to television, particularly to the reception of pictures or views transmitted by radio. An objective of my invention is to provide an apparatus for receiving radio television waves of the type generated by the apparatus described in my co-pending application.

With Farnsworth's patent applications pending, the inventor's idea was on its way out into the world. Contrary to what some people believe, a patent shrouds an invention in secrecy only for the very first part of the application process. For the rest of the process, and especially after the patent is issued, the idea is exposed to all. The very word patent comes from the Latin root *patens*, which means "open, accessible, exposed, and clearly evident." This openness is essential to general progress, as open disclosure reduces the chance that time and effort are wasted reinventing the wheel, so to speak. In filing these applications, Farnsworth was now revealing what he intended to produce and by exactly what method he was going to do it. Potential rivals would soon be able to view this application and not only learn from it but try to "interfere" with it or block it from being issued, on the grounds that prior patents cover the work in question. Or they could challenge the patent on the basis that Farnsworth really didn't have what he claimed to have.

If the application was approved, the inventor would be granted a limited period of time—seventeen years—to control the exploitation of his invention. To obtain an official patent, the idea in question needs to be original and useful. On these grounds, Farnsworth was confident. He didn't know of anyone who would question the originality or the usefulness of his electronic television. But the applicant also has to prove that his idea will work, and that's why his investors demanded a successful demonstration.

The lab journals in 1927 show Farnsworth moving at a furious pace. The small staff was working twelve hours a day, six days a week, trying out one technique after another, and doing their best to learn from their failures. "I'm a professional mistake maker," Phil told Pem.

By February, Farnsworth called in one of his cousins, Arthur Crawford, who happened to be the top geologist for the state of Utah, to help find a photoelectric coating that would work better than potassium. Crawford left Utah promising his pregnant wife he'd be back home in time for the birth of their baby and arrived in San Francisco promising Farnsworth that he'd get the job done. He, Cliff, and Phil tried everything from celestite to topaz to willemite, grinding rocks and crystals into powders and distilling them into gooey compounds.

They had so many failures that before they got very far, Crawford realized he was going to have to break one of his two promises. While he toiled away on Green Street, his child was born. Eventually, the lab staff hit on a compound made mainly from cesium, which later became known as the most electropositive element available. Since opposites attract, this turned out to be the best substance for luring the electrons emitted from the negatively charged cathode. With that success, Crawford went back to Utah.

Despite the heroic hours they all put in at the lab, Farnsworth insisted on taking Sundays off on religious grounds. They didn't go to church, but he and Pem relaxed, played music, and explored the neighborhood. One Sunday, on a walk with Cliff, they came upon Berkeley's Greek Theater, a stone stage surrounded by a massive semicircle of seats set in the hillside. The stage was practically inviting someone onto it, so Phil answered the call and launched into a performance of Shakespeare's *The Taming of the Shrew*, summoning a section of dialogue he memorized during his drama class at BYU. Pem and Cliff sat in amazement, watching Phil recall the lines of all the different roles.

One night, Phil and Pem gazed at the stars from the deck of the ferry crossing the bay.

"Did you ever wonder whether there's any life up there?" Phil asked.

"I know some of the names of the stars," Pem replied. "But no, I haven't thought much about it."

"It would be really egotistical of us to think we were the only ones. There must be others who have surpassed us in intelligence. I'm going to take an expedition out there someday and find them."

Pem could tell that he wasn't joking about this. "You don't expect me to go with you, do you?"

"Well," said Phil. "I wouldn't like to go without you."

Pem thought this over for a minute. "Well, I guess I'd go too," she said, finally. "I'd rather die with you in space than be stuck here alone on Earth."

Phil said he was glad to hear it, but that he first needed to commercialize television.

Back at the lab, the pressure was building. Everson and Gorrell were coming by for more and more frequent visits, and Gorrell in particular developed a routine. He'd saunter inside with a spring in his step, greet Farnsworth with a slap on the back, and cry out, "Hi Phil! Got the damned thing working yet?" He understood that Gorrell was joking, but the humor was wearing thin.

Before long, Farnsworth was resenting the time lost commuting back and forth by ferry from Berkeley, a round trip that ate up two hours each day, so he convinced Pem and Cliff to move with him to an apartment near the lab. They found a spacious flat on Vallejo Street. The original trio was soon joined by Pem's sister Ruth and Phil's sister Agnes. The economy was booming, so jobs were plentiful. They all chipped in for the rent and the food, and helped in running the household.

Stretching their budget thin, Phil hired two engineers to help out at the lab. One, a tall, square-jawed grad student named Carl Christensen, was given room and board at the apartment as part of his salary. Along with a curly redheaded radio technician named Bob Humphries, he was assigned the task of building an amplifier to boost the strength of the transmission signal, a big challenge that had been holding up everything else. Since there were no appropriate amplifier tubes for sale then, the staff had to make their own. "It's a little like having to make your own tires before inventing the car," Pem later said.

By August, the full-time workforce of five finally had all the pieces in place, and their energy level and sense of anticipation were rising every day. There were only two months to go before the original one-year deadline, a target date that loomed large in the minds of Farnsworth's investors. The lab staff was up to Experiment Numbers Seven and Eight, which involved shielding the Image Dissector tube in an iron casing to prevent outside interference, and that seemed to help. Experiment Numbers Nine and Ten, conducted at the end of August, involved hooking up the Image Dissector to the receiving tube for the first time. The complete system didn't work yet, but Farnsworth felt it was getting close.

"The morning of September 7, 1927, dawned with the high fog typical of San Francisco in autumn," wrote Pem, "but it had already begun to clear as we drove to the lab." This was the day they were to conduct Experiment Number Twelve, a test of the entire apparatus.

They had partitioned the room into two parts. Cliff placed a slide with the image of a triangle in front of the Image Dissector in one section of the lab, while everyone else gathered around the receiving tube behind the partition. The two tubes were connected by an amplifier and wires. Within a couple of seconds, "a line appeared across the small bluish square of light on the end of the tube," wrote Pem. "It was pretty fuzzy, but Phil adjusted the focusing coil, and the line became well-defined."

"Turn the slide, Cliff," shouted Phil. When he did so, the received line also turned ninety degrees. They didn't see the full triangle, but even so, this line represented a historic first. "That's it, folks!" Farnsworth exclaimed. "We've done it! There you have electronic television." Cliff came racing in, looked at it, and exclaimed, "Well, I'll be damned!" Carl Christensen seemed the most surprised. "If I wasn't seeing it with my own two eyes, I wouldn't believe it." Bob Humphries said nothing but wore a dreamy grin on his face. Pem, meanwhile, was jumping up and down in jubilation.

A short time later, George Everson arrived, after receiving an urgent call from Farnsworth. He rushed in to witness a repeat of the successful demonstration. When he saw the line, he slapped Phil on the back. "There's no doubt about it, Phil," he said. "My faith in you all this time has been justified." He added a pinch of caution, though. "Of course, you'll want more of a picture before you show it to the Crocker group."

Farnsworth nodded his head in agreement. Then the two of them raced to the telegraph office and sent a wire to Leslie Gorrell, who was working in Los Angeles. Just four words: THE DAMNED THING WORKS!

For the time being, Philo T. Farnsworth's demonstration of an all-electronic television signal was a secret kept among his staff, friends, and investors. Meanwhile, the press had become enchanted by the experimenters trying to achieve television through mechanical methods based on the early Nipkow disk, a spinning saucer that aimed to scan images by capturing flickers of light through a lineup of holes. Every public showing of a mechanical television system led to a flurry of publicity.

The first and probably the most colorful of the mechanical experimenters was a Scotsman living in England named John Logie Baird. A serial inventor whose greatest claim to fleeting success was an "undersock" to prevent damp feet, Baird had also racked up a number of total failures, including a method for preserving jam that fell through when a swarm of insects ate his inventory and a rustproof razor made from glass that cut his face rather badly.

Like Farnsworth, Baird was inspired to tackle the idea of television from reading scientific journals in the early 1920s. A few years later, while in his mid-thirties, he developed a system out of scattered items he bought or found in his attic, including an old tea chest, a bicycle-light lens, a hat box, and an old biscuit tin. He cut the round scanning disk out of cardboard, punched holes around its perimeter, and patched the entire contraption together with dabs of glue, sealing wax, and shoestring. The disk revolved around a knitting needle like a pinwheel, picking up light and relaying it to a selenium cell, which produced a current that lit neon lamps that sent the light patterns to an identical spinning disk that finally decoded the pattern and projected it to a screen two feet away.

Somehow, it all worked. He transmitted the shadow of a Maltese cross to his receiver across the room. Pretty soon, he was claiming he could convert pictures into fifty-line images, about one-tenth the resolution of the system Farnsworth intended to build. Shortly after Baird relayed his first shadows, he produced an electrical

explosion in which he nearly died. He survived the shock but created so much noise and commotion that his landlord evicted him.

By January of 1926, Baird secured a new place to live and work,
in London's Soho, and invited reporters from the *Times*, as well as
scientists from London's prestigious Royal Institute, up for a demonstration. Despite the fact that one of the senior scientists got his
long white beard caught in the spinning disk, the event went as well
as could be expected. The story in the morning paper described
how Baird "claims to have solved the problem of television," but it
warned that it "[remains] to be seen to what extent further developments will carry Mr. Baird's system toward practical use."

When American newspapers retold the story, however, they left
out the notes of caution. "The international race for television has
been won by Great Britain," reported the *New York Times*. Baird had
already received some publicity in 1925 from an ongoing demonstration in one of London's busiest department stores, Selfridge's,
for which he was paid twenty pounds per week, but his 1926 demonstration was his breakthrough.

No one covered Baird's activities more faithfully than Hugo
Gernsback's *Radio News*. The September 1926 issue ran a story under
the headline: "Television an Accomplished Fact." All prior articles
about television, Gernsback wrote, "were of a theoretical nature." With
a scarcely disguised pat on his own back, he recalled how he "came
in for a good deal of criticism" but that his "faith in television was
sufficiently persistent. Now the art has progressed to such an extent
that it is possible to see a moving face at a distance."

As a result of all this attention, Baird was eventually able to raise
about 1 million pounds to further develop his invention, and his
company soon grew to more than 200 employees.

But Baird knew, perhaps better than anyone, how limited his
system really was. It wasn't long before he began brainstorming for
a superior method of scanning images. Early in 1928, he hit upon

an idea: The best image scanner on Earth is the human eye! Why not use one of those! So he met with a surgeon at a London hospital and convinced him to call when he next came across a spare eyeball Baird could use. Sure enough, some time later, the surgeon came through, and Baird detailed the bizarre experiment in his journal:

> As soon as I was given the eye, I hurried in a taxicab to the laboratory. Within a few minutes I had the eye in the machine. The essential image for television passed through the eye [but] on the following day the sensitiveness of the eye's visual nerve was gone. . . . Nothing was gained from the experiment. It was gruesome and a waste of time.

Electronic television was to mechanical television what the telegraph was to smoke signals, yet in the late 1920s, even the top scientists at the top corporate labs didn't realize that electronic television would eclipse all other methods. At AT&T's Bell Telephone Laboratories in New Jersey, Herbert Ives was directing a large, well-funded research staff in the creation of a form of mechanical television to be transmitted over phone lines. In April of 1927, Ives staged an event for reporters, politicians, and scientists that was covered in virtually every major newspaper. Using a pair of Nipkow disks fifteen inches in diameter and punctured with fifty holes each, he transmitted the image of U.S. commerce secretary Herbert Hoover, who sat in Washington while a blurred approximation of his face flashed on a distant screen in New York as he spoke the words "Human genius has now destroyed the impediment of distance" over a separate telephone line connected to remote speakers. The *Times* echoed the proclamation in its front-page headline the next day: "More Than 200 Miles of Space Annihilated."

This method would soon prove to be as unworkable as Baird's, and finally, Bell Labs dropped television research altogether, claiming it wasn't interested in broadcasting, only in attaching a picture screen to a telephone, an idea that seemed too expensive and far off to develop any further.

Paying an increasing amount of attention to all this activity was RCA's David Sarnoff. He was keeping a watchful eye on Bell Labs because his old nemesis Walter Gifford was directly involved in the Bell Labs demonstration, and he wanted to be sure AT&T didn't beat RCA to the punch. But of even more interest to Sarnoff were the developments at RCA's parent company, General Electric. Sarnoff had inside access to all the research being done in GE's laboratory in Schenectady, New York, where the company was throwing more and more of its abundant laboratory resources into television.

The project was led by one of GE's most renowned scientists, Ernst Alexanderson, an absentminded professor-type who had a habit of suddenly switching to Swedish, his native tongue, in the middle of a conversation. He was by all accounts brilliant, but by the late 1920s he seemed to be resting on the laurels of his past success, including his invention of a breakthrough radio transmitter. In a memo to Sarnoff, Alexanderson wrote: "We have designed a very promising form of television projector. I believe that we will control this situation provided that we are the first to give a practical demonstration." Yet in a public speech in 1926, Alexanderson made a rather damning observation about the limits of mechanical television.

If we knew of any way of sweeping a ray of light back and forth without the use of mechanical motion, the solution of the problem would be simplified. Perhaps some such way will be discovered, but we are not willing to wait for a discovery that may never come.

Alexanderson certainly knew how to deflect electromagnetic waves, and he knew quite a bit about cathode rays, but he seemed unwilling to drop all of the company's prior television research and take up an entirely new approach. So he pressed on with the mechanical method, hoping that it would somehow lead to something. It never would.

Of all the rivals in that doomed field, the one who would have the most immediate effect on Farnsworth would be an inventor named Charles Francis Jenkins. Born in Dayton, Ohio, home of the Wright brothers, Jenkins had read about Edison's early Kinetoscope, a peepshow machine that crudely flashed a sequence of photographs but didn't work very well. By 1895, Jenkins had come up with a greatly improved variation, a projector that illuminated successive frames of film fast enough to fool the eye into seeing fluid movement. His invention would lead to the formation of the motion picture industry, but not under the Jenkins name.

The only working model was stolen from his home by his opportunistic financial backer, who sold it to a theater company which marketed it worldwide under the name Edison Vitascope, taking advantage of the famous inventor's name recognition. Thomas Edison himself didn't object because it resulted in the popular view that Edison was the one who invented the movies. To put an end to a drawn-out court battle, Jenkins eventually agreed to a $2,500 payment from the theater company.

"It's the old story over again," Jenkins later wrote. "The inventor gets the experience and the capitalist gets the invention."

Jenkins was determined never to let this happen again. By the early 1920s, living in Washington, D.C. so he could have close access to the library and the filing desk of the Patent Office, Jenkins came up with something he called the Radiovisor, which at first was concerned only with sending still photographs over the airwaves. When he achieved a demonstration of that, he sold the invention to the navy and went to work immediately on transmitting moving pictures. The transmission itself, as everyone in the field knew, was the trivial part. The hard part was scanning a moving image, and this is what he set out to do.

In 1925, shortly after Baird began demonstrating at Selfridge's department store in London, Jenkins had developed a mechanical system that he felt was ready for a public showing. From a local radio station, the inventor was able to broadcast the shadow of a turning windmill several miles through the air to a screen in his laboratory. Among the gathered dignitaries at the demonstration was Hugo Gernsback, who immediately raced back to New York to complete an article for *Radio News*. "I have just left the laboratory of Mr. C. Francis Jenkins," Gernsback gushed, "and am still under the influence of what I consider to be the most marvelous invention of the age."

Yet the Radiovisor produced images that were of even worse quality than Baird's. The scan produced an image of only forty-eight lines, not enough to recognize anything more than a vague silhouette. Nevertheless, Jenkins was determined not to be upstaged a second time. To prevent someone else from stealing the credit and the financial reward for his invention, Jenkins became a self-promotion machine, garnering publicity left and right, including a series of cover stories in *Radio News* that were illustrated by lurid cartoons that wildly exaggerated what the Jenkins system could actually do.

He also entered into a deal with Gernsback. Through ads in Gernsback's magazine, Jenkins began selling kits that would enable anyone to assemble a crude mechanical Radiovisor receiver at home. They included cathode ray screens and spinning drums that could be attached to existing living room radios. Inititally offered for $42.50 each, including postage, Jenkins lost money on every kit sold, especially as he cut the price. Jenkins broadcast his silhouettes from WRNY, Gernsback's New York radio station. For the time being, it was an interesting novelty. Soon, more than a dozen other radio stations began using the Jenkins system to transmit shadows of a little girl bouncing a ball and other so-called pantomime movies.

The radio announcer would explain to viewers what they were seeing, as it often wasn't entirely clear by looking at it.

For Jenkins, the terrible quality and the lack of profits were beside
the point. He would make money, tons of it, at least on paper, another
way: by offering stock in his company. At the height of the bull
market, the Jenkins Television Corporation became a Wall Street
darling, not by making money selling a product that many people
wanted, but by selling a promise to somehow do so in the future. To
stockbrokers and investors of all stripes, it made for an irresistible
story. Most of the people touting the stock never saw the Jenkins
system demonstrated; most didn't know how it worked or what it
really was, but based on the publicity and the promise, bankers
were able to form the company with an eye-popping initial market
capitalization of $10 million—such was the fervor for the future of
technology.

The financial euphoria surrounding Charles Francis Jenkins put
Philo T. Farnsworth in a knotty bind. After all, the bankers who
were backing his venture were not in the television business but in
the business of seeking the highest possible return on their money.
Farnsworth needed to get his electronic television system to a commercial stage as quickly as possible, but he didn't want to excite his
investors so much that they would want to sell the company out from
under him.

The lab journals from 1928 show Farnsworth immersed in attacking problem after problem. In January, he achieved a method of mag-
netically focusing the electron beams to present a two-dimensional
image on his receiving screen. He accomplished this by experimenting with different ways of winding the electromagnetic coils around
the camera tube, so that it would "sweep the image across the anode
of the Dissector a line at a time," according to Everson. This method
of focusing an image would become an indispensable piece of vir-

tually all commercial television systems for the rest of the century
and beyond.

By April, Farnsworth reported his Image Dissector to be "free of
past defects." By May, he brainstormed a theory for narrowing
the transmission wave band, so that picture signals wouldn't crowd
out sounds assigned to adjacent frequencies. "I have a plan for cutting this required band in half," he wrote. By August, all the small
improvements added up to something big. "It is conservative to say
that the picture which can be transmitted is improved 10-fold by
the use of this new tube," he wrote. His scan was now up to 150 lines
of resolution.

All year long, he still kept getting the same message from his
backers at the Crocker Bank. With his forefingers, Fagan would make
glasses around his eyes, and ask Everson: "When are we going to
see some dollars in Phil's gadget?" Fagan kept repeating this over
and over. Finally, Phil told Everson to invite the bankers over for a
demonstration, but he warned that he didn't want to get them too
aroused, as there was still much to do. The next morning, the bankers
paraded into the lab. Jesse McCargar, as seemed usual, was off on
vacation. But J. J. Fagan, Roy Bishop, plus William H. Crocker and
his son were all there in a high state of anticipation and in a rather
chipper mood to boot, especially when Fagan repeated once again,
"When are we going to see some dollars in this thing?"

As the assemblage stared into the receiving tube, Farnsworth
said, "Here's something a banker will understand." And at the center of the blue screen appeared the image of a dollar sign. The group
broke out into laughter, as the men began slapping their knees in
approval. Cliff, in the other room, then began smoking a cigarette
in front of the camera tube, and the men saw the vague outline of
smoke wafting on the screen. Fagan, in his day, had witnessed plenty
of people blowing smoke at him, but nothing like this. The demonstration, as Farnsworth had feared, was a huge hit with the bankers,

who had been privately referring to the project as the "Jonah," because this big black thing was swallowing all their cash.

After congratulating Farnsworth, Roy Bishop switched into a formal tone of voice. He said that the investors had lived up to their end of the bargain. By now, the bankers' investment had increased, to a total of $60,000. It was time to move forward, Bishop said. According to Everson's recollection of the meeting, this is how Bishop put it:

> It is of my opinion that it would take a pile of money as high as Telegraph Hill to carry this thing on to a successful conclusion, and I feel that we should take immediate steps to place it with one of the large electrical companies where there will be adequate facilities for its development. I think it is time to incorporate this undertaking and then take steps to dispose of it in some way or another.

Farnsworth didn't say a word in response to that, but Everson knew that Bishop's phrase "dispose of it" must have stirred in Farnsworth an incredible sadness. To stall the bankers, Everson proposed waiting at least until McCargar got back from vacation before a final decision would be made. No one wanted to appear unreasonable, so everyone agreed to convene again in a month, and the meeting was adjourned.

Farnsworth did, however, agree to one of the suggestions made by the bankers: to hold a demonstration for the press and get the invention out in the eye of the public at last. The bankers wanted to do this to attract a buyer. Farnsworth had his own reasons. The details in his patent applications were winding their way through scientific circles, and leading engineers were taking shots at his concept of electronic television in technical journals. In essence, they were saying it wouldn't work. Perhaps attention in the mainstream press would help silence his critics.

The press conference was set for September 1, 1928, a Saturday. A weekend day was not the most likely time to attract business reporters, who were well used to working Monday through Friday. Public relations was not Farnsworth's forte. Still, while few reporters managed to show up, one in particular, Earle Ennis from the *San Francisco Chronicle*, showed a keen interest and clearly understood the significance of Farnsworth's work. By now, Farnsworth was able to televise film clips picked up from a secondhand, modified movie projector that he placed in front of the Image Dissector. His favorite clip was a thirty-second cut of Mary Pickford combing her hair in the Hollywood adaptation of *The Taming of the Shrew*. The film loop ran over and over again, hundreds of times per day, and the sharp contrasts in the frames came through on the receiving screen. It made for the best demo to date, and Ennis was clearly impressed.

On Sunday night, Phil and Pem went out with Cliff and Lola (Cliff's high school sweetheart and new bride) to the movies at a downtown theater. Farnsworth was astonished when he stopped the car to pick up the Monday edition of the *Chronicle*. The following headline jumped off the front page of the second section: "S.F. Man's Invention to Revolutionize Television." And there was a clever little subhead: "New Plan Bans Rotating Disc in Black Light." Plus a smaller tagline after it: "W. W. Crocker, R.N. Bishop Head Local Capitalists Backing Genius."

> Two major advances in television were announced yesterday by a young inventor who has been quietly working away in his laboratory in San Francisco and has evolved a system of television basically different from any system yet placed in operation.... Farnsworth's system employs no moving parts whatever.... He varies the electric current that plays over the image and thus gets the necessary scanning. The system is thus simple in the extreme, and one of the major obstacles to the perfection of

television is thereby removed. Through this simplicity he achieved his second great advance, the cutting in half of the wave band length necessary to prevent broadcasts interfering with each other. . . . The sending tube is about the size of an ordinary quart jar that a housewife uses for preserving fruit, and the receiving tube containing the screen is even smaller. . . . It is a queer looking little image . . . but the basic principle is achieved and perfection is now a matter of engineering.

The horse was out of the barn. The *Chronicle* story was immediately picked up by newspapers all over the country and led to the recognition of the basic concept, as Farnsworth had wanted. It also heightened hopes to sell the venture at a big profit, as the bankers had wanted.

On the last Sunday in October, Phil and Pem were playing tennis with Cliff and Lola when a policeman drove up to the court.

"Are you Farnsworth?" the policeman asked.

"Yes," replied Phil, with hesitation. "I am."

"You might want to get down to your laboratory right away. The place is on fire!"

The policeman activated his siren, loaded everyone into the car, and rushed the entire group to the lab. When they arrived, Farnsworth met up with a perplexed fire chief. Water only seemed to add fuel to the fire, the chief said with a sigh. Farnsworth explained that the lab contained complex chemicals. The fire chief sounded pessimistic that anything inside would be recovered, and he was correct. The place was ruined. The charred remains of the interior included a burned-out floor that was dripping chemicals into the woodworking shop below.

After a sleepless night wondering whether the place was insured, Farnsworth found out the next morning that indeed it was, and in a stroke of extreme luck, Pem had brought the lab journals home where they were safe. The staff spent the next month doing theoretical research while the place was rebuilt, and they were back in business by early December, with better lab equipment and an improved picture on the reception screen.

Soon after, the fledgling company was officially incorporated and organized as Television Laboratories, with shares issued to Everson, Farnsworth, Gorrell, and the Crocker group. No one wanted to bring the shares public at this time, for the very real fear that Wall Street's rabid speculators would bring the company to ruin. Yet they needed to behave as if they were public, and to make the enterprise seem more professional, the bankers insisted that Farnsworth couldn't keep such a close relative on staff. Pem had to quit.

That was perfectly fine by her. She felt her relationship with Phil had become too complex. "I was Phil's personal secretary, his draftsman, his friend, his confidante, and his lover," Pem recalled. Now she assumed a more traditional role and also found a part-time job in a lamp shade factory. By Christmas, things got even more traditional. She was pregnant.

One day, Gorrell showed up at the laboratory with the news that he had sold a tenth of his 10 percent stake for $5,000. Although it wasn't listed on an exchange, the company's shares could be bought and sold at whatever price the market would bear at any given moment. By now, Gorrell was working full-time as a research analyst at a local brokerage house, issuing buy and sell recommendations. He said the financial community in San Francisco was abuzz over Farnsworth. Due to the recent publicity as well as the success of the Jenkins stock, *television* was now a magic word, even more so than *radio*.

At the time of Gorrell's first stock sale, investors were valuing the company at $500,000. But soon after, Gorrell heard a rumor that the total value had doubled, to $1 million. Gorrell used some of the proceeds to pay Everson back the original $3,000 loan. He also bought a few nice things, then began playing the stock market with the rest of his money. Within a few months, after liquidating all of his holdings in Television Laboratories, he lost almost everything when stock prices broke badly for him. He still kept his job as a research analyst, though, recommending stocks for other people.

With the price of shares in Television Laboratories valued so highly, Farnsworth decided to sell off some of his stock. He initially sold less than 5 percent of his holdings, but the money went far. He bought a boxy black Chrysler roadster, which he promptly drove to the factory where Pem was working. He took her hand and led her out to the shiny new car. He told her that she could quit her job now, and she gladly did. Soon after, they went looking for a home to buy and came across a newly developed set of row houses on Lyon Street, right across from the Presidio, on the marina, not far from the water. Phil signed over some shares to the developer as a down payment. He also gave shares to his siblings, Pem's siblings, Pem's father, and his own mother back in Utah, making her financially independent for the rest of her life. Mother Farnsworth soon got lonely, though, and decided to move in with them and help Pem with the baby.

Pem nested nicely. Neither she nor Phil had ever experienced much more than bare subsistence living, so this was a welcome change. They bought an alabaster female figure to hang over the fireplace in the living room, and Pem worked with her mother-in-law to set up the baby's room with homemade ruffled curtains, a wicker bassinet, and a rocking chair, and helped Phil set up his study upstairs. He called it the "airplane room" because it offered a view of aircraft taking off and swooping in over the sea. In those days, when you heard an airplane humming overhead, you stopped to watch, and Phil was as fascinated as anyone. After just a few weeks in the new home, they agreed that there was one thing lacking in the living room: a piano. Phil had one delivered the very next day.

George Everson was especially happy for Pem. "She was a lovely girl and is now a beautiful woman," he wrote. "She has instinctive good taste and a fine feeling for gracious living. Phil is inordinately proud of her and is happy to give her the means to dress well and have a fine home."

In September of 1929, Pem gave birth to a healthy baby boy. They named him Philo Taylor Farnsworth III. On the first night they were all back home, Phil waltzed into the baby's room singing his own version of "My Blue Heaven," with the words "just Pemmie and me, and our baby makes three, we're happy in our blue heaven." Everything was going as well as could possibly be expected. Life on Green Street was good. In more ways than one, Farnsworth's stock was high.

Vladimir Zworykin, RCA's top television scientist, poses with his Kinescope television receiver tube, in 1929. (DAVID SARNOFF LIBRARY)

CHAPTER EIGHT

Confrontation

Sitting at his gigantic, gleaming desk at RCA headquarters in New York, David Sarnoff glanced at a terse but spectacularly timed note from his secretary. The message stated that a certain engineer from Westinghouse had called and wanted to meet with him to discuss a new and all-electronic approach to television. By now, Sarnoff had grown to resent the mechanical contraptions on the market. He knew the public would develop higher and higher expectations, and if the industry couldn't produce a major break-through soon, television would soon become a punch line, just another failed novelty item.

It was December of 1928. Only a few months earlier, Sarnoff had read the news reports about Philo T. Farnsworth and his electronic tubes. To Sarnoff, it must have seemed far-fetched that some kid from California, working independently, would be anywhere near getting so complex an invention to a commercial stage. Still, Sarnoff was worried about the television situation in general, evidenced by the press interviews he granted at this time, during which he pontificated about the future of the medium. So without hesitation, he agreed to the appointment request, setting it for a day in early January 1929. He wanted to find out what this Westinghouse engineer had in mind.

Vladimir Kosma Zworykin walked in at the appointed hour. A thin man of medium height, with sandy hair and thick glasses, Zworykin was, at thirty-nine, only two years older than Sarnoff, and he too had emigrated from Russia. While Sarnoff was from a poor, rural, Jewish family, Zworykin was from a prosperous, bourgeois, urban one and had fled his homeland after the Bolsheviks seized his family's mansion during the Russian Revolution of 1917. The Russian connection meant practically nothing to Sarnoff. While Zworykin spoke in heavily accented English, Sarnoff had rid his speech of all traces of his heritage. Sarnoff considered himself as American as Henry God-damn Ford. He was interested not in this engineer's background but in the ideas in his head at this very moment.

He invited Zworykin to have a seat, then lit up a fat cigar, sat back in his soft leather chair, and listened to his guest's story without interruption. As a student in St. Petersburg, Zworykin explained, he had helped his physics professor conduct experiments with cathode ray tubes, which sparked his own research into transmitting images using electricity. He wasn't able to resume any such work until the early 1920s when he joined Westinghouse in Pittsburgh, Pennsylvania. Even then, he often had to hide his experiments or camouflage them as parts of other projects he was supposed to be working on. In 1923, he had filed for a U.S. patent on his ideas, but he hadn't been able to demonstrate that his electronic television concept operated as described. Thus far, the Patent Office had refused to grant that application.

After asking a few questions to clear up some points, Sarnoff needed to know only two things: How long would it take to develop a working electronic television system? And how much would it cost?

Zworykin immediately came back with an estimate: Two years. And $100,000.

Since Westinghouse was part of the radio combine that pooled patent rights, it wouldn't be all that unusual for RCA to fund the work at its sister company, provided it got top-level approval. In Sarnoff's mind, such approval wouldn't be necessary. Sarnoff had designs on unifying the laboratories of Westinghouse and RCA at the company's recently acquired Victor Talking Machines facility in Camden, New Jersey. He was planning on cherry-picking the top scientists at Westinghouse anyway, so this meeting was quite convenient for both men. Each needed the other. They struck a deal, setting up the budget and time frame that Zworykin requested without running this by the bureaucracy. By the first of February, Zworykin was back in Pittsburgh conducting experiments under direct orders from Sarnoff. The operation was to be carried out in secrecy.

In late February of 1929, Hugo Gernsback's publishing empire was forced into bankruptcy. "Radio News Publisher in Hands of Receiver— Gernsback's Concern Is Called Insolvent," said a headline in the *Times*.

To Philo T. Farnsworth, Hugo Gernsback was the personification of the future. Gernsback's magazines had been the first to advertise and sell kits for building the original homemade radios that so excited Farnsworth as a boy, and the editor had prided himself on making bold predictions across the entire spectrum of scientific and technological progress, printing prophesies about magnetic memory cells, radar, solar energy, atomic power, flying cars, transatlantic flight, telemedicine, electronic dating services, pills for controlling human reproduction, jukeboxes, night baseball, vending machines, and newspapers that could be transmitted and re-created in homes. Whenever someone actually made progress on one of these things, Gernsback's response was always "What took you so long?"

In recent years, Gernsback's mind had became fixated on more spectacular topics, such as space exploration, teleportation, floating cities in the sky, saucers from space, life on Mars, and human colonies beneath the sea. His most talked about magazine now was called *Amazing Stories*, and on the cover each month was a lurid painting—giant spiders attacking pedestrians or glowing spaceships and the like. He was now bringing esteemed writers such as Jules Verne and H. G. Wells to the masses, and he had a name for his new genre: *scientifiction*, which he later modified to *science fiction*, which he defined as stories of the scientifically feasible. Yet no other prediction had become more identified with Gernsback's magazines than television. Many of his readers even gave him credit for coining the term (although that honor usually is attributed to an obscure French scientist who used it in a speech at the Paris Exposition in 1900 to describe something like a fax machine). If Gernsback, a man with such an encompassing vision for the future, were to go bankrupt, what would that mean to Farnsworth and his fledgling invention?

As it turned out, Gernsback's troubles had more to say about the precarious state of business in 1929 than they did about technology. His Experimenter Publishing Company had been expanding rapidly and spending extravagantly, operating from its plush offices on Fifth Avenue and even going so far as to mail out, free of charge, tens of thousands of radio blueprints, detailed circuit and wiring diagrams for do-it-yourself radio making. Giving those materials away only led to huge printing and postage bills. Gernsback was now stuck in a financial tar pit. His company listed assets of $182,000 and liabilities of $600,000, and creditors were demanding payment. "Plans are being formulated to reorganize and continue publication," Gernsback told the press. "I am authorized to say this by the receiver."

To survive, the company had to auction off core assets, most notably its three flagship magazines, which then continued publication under their new owners. *Amazing Stories* remained a leading science fiction journal for many years. *Radio News* was repositioned as a more sober trade journal for technical professionals, and the new owners of *Science and Invention* merged the magazine with *Popular Mechanics*, a glossy consumer monthly that would survive the century. In the reorganization, Gernsback kept hold of his radio station, WYNY. He then let most of his employees go, packed up his Fifth Avenue offices, and retreated to cheaper digs in a more modest part of town.

As he emerged from bankruptcy protection a few months later, Gernsback once again grew ambitious. He launched a new science fiction magazine called *Science Wonder Stories* and, most significantly, put a brand-new technical publication on the drawing boards. Called *Television News*, it would be dedicated to the potential millions of experimenters who yearned to send and receive moving images.

Gernsback's plight was emblematic of the wrenching changes happening in the financial markets and the economy at large. The boom years of the 1920s had produced thousands of fast-moving, fast-growing ventures that simply didn't make any money. The public was enthralled by radio, electronics, automobiles, airplanes— all the wondrous new technology. Gernsback, more than anyone else, was pushing the outer limits of what all this technology would be able to do in the future. As a result, he played a leading role in focusing the public on the limitless, blue-sky opportunities that lie ahead.

Other business "journalists" and columnists were doing far worse, taking outright bribes from executives to write glowing stories about new companies and their shares. In addition, there were little or no restrictions on stock pools and other forms of market manipulation. It was no surprise that the public was speculating on dubious new companies, regardless of the price and regardless of whether revenue exceeded expenses.

All the warning signs were there. Average investors were buying stock on margin, with brokers acting as banks, allowing consumers to put down 10 percent and pay off the rest in monthly installments, plus interest on the loan. If the stock continued to go up, it was a snap to pay off the balance right away. If the stock went down, it was another story. In minicrashes and quick rebounds that began in late March 1929—right after the inauguration of President Hoover—investors began to see the pain this could cause. Instead of free money, many now had crushing debt. The wild volatility caused widespread nervousness, but the new administration didn't move to restrict margin trading, fearing that any remedy would be worse than the disease. In a misguided attempt to salvage their money, many investors bought more stock as the prices dipped.

By the summer, even Philo T. Farnsworth was playing the market, although he refused to buy on margin. He invested $4,000 in a few stocks, made a modest profit, and quickly got out. David Sarnoff also liquidated all of his stock holdings, acting on a hunch that may have been inspired by his well-connected associates. Joseph P. Kennedy did the same, later saying that only "dumb people" were left in the game. Indeed, Kennedy reportedly made more than $1 million during the last few months of the great bull market by short selling, betting stocks would soon drop. Insiders like him knew that the speculation didn't make any sense. Eventually, it had to end badly.

By the start of the Labor Day weekend, 1929, the Dow Jones Industrial Average had climbed back to reach an all-time high. RCA in recent years had become a component of this esteemed index of thirty industrial corporations, and after splitting five for one, RCA's shares were now trading close to its split-adjusted peak of 110.

After the weekend, the market began its slide. A big banking pool organized by J. P. Morgan & Company tried to stabilize the sell-off by pumping money in, but the temporary rallies quickly faltered. On the morning of October 29, 1929, panic set in. As brokers unloaded the highly margined shares of their clients, a huge order imbalance developed at the opening bell. Everyone wanted to get out, and no one seemed to be buying. On this day of reckoning, Black Tuesday, more than $15 billion in market value was wiped out. RCA plunged below twenty dollars per share. Failure to respond to a big margin call could mean losing your home and your life savings. There were at least eleven reports of suicides among various Wall Street figures over the following days. Out of the $80 billion in shares listed on the New York Stock Exchange, close to half had been vaporized in just two months, a sum equivalent to what the United States had spent to fight the Great War.

The market implosion changed everything, and the repercussions were even felt within the insular world of Television Laboratories. Facing a cash crunch, the investors at Crocker Bank were exerting increased pressure on the company to find a buyer, flatly refusing to pump any more money into the venture. One day, Jesse McCargar called George Everson and told him that he was going to shut down the whole operation. He was going to fire everyone and padlock the door until someone stepped in to take it off their hands.

Everson raced over to Green Street to warn Farnsworth and head off the anxious banker. When McCargar arrived, he found a defiant Farnsworth standing at the door, with Everson behind him. McCargar explained that he needed to do this, that the bank couldn't keep sinking its money down a hole without a return.

When he ordered Farnsworth to fire everyone, Farnsworth flatly refused. "This is my laboratory!" Farnsworth exploded, in a fit of anger that no one had ever before witnessed coming from him. "No one comes in here giving me orders as to what is to be done!"

McCargar shot back at him, declaring that *he* was the president of the company. It was true. When the formal charter was drawn up,

McCargar was appointed the top executive, Farnsworth the vice president of research, and Everson the treasurer.

Before McCargar could do something drastic, Everson stepped in between the two to cool things off and propose a solution. Cliff Gardner and the other members of the laboratory staff watching the blowup all stepped forward and agreed on the spot to work without pay. Perhaps, suggested Everson, the employees could be granted shares in the company instead of a salary.

By 1929, the original members of the ragtag staff had burned out from the long hours with little pay. As replacements, Farnsworth had hired the most gifted electrical engineers he could find. One of them, Archie "Arch" Brolly, had a degree from MIT, while another, Russell Varian, was a Stanford graduate who later developed an indispensable radar tube that helped win the Second World War. After the war, Varian became a famous pioneer of a new industrial zone called Silicon Valley. A third employee, Harry Lubcke, was a graduate of Berkeley and the future president of an organization called the Academy of Television Arts and Sciences, which would host the annual Emmy Awards. That young men of this caliber and such promise would forgo paychecks made a powerful statement.

Of course, the investors would have found it difficult to sell a closed company. McCargar was forced to admit that a business that was actually doing something was more valuable than one that was shut down. He granted Farnsworth a temporary reprieve, with the understanding that everyone needed to widen the search for a buyer. Everson said he would do his best to sell some of his shares to generate operating cash, which he soon did even though prices were greatly depressed.

Farnsworth had no intention of selling the company. He was an inventor. An inventor doesn't sell out and go to work for someone else. An inventor doesn't sign his patent rights away to a big corporation. An inventor *licenses* patent rights to other companies, and uses the ongoing *royalties* to finance new inventions. Of course, it would be no use explaining this to McCargar, especially at such a financially desperate moment. Still, Farnsworth had hopes that his business partner would catch on soon.

As the bankers sought their exit from the venture and as Farnsworth received more and more publicity, the promise of electronic television attracted a procession of prominent visitors to 202 Green Street.

By now, the demonstrations that Farnsworth could conduct were quite impressive. He was transmitting visual signals a mile away by radio to an office called the Hobart Building. He secured a copy of the first talking cartoon, Walt Disney's *Steamboat Willie*, plus footage of the famous Dempsey-Tunney fight, and he was able to show these entertaining snippets on his reception tube. Staff members built their first floor-model console receiver, which was housed in a handsome wooden cabinet and sported a circular screen seven inches in diameter. Farnsworth told visitors that these units could be made and sold profitably for $300 each. Around this time, he became the first television pioneer to transmit the image of a live face and have it be recognizable to the viewer. The first face he chose to televise was that of Pem, and the fuzzy screen shot of her smiling and wearing a stylish hat was soon reproduced in a leading technical journal.

Among those swinging by the lab in early 1930 was Guglielmo Marconi, by now a bona fide Nobel laureate. He seemed quite impressed by Farnsworth's demonstration, as did another famous inventor who stopped in, Lee De Forest, the creator of the Audion, the vacuum tube that transformed Marconi's discovery into modern radio. The California representative from the Federal Radio Commission came by and took notes, as did Herbert Hoover Jr., eldest son of the president and a well-known technology buff.

A young Berkeley scientist named Ernest Lawrence paid several visits. Lawrence was most fascinated with a device Farnsworth invented to boost the strength of his transmission signal. It was an electron multiplier, and it worked by bouncing electron beams inside a metal chamber, which dislodged more electrons from the metal plates, creating a feedback loop so powerful that the resulting energy had to be released in bursts within a fantastically tiny fraction of a second, or the circuits would fry. Farnsworth called this device the Multipactor, and he filed for his first patent on it that March. Lawrence's name would later grace a famous Berkeley laboratory that housed his first cyclotron, a particle accelerator for advanced physics research. Lawrence won the Nobel Prize for this work, and he gave public credit to Farnsworth for inspiring parts of it.

The most frantic of these visits in early 1930 began with a call from the offices of United Artists, a company formed to counter the power of the major Hollywood studios. The caller said that the head of the company, producer Joseph Schenck, wanted to come by with two of the UA founders, Douglas Fairbanks Sr. and his wife, Mary Pickford. They were at that time one of the world's most celebrated and famous couples. Pickford in particular had just picked up an Oscar for best actress at the second annual Academy Awards ceremony, although only a few hundred people saw the ceremony. The caller said that a third UA founder, Charlie Chaplin, also wanted to visit but was away in Europe.

The call sent Farnsworth and staff into a frenzy. On the afternoon before their arrival, Farnsworth made some changes to the setup to improve the picture, but for some reason, one of his adjustments rendered the system inoperative. No picture was coming through at all. He called Pem and told her he wouldn't be coming home for dinner. The staff would be troubleshooting into the night.

At seven the next morning, Phil called from the lab to see if Pem could cook some breakfast for the boys. They also needed to shave and wash up while they were at the house before going back to the lab to meet the movie stars. Pem served bacon and eggs, pointed them to the washroom, and then saw them off. The appointment had been set for 10 A.M., and Fairbanks called a few minutes earlier from the Mark Hopkins Hotel on California Street to check whether everything was on schedule. Farnsworth told him to please wait a little while. He had to correct a little problem and would call back shortly.

The men were exhausted and in a panic as they worked the better part of the day to no avail. Meanwhile, the afternoon newspapers had caught word of the appointment and ran a story with the headline: "Mary, Doug Here to Test Television" below a photo of the dashing Fairbanks and the adorable Pickford talking on the telephone, supposedly with Maurice Chevalier. At 3 P.M. Fairbanks called to ask if they could just see whatever Farnsworth had, as they had to take the evening train back to Los Angeles.

With dark circles around their eyes, the lab staff kept working while Hollywood's leading man stood with his arms folded and America's sweetheart sat on a lab bench looking a little glum. Cliff tried and failed to keep them entertained with glassblowing tricks. When Fairbanks mentioned that he had recently imported from Vienna the world's leading glassblowing artists for work in a film, Cliff sucked in the remains of his pride and put down his equipment.

Trying not to look too embarrassed, Farnsworth switched on the system and demonstrated to them a blurry, substandard picture that obviously didn't impress anyone. Pickford was especially gracious through the whole debacle. Before leaving, she invited Farnsworth to bring his wife to visit them at Pickfair, their palatial estate, but Farnsworth couldn't help but feel humiliated as he escorted his guests to the door. As soon as the Hollywood icons were gone, of course, a member of the lab staff located a faulty wire that was quickly repaired, leading to the sharpest picture they had to date.

.   .   .

The tobacco-spitting J. J. Fagan and the other executives at the Crocker Bank were not awed or amused by the big names trotting through the laboratory door. This was a struggling company, not some tourist attraction or some glamorous salon. They wanted a visitor who was capable of swallowing the entire outfit, someone from one of the big electrical concerns, someone serious about pioneering the future, someone with real money behind them.

The next guest fit the bill. The head of television research at the Westinghouse Electric Corporation had called to make an appointment for an extended stay. His name was Vladimir Zworykin. Westinghouse was not only a successful maker of household appliances but a pioneer of radio broadcasting. For that company to make a bold move into television made perfect sense. While Farnsworth knew some of Zworykin's past accomplishments from reading technical journals, he hardly knew anything at all about the state of television research inside Westinghouse, and he knew nothing about Zworykin's arrangement with David Sarnoff.

Backed by Sarnoff's resources, Zworykin had been working feverishly. By the summer of 1929, Zworykin had developed his own electronic receiving tube. In one sense, it was an improvement over Farnsworth's receiver, in that it employed the principle of a "cache," or a set of circuits that temporarily stored parts of the incoming picture, which would help reduce the need for hot, intense light while scanning the subject. Zworykin filed for a patent on his so-called Kinescope by November, and the legal eagles at the radio combine were already using his application to interfere with Farnsworth's pending patents. Yet Zworykin's electronic image had a resolution of only twelve lines at this point, mainly because he had yet to tackle the harder problem of building an electronic television camera. Thus he was still relying on mechanical scanning, meaning he was for all intents and purposes way behind Farnsworth.

Zworykin arrived at Green Street in the middle of April 1930. For three days, all of the activity at the laboratory was centered on impressing this esteemed visitor. Farnsworth simply wanted to license his patents to Westinghouse, while the bankers wanted to sell the company outright. In any case, they showed him every courtesy as they revealed to him everything in the lab. No one was especially concerned that Zworykin would try to swipe any intellectual property. Engineers at Zworykin's level were all members of international professional societies that promoted clear codes of ethics. Besides, virtually all the demonstrations at the lab were already described in officially filed patent applications and technical journals.

Farnsworth enjoyed having such a knowledgeable colleague on hand, someone he could talk to and exchange ideas with. One evening, he invited Zworykin back to his house across from the Presidio for a home-cooked dinner with Pem. The laboratory journal for the week ending April 19 states in technical terms some of what Zworykin witnessed: "Dr. Zworykin spent three days at the laboratory. Demonstrations were given on moving-picture transmission, admittance-neutralized receiver, slope wave, deltatron, mutual conductance, etc. The demonstrations were all successful."

Like Lawrence, Dr. Zworykin seemed especially impressed by the electron multiplier, which amplified transmissions. Most significantly, Phil asked Cliff to build an Image Dissector tube from scratch right before Zworykin's eyes. Indeed, Zworykin insisted on this demonstration. Afterward, Zworykin marveled at it as he held it in his hands. "This is a beautiful instrument," he remarked. "I wish I had invented it myself."

Everything seemed to go extremely well. But after the visit, no offer from Westinghouse was forthcoming. In early May, the laboratory hosted another pair of visitors, Albert Murray, RCA's head of advanced development in Camden, New Jersey, and a patent attorney only identified in the Farnsworth lab journal as "Mr. Porter from RCA." Farnsworth didn't learn the real motivation behind these two visits until later, when it would become clear that they were coordinated by David Sarnoff.

In a letter dated July 8, 1930, to Farnsworth after his visit, Albert Murray revealed just how interested RCA was in every aspect of Farnsworth's work:

> I greatly enjoyed our visit to your laboratory, the demonstrations which you made for us and our conferences. . . . After going over my notes taken in your laboratory, I found that you were kind enough to say you would send us a bread board model of a two or three stage amplifier. . . . In making our reports to Mr. Otto Schairer, [the patent chief] of the Radio Corporation of America, we would like to report as fully as possible concerning your amplifier and before doing so, I would like to have an opportunity to test [it]. . . . We would be pleased to hear of any recent advances made since our visit in your laboratory in which you might wish to interest the RCA. Very truly yours, A. F. Murray

What the RCA visitors and the letter didn't reveal was Sarnoff's plan. Shortly before the Zworykin visit itself, Sarnoff had quietly hired the Russian scientist away from RCA's sister company, Westinghouse. No longer would he be operating in Pittsburgh. The plan was for Zworykin to visit Farnsworth, then move to the RCA lab in Camden. Zworykin's work, all his television research and related patent applications, would now become the property of RCA itself. Under orders from Sarnoff, most of the television personnel and equipment—not only from Westinghouse but from GE in Schenectady as well—were already in the process of being transferred and consolidated in Camden.

After visiting Farnsworth, Zworykin took the train back to Pittsburgh, where he and his assistants re-created, as best they could, a replica of Farnsworth's Image Dissector while it was still fresh in his mind. Then Zworykin packed it up, collected the rest of his things, and boarded another train to New York, where he reported to Sarnoff.

Upon receiving the letter from Murray and hearing scattered details about the reorganization at the radio combine, Farnsworth's backers at the Crocker Bank switched into a defensive position, sending a letter to Farnsworth requesting a full account of Zworykin's stay, including details on

all time spent with Zworykin, both at the laboratory and elsewhere, mentioning subjects discussed generally and the tests and observations made at the laboratory. We want your signature witnessed by a notary. If any data or photographs were furnished him, attach copies to your report; if any apparatus was given him, include descriptions.

Any pretense that Zworykin had come to see Farnsworth as a colleague, on a cooperative scientific mission, was now shattered. This bit of corporate espionage was a clear act of aggression. The war over television was hereby declared.

By now, David Sarnoff was no longer a rising executive; he had officially arrived at the top of one of the highest ladders in corporate America. Earlier in the year, RCA's founding chairman, Owen Young, reeling from personal debt in the wake of the market crash, resigned from his post. He appointed General Harbord the new chairman and selected Sarnoff to become RCA's new president. The choice was affirmed by a unanimous vote of the board of directors.

Just as important, Sarnoff's own vision of himself was duly ratified by the press. Here was someone who didn't know a word of English as a young boy yet was now "doing more than any man who ever lived to make English the language of the world," wrote the *New York Times*. The profile continued at length in this tone:

> Between the boy and the executive lies a quarter of a century filled with years of struggle in the face of great odds, of obstacles surmounted, of enormous energy, tremendous perseverance, and hardships endured before the heights of success were scaled. He now sits behind a glass-topped desk in one of the world's tallest skyscrapers as head of a gigantic organization whose worldwide influence is a byword on two continents.

In his own mind, however, he had only just begun. Sarnoff not only moved to consolidate all research and development in Camden but also acted to seize absolute control of RCA's other ventures. He traded large blocks of RCA stock—now at a new low of $11.50—to GE and Westinghouse in exchange for their interests in RCA Victor and NBC, finally freeing both subsidiaries from the bureaucracy of the radio combine, although GE and Westinghouse had become even larger stakeholders in RCA itself. For Sarnoff, breaking away from his corporate partners was like untangling a ball of yarn.

Just as he was beginning to concentrate his power and focus it on the new field of television, Sarnoff was torpedoed by his longtime enemies. After the market took its dive, the same horde of investors that had been euphoric beforehand was now livid over losing their life's savings, and no company symbolized the great boom-to-bust nightmare more than RCA. As a result, when banks began to fail, when consumer spending began to collapse, when the prices of everything began to plummet, when masses of jobs began to disappear, the old antitrust issues that the Federal Trade Commission had dropped years earlier were now revived, more forcefully than ever. A newly cynical public was eager to punish corporations for their sins, and members of Congress were eager to oblige.

When the U.S. Senate's Interstate Commerce Committee began holding hearings, RCA rivals such as Zenith and Philco lined up to fire barbs at the radio combine. Sales of radios, like everything else, were plunging, triggering massive price cuts that were threatening to put many manufacturers out of business, leading to further job losses. One radio maker, Grigsby-Grunow, testified that it was being forced to pay $5 million to RCA for patent licensing but was never told what patents were covered. The outrageous payment seemed to serve only as insurance against being sued by RCA, something akin to paying protection money to the mob. Everyone was afraid of saying no to RCA because bankers wouldn't finance an unlicensed company. The senators were being told that RCA's patent policies were simply a way of terrorizing competitors.

On the evening of May 30, 1930, Sarnoff was arriving by limo at a dinner party celebrating his election as president of RCA. The event was being held at a luxurious Fifth Avenue town house owned by the chief of Lazard Frères, the investment banking powerhouse. As Sarnoff stepped out of the car and began to walk into the doors being held open for him, a man in a trench coat emerged from the darkness to block his entrance. It was a U.S. marshal serving him with a formal lawsuit filed by the Department of Justice. The government had finally turned on its own creation, charging RCA and the other members of the radio combine with antitrust violations. The summons asserted that the patent pool constituted an illegal restraint of trade.

After scanning the papers briefly, Sarnoff put them in his breast pocket and proceeded through the doors. He managed to make it through the evening's revelries without mentioning the suit, but afterward, he conferred all night long at his office with a group of RCA executives to discuss the potential consequences. Could the government dissolve the radio monopoly? Could it drain the patent pool? Could it invalidate RCA's license agreements? Could the feds take away its radio stations? Could it force RCA to divest itself of NBC?

While Sarnoff tried to seem cool and confident in public as the monopoly charges blared in headlines across the country, behind the scenes he was anything but. "Privately," wrote RCA executive Kenneth Bilby, "a sense of outrage swept through the organization that a business-oriented Republican administration would thus betray them." President Hoover was considered a personal friend of Young, Harbord, and Sarnoff. How could he have not stopped his attorney general and antitrust chief from doing this? "Later they would learn that Hoover had actually encouraged [the lawsuit]. Already under siege for his Depression policies, he was not prepared to risk a further political explosion."

As the battle lines against the government were drawn, and the legal expenses piled up, radio sales continued to drop, and RCA's profits literally dwindled to zero. Yet Sarnoff didn't back off from the other war being waged on another front. He oversaw the remodeling and expansion of the Camden plant, now christened RCA Laboratories, and he began making frequent visits down there, rolling up his shirtsleeves, observing experiments, having technical conversations with the engineers, and above all, meeting with Vladimir Zworykin to plot the company's strategy to dominate the new medium.

He even saw to it that the money being spent on the development of mechanical television at GE, under Ernst Alexanderson, was diverted to RCA's new electronic effort. In July 1930, after conducting side-by-side demos between GE's apparatus and Zworykin's system, the electronic approach clearly showed more promise. Sarnoff transferred to Camden some of Alexanderson's brightest colleagues, leaving the aging engineer stranded in Schenectady, with virtually no budget for improving what was perhaps the world's best spinning disk setup. Alexanderson soon phased out his television work and turned to other projects.

In Sarnoff's view, not only would electronic television save the company from ruin, it would be his own personal salvation as well. He would build a new television industry, not because RCA was handed a monopoly by the government, as it was with radio. This empire would be crafted out of sheer ingenuity, hard work, and Sarnoff's own penetrating vision. He now focused his sharpest rhetorical flourishes on visual broadcasting. "When television has fulfilled its ultimate destiny, man's sense of physical limitation will be swept away," Sarnoff proclaimed in a 1930 speech. "With this may come a new horizon, a new philosophy, and greatest of all, perhaps, a finer and broader understanding between all the peoples of the world."

Of course, all this bluster meant that RCA was willing to do whatever it took to win. Nothing would ever stand between RCA and television, especially not a young inventor who had designs on controlling the patent structure of the new art. As a result, Sarnoff established a clandestine task force. Composed of both engineers and patent attorneys, this new team became known, informally, as the "Get-Around-Farnsworth Department."

At the end of August 1930, Farnsworth received a notice from the U.S. Patent Office. The news was stupendous. His two key applications for establishing the new art of electronic television had officially been issued. Farnsworth's television scanning system was assigned patent number 1,773,980, and his television receiving system was assigned number 1,773,981. A relatively minor patent on his oscillator had already been issued months earlier, and about a dozen of his other applications were still pending.

This triumph should have been cause for major merriment at Green Street. After all, Zworykin's television patent application from 1923 had still not been granted, and the interferences that RCA ran to try to block Farnsworth's patents had obviously failed. Number 980 and Number 981, as Farnsworth and company called them, meant that Farnsworth was the inventor of electronic television, which was proving to be the only practical form of television possible. Patents can always be challenged and appealed, of course, but for now, it appeared that the field belonged to Farnsworth for the next seventeen years, the time period Congress granted to all inventors before their patents expired.

In the midst of what should have been a celebration, though, Jesse McCargar clamped down once again on the budget, this time with such might that Farnsworth was forced to tell his star engineers Brolly, Varian, and Lubcke that he had to let them go. The relentless pressure from his investors and their reluctance to further finance the lab represented a major social and economic change that even Farnsworth himself didn't fully recognize.

By 1930, the role of the lone inventor had been marginalized. Independent inventors could no longer compete with the well-financed, well-organized laboratories owned by corporations practiced in the art of modern mass marketing. RCA Laboratories was only one of many that had sprung up in virtually every major industry. These operations were so vast that would-be inventors no longer had the heart to go it alone.

One independent inventor who made his mark at the turn of the century, a creator of many great radio improvements, a onetime associate in Thomas Edison's laboratory named Reginald Aubrey Fessenden, was arrogant enough to devise a definition for invention, building upon the old adage that "necessity is the mother of invention," a phrase typically attributed to an obscure seventeenth-century writer named Richard Franck. As the saying implies, if there isn't a preexisting demand for what you have invented, then it isn't an invention, per se, even if people buy it. Think of the yo-yo. Someone created it. People liked it. People bought it. But it wasn't as if humankind needed it and was sitting around waiting for it. It may be a new, well-marketed product, but it isn't an invention, at least according to what Fessenden wrote in a 1925 article for *Radio News:*

> When a demand has existed for more than five years, and when
> it has been known for more than five years that there would be
> adequate financial reward for supplying [i.e. satisfying] the
> demand, and when the means for doing so have been in known
> existence for more than five years, then the application of the
> means to the demand will be presumed to involve invention.

Fessenden stressed that the "means" for performing the invention cannot be new. For instance, when Edison invented the incandescent electric light in 1879 (whether he was really the first was later disputed by two rival inventors), he was not only fulfilling a long-standing and obvious demand, but using materials (such as the vacuum pump) and principles (such as direct electric current) that had been around for over a decade. But, according to this definition, using Edison's lightbulb in different ways, such as in electric street lamps—the mere application of an invention to create a related device—is often too obvious and therefore is not typically an invention in itself, though it might merit a patent. Therefore, not all patents represent true inventions. In fact, few do.

A dramatic improvement of a prior invention, or a new take on an old one, could very well be considered an invention itself. As an example, consider William Coolidge, a GE Labs engineer, and his 1910 invention of the long-lasting tungsten filament, replacing the messy and unreliable carbon one used by Edison. Or Coolidge again in 1913, this time adapting the vacuum tube to produce X rays. Sometimes, new inventions make prior ones obsolete. In fact, this is exactly what happened to several of Fessenden's radio inventions when Lee De Forest came up with the vacuum tube. The same thing happened to De Forest decades later when Bell Labs developed the transistor.

The five-year time period in this definition is quite arbitrary, but having some kind of time period is highly significant. Fessenden probably thought ten years was too high a threshold, and that one year was too low, so he arrived at a compromise based on his own reading of history. The "demand" needs to be evident, the "means" needs to have been available for some time, and the invention itself needs to be original. The longer the jump the inventor has on others in the field, the more ingenious the invention will seem, as Fessenden continues: "An inventor is one who can see the applicability of means to supplying demand five years before it is obvious to those skilled in the art."

Invention, of course, has been going on since the beginning of the human race. But until a system of patents came along, there was no way to provide credit and economic incentive to the inventor. Whoever invented the wheel or the candle, for instance, probably didn't get very rich. The notion of a government granting a license to market a creation for a limited period of time can be traced to the Renaissance—more specifically to Florence in 1421—with the idea then spreading to other European countries. Some of America's founding fathers—most notably Benjamin Franklin—were lone inventors, so it became imperative that the U.S. Constitution would call for the creation of a patent system and that this would be one of the first acts of the first Congress of the United States, producing a statute signed by President George Washington on April 10, 1790. As the first secretary of state, Thomas Jefferson was charged with examining patent applications, and he reviewed them personally, including one issued to Eli Whitney for the cotton gin.

However, the year 1838 was the big breakthrough as far as patents were concerned. Until then, the U.S. Patent Office simply granted a patent to anyone who claimed one, even if the device in question was in fact already patented. If one inventor received a patent on something similar to something already patented, the two parties would have to resolve their dispute in civil court. The patent law of 1838 established the principle of "search," meaning that the Patent Office was now responsible for sifting through past claims and examining each application to determine originality. In addition, the United States became unique because of its system to resolve complex appeals. Whereas other countries grant a patent to the party that was the *first to file* an application covering the invention, the United States grants the patent to the party that can prove that it was the *first to demonstrate* the invention, regardless of the time the application was filed.

This more rigorous approach to granting patents suddenly made patents, and therefore inventions themselves, much more valuable. Now the patent office could eliminate the most basic of disputes by establishing priority over inventions. As patents became more valuable, people naturally wanted them much more badly. Before 1838, fewer than 500 U.S. patents were granted. From then until 1900, about 700,000 patents were issued.

This golden age of invention produced a parade of great lone innovators: Samuel F. B. Morse and the telegraph, Charles Goodyear and vulcanized rubber, Elias Howe and the hand-cranked sewing machine, Isaac Singer and the foot-powered one, George Washington Carver's agricultural innovations, the prolific George Westinghouse's railroad breaking and signaling systems, George Eastman and photographic film, Elisha Otis and the elevator, and, of course, Alexander Graham Bell and Thomas Edison, who had been born just weeks apart in 1847. Many of the great European individualists, such as Guglielmo Marconi and Nikola Tesla, came to America to establish laboratories. The new century saw the Wright brothers and the flying machine, King Camp Gillette and the safety razor, Leo Baekeland and plastics, Henry Ford and the assembly line, Lee De Forest and the vacuum tube, Edwin Howard Armstrong and radio amplification, Willis Haviland Carrier and the air conditioner,

Clarence Birdseye and flash-freezing, Edwin H. Land and polarized photography.

Many lone inventors, especially those who achieved miraculous electrical and chemical breakthroughs, believed that they were chosen by God to deliver their developments to man, a conviction that endured for decades. "Americans believed the great natural truths of the world were being revealed to men through God's goodness," wrote Mitchell Wilson, author of *American Science and Invention*. "When all the secrets had been revealed, then men would live in perfect peace and perfect happiness."

This utopian fantasy gave way to the harsh and exhilarating forces of corporate capitalism. At the turn of the century, it had become entirely obvious that great inventions were, more than anything else, worth untold millions of dollars. Corporations and entire industries could be built around them. Often, the lone inventors themselves remained in charge of those corporations. When they burned out, retired, or died, however, their companies were taken over by professional managers who feared that another technological breakthrough would topple their empire. So these companies began hiring scientists and engineers by the hundreds or thousands in an attempt to come up with those breakthroughs themselves.

In the year 1900, fearing that Edison's expiring patents would open up the electric lighting industry to outsiders, General Electric, the company originally formed by Edison, opened its Schenectady laboratory. Following on GE's heels were Westinghouse, DuPont, Eastman Kodak, General Motors, and AT&T, which opened its Bell Telephone Laboratories in 1925. If an outside inventor came along with something that threatened one of these companies, the corporation simply made an offer that the inventor could not refuse. Once the process of invention could be defined, quantified, understood, and controlled, corporations became hungry to feed their

new laboratories with new minds that could come up with new gizmos before anyone else.

Corporations now saw scientists, engineers, and inventors as
property whose minds could be systematically milked for their ideas.
As a result, the patent rate accelerated further; soon hundreds of
thousands were being filed every year. The corporations owned the
patents, while the engineers got steady salaries and sometimes a modest bonus for each application. At GE and RCA, the bonus was only
$1 per patent, but at Bell Laboratories, it was $100, enough for a team
of engineers to split inventions into many different claims so that
each member of the team could file a patent application and collect
a bonus.

For individuals in the nineteenth-century mold, invention had
sometimes led to great wealth and fame, but that game was over by
1930. The new corporate control of invention led to fame not for
individuals but for the companies and their CEOs, and it helped
consolidate wealth among a handful of those corporations. "A man
born in 1900 was shocked to read in 1930 that half the national
wealth was controlled by corporations, of which half again was owned
by only two hundred companies," wrote author Mitchell Wilson.
"His daughter, born in 1930, looked askance in 1954 when the point
of consolidation was raised. 'Wasn't it always this way?' she asked in
innocence."

Fame and glory were no longer an option for individual inventors. They had a new choice: they could be paid a modest sum of
money by a corporation or make nothing at all. The problem for
many of these individualists was that the money often didn't provide much in the way of happiness. They really were in it for the
greater glory of it—not just for the fame but for the intrinsic plea-
sure of being able to shape the future course of human events with
their own hands.

.   .   .

Around Thanksgiving, Farnsworth received an urgent telegram summoning him to appear before the Federal Radio Commission in Washington, D.C., at 9 A.M. on the morning of December 3, 1930. He was to testify on the matter of whether the FRC should change the official status of television from experimental to commercial. Before it rendered a decision, the commission had to know the full implications of Farnsworth's invention.

Farnsworth was so anxious to attend the hearing that he couldn't bear the notion of stewing in his thoughts for four days and nights on the transcontinental train. He had heard that the U.S. Airmail Service had started carrying in their planes small numbers of passengers to defray costs. Later, when he told his wife of his idea, she got a cold look on her face. She was eight months pregnant, and she pleaded with him not to fly. There was a damn good reason why aviators were among the greatest heroes in America. The newspapers were so filled with plane crashes that it also made headlines when a pilot successfully weathered a storm. But she knew she couldn't stop him. Television was going to get its place in the electromagnetic spectrum, he told her, in a buoyant tone, at home that evening. "They're about to slice up the pie in the sky."

Farnsworth's friend and patent attorney, Donald Lippincott, agreed to accompany him on the trip, and so the two men kissed their wives good-bye and climbed into a Lockheed 5C Vega, a five-passenger, single-engine, turbo-prop aircraft with a full-cantilever wing. As they took their seats, sandwiched between sacks of letters and parcels, they must have been enthralled by the novelty of traveling this way. Flying at speeds up to 165 miles per hour, the trip was scheduled to take just twenty-four hours.

They encountered smooth skies until a violent blizzard over Kansas City forced the aircraft down. After enduring an emergency landing, Farnsworth and Lippincott found an inn for the night. They boarded the plane again the next day, only to hurtle into another whiteout that drove the aircraft to a second hasty landing, this time in St. Louis. After an overnight train to Indianapolis, they chanced upon another mail pilot and agreed to take another shot at air travel. Finally, the two men flew to Washington, beating by only a few hours the transcontinental train they could have taken in the first place.

On the day of Farnsworth's scheduled testimony, a cartoon in the *Washington Evening Star* captured the current state of political affairs in town. A donkey was saying, "I see nothing but clouds," while President Hoover was exclaiming, "See the silver lining!" and pointing up at the darkest cloud in the sky, which displayed in giant bold letters the word *Depression*. Topping the news was the latest national unemployment tally: "4,860,000 Listed as Out of Work," according to one headline. Economists predicted that this number would double within the coming months, and they were right.

The hearing was held at the newly constructed Commerce Building, a five-story, stone block fortress surrounded by massive pillars, and the Federal Radio Commission wing was buzzing with activity that morning. The hallway was jammed with men in expensive suits who were dead set against television on the grounds that it would crowd out everything else on the radio spectrum. Among the crowd were lobbyists from the Radio Amateurs Association, lawyers for the professional radio station owners, Western Union telegraph executives, and facsimile zealots who dreamed of transmitting memos through the airwaves. All these factions were lined up against television because it was thought of as a bandwidth hog. They believed that transmitting visual signals would take up at least ten times the space of sound signals. If the government approved television, it might spell the end of their own industries.

Farnsworth would also encounter a surprise guest at the hearing. As he stepped inside the hearing room and took his seat in the front row beside Lippincott, he watched in wonder as David Sarnoff entered the room, trailed by his minions. Sarnoff wasn't scheduled to testify. He would let his engineers do that. He came to the hearing to size up this peculiar kid from California. As the hearing got under way, the skinny inventor and the overbearing baron shot quick glances at each other from across the room, taking mental measurements with each no doubt wondering what the other would do next.

When Farnsworth was called to speak, the gathered throng of engineers, executives, politicians, lobbyists, and reporters watched a young, shy scientist stand up at the witness table and transform himself into a passionate advocate of a single technological idea, and that idea was *electronic* television. He had explained his approach to television many times before, but this was his chance to recite it for the public record.

Everything Farnsworth knew told him that so-called mechanical television would never work. It was a scientific dead end, yet the commission had begun to hand out experimental licenses to people developing those very systems. Most everyone in the room knew that mechanical television was capable of producing only about sixty lines of on-screen resolution. The disk could never spin fast enough to scan an image in enough detail to create a clear picture. The quality was so poor that viewing screens could be made no larger than postage stamps, and this blur would take up a massive 100 kilocycles of frequency, ten times the bandwidth of sound, just as the radio executives feared.

What Farnsworth would say would intrigue many people in the room. He spoke about doing away with the spinning disk—and all moving parts—entirely. Electrons would do the work instead, at speeds that surpassed anything the human eye could perceive. His apparatus would scan a moving image by directly converting patterns of light energy into electric current. This purely electronic system would use electromagnets to manipulate rays of light energy,

projecting an image with 300 lines of resolution, five times the clarity of the mechanical systems.

Sarnoff, for one, didn't need convincing. Based on what Zworykin and the other RCA visitors had already reported they'd seen at Farnsworth's lab, Sarnoff already knew that the kid's breakthrough spelled the end of the mechanical approach. He also knew he either had to propose a buyout of Farnsworth's patents or had to find a way around them. While RCA attempted to re-create an all-electronic prototype in Camden, Sarnoff needed to stall Farnsworth, so he had his engineers argue vigorously at this hearing that television wasn't ready to enter the commercial stage.

The members of the Federal Radio Commission didn't particularly care whether Farnsworth's invention worked or not; they just wanted to know if it was politically feasible, given the opposition by everyone else in the room. And most of the opposition was concerned with the bandwidth problem. If what Farnsworth was saying was true, that he could achieve five times the picture quality with his all-electronic system, wouldn't such transmissions take up five times the space on the spectrum?

Farnsworth was well aware of the bandwidth problem. In fact, he had focused on this obstacle for months. He had even published an article on a complex mathematical formula for compressing the wavelengths of image signals, but he knew that it was just a theory, and he was probably a long way from devising something that actually worked.

What Farnsworth did next surprised everyone, perhaps even himself. He especially surprised—and alarmed—Sarnoff. Farnsworth claimed that his electronic television could transmit signals in a six-kilocycle band, about half that of radio. It was a brazen claim, and by making it, Farnsworth was stepping over an imaginary line. He was no longer just a scientist, no longer just an engineer, no longer just an inventor. He was now a businessman too. He really did want

to be the Thomas Edison of television. At that point, Sarnoff knew he had a big problem on his hands.

The engineers on the Federal Radio Commission remained skeptical and steadfast. A few days later, the commission's chief engineer, Charles Jolliffe, recommended exactly what RCA was hoping for: that television should remain experimental for the time being, despite what Farnsworth had done and said. The FRC adopted the recommendation unanimously. Not long afterward, Sarnoff hired Jolliffe, paid him a salary far greater than his government job, and installed him as the engineering chief of RCA.

Nevertheless, Farnsworth's testimony set off a minor media sensation. Hugo Gernsback was at the hearing too, and he introduced himself to Farnsworth and invited him to New York to discuss submitting an article on his invention, to appear in the debut issue of *Television News*. Forty-six years old, this diminutive gentleman wore a monocle in his left eye, a silk bowtie, and a European-cut suit. He reeked of expensive toilet water, piled his graying hair in a wet comb-over, and spoke in an eccentric, Luxembourgian accent that few Americans were able to place. Farnsworth was honored to finally meet the man who edited all those magazines and made all those predictions that had such an impact on his life.

In Farnsworth, Gernsback saw everything he himself treasured. Gernsback had spent his career encouraging his readers to experiment by putting together and taking apart radios, car engines, and the like. His dream was that his words would inspire the next generation of inventors. In the early 1920s, in a speech before the National Institute of Inventors, Gernsback told a story about the plight of the prototypical inventor:

The inventor, who as a rule, is poor or without means tries to interest someone in his invention, but nine times out of ten he

does not succeed. Often he does not have the money to develop the invention himself and frequently he dies of a broken heart, for the reason that he has not been able to realize the fruits of his labor. In that case, the world has lost a man who might have enriched it by untold thousands.

Gernsback really did have a soft spot in his heart for geniuses like Farnsworth, whom he saw as throwbacks to an earlier age, an era he yearned to keep alive, but the generation of boys he tried to inspire all seemed to be growing up and going to work for the big corporations, and who could blame them?

David Sarnoff saw something completely different in Philo T. Farnsworth. The kid was clever, for sure, but when Sarnoff glanced briefly at Farnsworth during the hearing that morning, all he saw was yet another obstacle on his own path to greater glory. When Sarnoff peered into the future, as evidenced by all of his speeches at the time, he saw himself as the Moses of a great new industry, the television industry, developed around an invention that would lead humankind toward fulfilling its destiny. Anything that would interfere with that had to be shoved aside.

This goal would be more difficult to achieve now that stories on Farnsworth were appearing in major newspapers. The headline in the *Evening Star* trumpeted, "Television Is Here, Inventor Claims." The article went on to describe how this "24-year-old youth of San Francisco unfolded a story of revolutionary claims that makes commercial television a reality. It lifts it boldly from the field of experimentation, in which it has so long wallowed, and makes it practicable." As for the bandwidth claim, the story said, "the Farnsworth revelation was unexpected." Yet the inventor wasn't exactly a celebrity just yet. The *Star* reporter had spelled Farnsworth's first name as "Phila."

After the hearing, Farnsworth and Lippincott took the train to New York City. Farnsworth met with editors of the *New York Times*, which led to a major piece, in the Sunday edition on December 14, 1930, that quoted him at length describing in plain terms how his invention worked. The headline read, "A Radio Idea from the West," and unlike the newspaper in Washington, this one spelled his entire name right.

> A young man, Philo T. Farnsworth, noted for his television experiments in California, came to New York during the past week after a visit in Washington, where he reported to the Federal Radio Commission that he has developed a vacuum tube that makes commercial television practical at once.

Farnsworth's visit to New York was overshadowed by the near simultaneous arrival of Farnsworth's hero and by now one of the most famous men in the world, Albert Einstein. Farnsworth extended his stay in the city, as he desperately yearned to speak with the fifty-one-year-old physics professor, if only to confirm that his latest ideas for television were aligned with Einstein's thinking.

Einstein happened to be arriving in New York at an especially auspicious time, when the planet itself was teetering on the edge of a precipice, about to tumble into modern history's deepest, darkest abyss. The economic depression had spread across the Atlantic to Europe. In Germany, Adolf Hitler was not yet in power, but his lunatic fringe Nazi Party won 18 percent of the vote in the recent national election, enough to set off serious concern. When Einstein, a dual citizen of Switzerland and Germany, was asked to comment on the situation, he likened Hitler to a temporary virus. "I do not enjoy Mr. Hitler's acquaintance," said the distinguished professor from the University of Berlin. "Hitler is living on the empty stomach of Germany. As soon as economic conditions improve, he will cease to be important." Yet Einstein also issued a remarkably prescient challenge to Americans, in a speech that he broadcast from his ship over the NBC radio network and other radio stations nationwide.

> It is in your country, my friends, that those latent forces which eventually will kill any serious monster of professional militarism will be able to make themselves felt more clearly and definitely. Your political and economic condition today is such that if you ever set your hand to this job in all seriousness you will be able entirely to destroy the dreadful tradition of military violence under which the sad memories of the past—and to a certain extent—of the world continue to suffer even after the terrific warning of the Great War. It is along these lines of endeavor that your mission lies at the present moment, and should you be able and willing to accept this high duty, I know that you will build for yourself an enduring monument.

With that message delivered, Einstein engaged in five frenzied days of giving lectures and seeing the sights. The biggest event of the week was his featured appearance at a Zionist rally and Hanukkah celebration at Madison Square Garden. Even if Farnsworth had managed his way into one of the back rows to see and hear Einstein, it's likely that the awestruck inventor would have surveyed the huge crowd, saw how Einstein was besieged by well-wishers and interviewers afterward, and realized that a one-on-one encounter with the halo-haired scientist would be all but impossible now. The time would come, years later, when the two would be introduced by a common friend.

After his East Coast swing, Farnsworth took a rather uneventful flight back home to San Francisco. He had clearly left his mark on Sarnoff's home turf. Farnsworth's big-city media splash was small, relatively speaking, but it was big enough to worry Sarnoff.

.   .   .

The two-year deadline that Sarnoff had given Zworykin was now looming. In Camden, Zworykin had organized his engineering staff into two teams, one that was working to reverse-engineer and improve Farnsworth's Image Dissector and another that was trying to build a television camera based on Zworykin's own concepts. Not only was the team working with the Farnsworth design getting greater results than the other group, but it was getting even better results than Farnsworth himself. By the beginning of 1931, the RCA engineers with the replica of the Image Dissector were able to pick up good pictures in outdoor sunlight, something Farnsworth had yet to achieve. Zworykin simply wrote in his journal that one staff engineer "got very nice results with the transmitting tube, which is a modified Farnsworth type."

Yet there was no hiding from Sarnoff the fact that Zworykin did not yet have a complete working television system based on an original, non-patent-infringing design. When Sarnoff's original two-year deadline for Zworykin—set at their first meeting in January 1929—came and went, Farnsworth was still way out in front.

In March of 1931, Gernsback's new magazine, *Television News*, made its debut. True to its name, the issue was filled entirely with articles about the latest progress in television, including a brief article, by an anonymous writer, describing Zworykin's Kinescope receiver as well as Farnsworth's piece describing his electronic Image Dissector camera. Aside from these two pieces, the magazine focused overwhelmingly on the doomed mechanical approach. The title given to Farnsworth's article, "Scanning Images with an Electronic Pencil," made his breakthrough sound rather trivial, but it was the most detailed and up-to-date description of the Farnsworth system available, complete with photos and drawings. In reading it, Sarnoff could see very well what that "pencil" was; it was a ray of electrons, and he wanted it badly.

RCA's halting progress on creating a complete electronic system was driving Sarnoff to the brink. For the first time in his career, the overall outlook was grim. RCA's stock was trading for a pittance. The Justice Department was on his back, and it won a court injunction that forced Sarnoff to slash licensing fees for the radio combine's patents. As a result of this and the drop in radio sales, funds were getting scarce. It didn't help that the RKO deal that Joe Kennedy put together had left Sarnoff with a complete mess on his hands. The movie company had to be put into receivership and restructured at a cost of $16 million to RCA. In addition, Sarnoff had already agreed with the Rockefeller family to break ground on a new headquarters. The office tower was to be the centerpiece of a new architectural landmark smack dab in the middle of Manhattan. Only a great company would be worthy of such a building—and only a prosperous company could afford it. RCA was in danger of letting its greatness and prosperity slip from its hands.

Sarnoff needed to do something. In April of 1931, he told his secretary to charter a private airplane with an experienced pilot. He then flew across the country and checked into San Francisco's Palace Hotel. The next morning, he took a taxi to 202 Green Street.

There David Sarnoff found himself, impeccably dressed in his custom-tailored suit and dark hat, enveloped by the rolling fog of a spring morning in San Francisco, knocking on the door of a shabby garage. Not realizing that Farnsworth's laboratory was located on the second floor, he began knocking on the front door at street level. At first, no one heard the knocking. So he began pounding harder and harder, then raising his voice. *Open this door!* Inside, someone's ears perked up and heard a faint sense of desperation in the voice coming from outside. *Please, please, open this door!*

David Sarnoff, chairman of NBC as well as president of RCA, sits in his office in Rockefeller Center, showing off the telegraph key built into his desk, 1934. (DAVID SARNOFF LIBRARY)

CHAPTER NINE

End Run

Farnsworth's staff did have some time to prepare for the visit. Sarnoff had telephoned the lab upon his arrival in San Francisco, setting off a frenzy of activity at 202 Green Street. The staff grew tense and nervous waiting for his arrival. Sarnoff, more than anyone else in the world, had the money and the incentive to make everyone at Television Laboratories rich and comfortable for the rest of their lives, if he chose to do so.

The door was answered by a cordial George Everson. He shook Sarnoff's large, well-manicured hand and escorted him up the creaky wooden stairs to the lab, where Cliff Gardner and the men were ready to demonstrate the equipment for their curious guest. Everson had already informed Sarnoff that Philo T. Farnsworth was away on urgent business and unfortunately could not join them, but he didn't tell Sarnoff exactly where the young inventor was or what he was doing.

Sarnoff witnessed televised film clips as well as live shots that were scanned with the Image Dissector and transmitted to the nearby console receiver, the one with the seven-inch circular screen housed in a wooden cabinet. Everson later wrote that Sarnoff "seemed impressed" with everything and "expressed a great deal of interest" in the TV set, perhaps because it was different from all the lab experiments with unfinished equipment he was accustomed to viewing. This seemed pretty close to a marketable product that a consumer could buy in a store. It wasn't the science of television that intrigued Sarnoff the most that day, but rather the prospect of commercial production.

After the demonstration, Sarnoff cut his visit short. "At the end of the visit, his tone changed abruptly," Everson noted. The mogul mentioned the reorganization at Camden and the stepped-up effort to create RCA's own brand of television there. He asserted that Vladimir Zworykin's work on his own television receiver made it "possible to avoid Farnsworth's patents." As for a television camera, he said that RCA was working on something that could equal Farnsworth's Image Dissector.

"There's nothing here we'll need," Sarnoff concluded.

With that bit of wishful thinking, the president of RCA picked up his hat and coat and motioned to Everson to escort him downstairs. Sarnoff offered a curt farewell before ducking back into the taxi that had been waiting at the curb.

"After this visit," Everson remarked, "we felt more certain than ever that RCA Laboratories would give us stiff competition."

A short time later, Everson received the bombshell: a verbal offer from RCA proposing to buy the company lock, stock, and barrel. Under the terms of the deal, RCA would own Farnsworth's television patents, both issued and pending, and Farnsworth himself would come to work for RCA in Camden under a salary to be negotiated. The price: $100,000.

The offer was so low that it could only be taken as an insult. By now, investors had already sunk at least that amount of money into the company. While $100,000 was a large sum during the grinding economic depression of the time, it would be absurd to accept no return on their investment.

When Everson contacted Farnsworth in New York by telegram with the news of the RCA offer, Farnsworth rejected it out of hand. He had absolutely no interest in selling the company or going to work at RCA, and the investors at Crocker Bank backed Farnsworth's decision. They desperately wanted to sell the enterprise as quickly as possible, but they also knew that Farnsworth's patents had real value and they knew from the press reports on Farnsworth that this was no ordinary invention. It was simply unthinkable to receive no premium on something so promising, especially at this advanced stage.

When Donald Lippincott, Farnsworth's patent attorney, got in touch with RCA's patent department to ask whether the corporation would be interested in licensing the patents, rather than buying them, he was rejected in no uncertain terms: RCA was formed to *collect* royalties, he was told, not to *pay* them.

On a purely financial level, Sarnoff's offer was hard to understand. He knew full well that it would cost far more than $100,000 to re-create what Farnsworth had built and somehow avoid infringement of the patents, if that was at all possible. Compared to what RCA would eventually spend on the endeavor, even $1 million would have been a bargain, and if Sarnoff bid that amount, the executives at Crocker Bank would have jumped at the offer. If Farnsworth objected, the bankers most certainly would have outvoted him. Even if Sarnoff offered only $500,000, it probably would have served as the starting point of a good-faith negotiation.

Sarnoff, however, had made up his mind about Farnsworth even before visiting Green Street. It wasn't a matter of money, but of pride. Sarnoff remembered very well the attention and acclaim that Edwin Howard Armstrong had received after RCA paid a large sum for his super-regeneration patent. To Sarnoff, the resulting publicity around Farnsworth would be far worse. A large payment to

Farnsworth could be interpreted by the press as a validation of this kid's status as the father of television. Sarnoff believed that television was destined to be invented at RCA under his own command, even if it had already been invented somewhere else. Sarnoff, it seemed, visited Green Street only to be able to claim that he satisfied his basic curiosity.

Just a few weeks later, on May 6, 1931, while presiding over RCA's annual meeting, Sarnoff made a bold announcement. He disclosed to shareholders that he was increasing RCA's investment in television research and development, to $1 million per year. In addition, he was promoting Zworykin to director of electronics research, expanding his research staff to twenty men, and building a bigger and better-equipped facility at the Camden lab for his television team.

During Sarnoff's visit to his lab, not only was Philo T. Farnsworth in New York City, he was trapped there. Jesse McCargar, the president of Television Laboratories, had been camped out for months at the Savoy-Plaza Hotel trying to piece together a pact with a smooth-talking wheeler-dealer named Mr. Cox. The idea was to assemble a large media conglomerate out of several television, radio, and movie companies, and Cox was the only one who knew all the details. But shortly after Farnsworth reached New York to join McCargar, they learned that Cox was bluffing more than anything else and that several participants either had lost interest or never had any. When they also discovered that Cox himself had a shady past, the whole deal collapsed.

As the Farnsworth party withdrew, Cox filed a breach of contract suit and somehow won an injunction from a judge ordering McCargar and Farnsworth to remain in New York until the issue was resolved. Eventually, McCargar and Cox settled on an amount of money, which Television Laboratories paid to Cox to dissolve the deal.

During this time in limbo, in May 1931, Phil and Pem's fifth wedding anniversary was approaching, and he invited her to join him in the big city to celebrate. By now, their second son, Kenneth Gardner Farnsworth, was four months old. Pem got an aunt to baby-sit for their two baby boys, and then she boarded a train eastward. Phil had made elaborate anniversary plans. With the depression forcing prices of everything lower and lower, people with a modest amount of money could live like kings and queens. First-rate hotel rooms could be had for six dollars per night, and the service was impeccable because anyone with a job was terrified of losing it.

Phil took Pem to Lord & Taylor, where she was fitted like Cinderella with a flowing powder blue, silk chiffon evening gown and a matching velvet and fox fur wrap, along with silver slippers and a stylish purse. For himself, Phil bought a sharp dinner jacket and black bow tie. They hailed a cab, which motored them over to the St. Regis Hotel for fine dining and dancing to the Vincent Lopez Orchestra. The following afternoon, McCargar treated the couple to a baseball game at the Polo Grounds, where they watched the Boston Braves edge the New York Giants seven to six. They went out for Italian food in Greenwich Village, visited the Statue of Liberty, and took an elevator to the top of the newly constructed Alfred Smith Building, soon to be renamed the Empire State Building, which offered a clear view of the sparkling Chrysler Building and all the bridges that connected Manhattan to the outer boroughs.

After their celebration, they boarded the train to Philadelphia and checked into the historic Benjamin Franklin Hotel. The city of brotherly love was the home of Philco, then the world's largest manufacturer of radios. The top executives there wanted to discuss a possible deal, and McCargar and Farnsworth were eager to see what they had in mind.

Philco had demonstrated a keen ability to make radios more quickly, more cheaply, and with greater style than RCA, and the company was rewarded with greater market share. Yet its profit margins were slim because it had to pay a fixed percentage of sales to RCA to cover the patent licensing. Now, with radio sales plunging, further depressing profits, the company was in search of a new market. For Philco, it was clearly time to diversify and pioneer the next wave of mass communication. Philco's vice president of engineering, Walter Holland, had already been out to visit the Green Street lab, and he had already persuaded top management of the need to act.

Both Farnsworth and McCargar were pleased to perceive this sense of urgency. In short order, the men hammered out an agreement. To Farnsworth's delight, Philco was not offering to buy the company, but rather to take out a broad, nonexclusive license on all of Farnsworth's patents. Although the proposed financial terms weren't very favorable, this was exactly the type of deal he wanted all along. The two companies also agreed to embark on a crash project to commercialize television as quickly as possible.

In doing so, they were forming an alliance against their common enemy. Philco was one of many radio companies that had filed formal complaints about RCA's patent-licensing terms to the Justice Department. "Philco was hoping to use Farnsworth's strong patent position to prevent RCA from spreading its control to television," noted Pem. "The whole arrangement was kept strictly confidential in order to avoid raising eyebrows at RCA."

Under the terms of the secret deal, Philco would fund all of the expenses of Television Laboratories. In addition, it would pay for the relocation of Farnsworth's family plus five engineers and their families from San Francisco to Philadelphia. Philco would carry the cost of maintaining the Green Street location, but the real action would now be happening here in Pennsylvania. Philco agreed to set up a new television lab on the top floor of the company's plant at the corner of Ontario and C Streets, and it would also fund the opening of an experimental television station. This meant that Farnsworth could rehire his star engineers, Russell Varian and Arch Brolly. When they each accepted, he told them to get ready for the big move east. The question for Farnsworth was whether his team could sweep by RCA before Sarnoff detected that the end run was in play.

The move to Philadelphia took place in the middle of July, while much of the continent was in the grip of the worst heat wave in years. Cliff and his wife, Lola, decided to drive their new Plymouth across the country, and so they escaped the worst of it. Everyone else from the Green Street lab made the trip in a rented Pullman railroad car. Traveling this way, in the days before air-conditioning, could be hellish. It got so hot inside the train that the thermometer registered 140 degrees before popping. Pem started developing symptoms of asthma, while baby Kenny broke out in a wicked heat rash. Phil kept the porters flush with tips to keep the drinks and ice coming.

The heat hovered over Philadelphia and remained blistering for the rest of the summer. The families took apartments downtown, and the men reported for work at the top floor of the plant, where secrecy was so paramount that even Philco employees weren't permitted to go up there. The three Philco bigwigs who were allowed access all wore three-piece suits, ties, and hats, and they expected their new colleagues to do the same, even though there were no exhaust fans installed in the lab.

All of this caused frequent clashes, as Farnsworth and his men not only refused to wear ties but rolled up their sleeves and sometimes simply stripped to the waist for relief from the sweltering heat, which was made worse by Cliff's constant use of the blowtorch. The Philco executives thought this behavior barbarian and referred to them as "those mavericks from the west." At one point, a Philco executive named Mr. Grimditch, annoyed beyond reason at seeing these shirtless "animals," as he called them, ordered the men to put their tops back on.

"Mr. Grimditch," Cliff shouted, turning down his torch. "Not only will we not put on our shirts, if we don't get exhaust fans within the hour, I quit!" The fans arrived shortly thereafter.

Directly across a mile-wide section of the Delaware River in Camden, New Jersey, Vladimir Zworykin and the RCA Laboratories team were making steady strides and hitting upon sporadic breakthroughs while working in well-ventilated comfort.

One of their leaps forward happened by accident. In an attempt to create an original television camera not based on a Farnsworth design, an RCA engineer named Sanford Essig was experimenting with various surfaces that could temporarily store electronic representations of images. At one point, he coated with silver a sheet of mica crystals attached to a wire mesh, then put it in the oven to bake. He forgot all about it and left it in way too long. By the time he got to it, he felt like a failed pastry chef, figuring his creation was ruined and that he'd have to start all over. When he looked at the result, however, he saw that his concoction had crystallized into what he described as a "beautiful uniform mosaic of insulated silver."

When Zworykin tested it, he found that this new photoelectric surface worked wonderfully. He called it the "final link" in his plan to create the first electronic television camera using the principle of temporary storage, which made the camera far more sensitive and reduced the need for bright lights. Zworykin called the newfangled instrument the Iconoscope. By the fall, his version of a complete electronic scanning, transmission, and viewing system was tested, working, and described in a new patent application. The picture wasn't as clear as Farnsworth's, and the viewing screen on the RCA receiver was only four inches, compared to Farnsworth's seven. Still, it worked.

Sarnoff was excited, but any enthusiasm had to be tempered by the fact that he was deep into the most intense phase of defending

RCA against the government's antitrust litigation. He decided any announcement of Zworykin's achievement would be ill timed for the moment.

Over at the Philco plant, Farnsworth and his crew knew that something was up at RCA. Camden was home to RCA's new experimental TV station, and so when test broadcasts were carried out, Farnsworth's men could easily pick up the signals, watching and listening to the RCA engineers on their sets. The broadcasts were nothing fancy, but Farnsworth was able to see that RCA's pictures were getting much clearer, and he could see that RCA had achieved a breakthrough in scanning.

Philco also won approval to open an experimental television station of its own, and it installed a broadcasting tower on the top of the plant. When Farnsworth used the tower to transmit his own pictures, the RCA team on the other side of the river were able to pick up those signals in the same way.

Occasionally, interesting things would show up on these broadcasts. One time, RCA had its Iconoscope "aimed out the window," recalled one RCA engineer, "and a building across the street caught fire. The cameraman called the fire department, and the receiver showed the whole thing. That was our first news broadcast." For its part, the Philco team stationed a camera at the University of Pennsylvania's swimming pool, and they kept it running live for their ongoing test picture. RCA soon tuned in to this broadcast as well, and at one point an RCA engineer actually telephoned Philco and said: "You know your camera at the swimming pool? Do you know that some of the students are swimming without bathing suits?"

The jig was up. RCA had learned for sure that Philco was getting into the television game, and that Farnsworth was behind the plan. There were all kinds of rumors around this time about RCA men hanging out in bars around the Philco plant, trying to meet Philco secretaries, buying them drinks, and getting some inside information out of them. In fact, Philco later filed suit against RCA, accusing its executives of gaining confidential information by plying Philco's female employees with "intoxicating liquors at hotels, restaurants and nightclubs," luring the women into "compromising situations," and attempting to "induce, incite and bribe said employees." RCA denied the charges, and the suit was ultimately dropped.

In the wee hours of the morning on October 18, 1931, the heart of Thomas Alva Edison stopped beating. The great inventor died at age eighty-four at his home in West Orange, New Jersey. "He will be buried on Wednesday, the fifty-second anniversary of his perfection of the incandescent light, which has been termed by many his greatest gift to humanity," said the front page of the *New York Times*. "Today and tomorrow, his body will lie in state in the library of his laboratory, surrounded by the mementos of his many winning struggles for the mastery of man over the elements about him. Flags on all Edison Company buildings will be flown at half-staff out of respect to the memory of the man whose genius brought them into being."

Tributes poured in from seemingly every prominent person in the world. Albert Einstein saw a chance to pose a challenge. "Thankfully we accept his legacy, not only as a gift of his genius, but also as a mission placed in our hands," Einstein wrote. "For to the new generation falls the task of finding the way for the right use of the gift given to us. Only if it solves this task will the new generation be worthy of its inheritance and become really happier than former generations."

David Sarnoff seized the occasion as an opportunity to imply that RCA Laboratories and other corporate labs were the rightful heirs to Edison's legacy. "Edison always had an objective in his research, and he taught that achievement results from perseverance," wrote Sarnoff. "Our modern laboratories are a heritage from his early labors at Menlo Park." Of course, Sarnoff's notion of "modern laboratories" differed from Menlo Park in key ways. At independent labs, individual inventors owned their patents and tended to benefit proportionately from their own labor. In company labs, the *corporation* owned the patents, and top management typically benefited disproportionately as compared to the engineers.

In 1932 the country entered the most ghastly phase of the Great Depression. Unemployment soared to 25 percent, and every fleeting rally in stocks gave way to a new plunge. From its apex of 381, the Dow Jones index had collapsed to 198 on Black Tuesday, October 29, 1929. Now free-falling to an unthinkable bottom of 41, the market at this moment seemed no longer to exist. Some people were still holding shares, but virtually no one was buying. People were defaulting on loans, hoarding cash, and simply scraping up enough money to buy food and other necessities. Since Farnsworth had arrived in Philadelphia the previous summer, ten banks had failed in that city alone.

One late afternoon, while Phil and Pem were at their unfurnished, rented home in the suburb of Chestnut Hill, the woman who lived next door came running over to knock on their door. She had been told by her husband that she needed to race to the Franklin Trust at once and withdraw all of their money. That was the bank where the Farnsworths kept all of their savings, and Phil had just made a sizable deposit. Out of guilt, she was inviting them to come along. "Do whatever you think is best," Phil told the neighbor. "I will not contribute to a run on the bank."

The next morning, the bank failed to open for business. All the depositors' money had vanished. An investigation later showed that the bank's top executives made off with much of it. Phil and Pem counted up the remains of their pooled pocket change. They arrived at the figure of $1.57. That was all they had, and there wasn't much food left in the house.

The very next day, Farnsworth miraculously received a check in the mail for $700. As it turned out, an executive at the Crocker Bank who was managing the Farnsworth company account had failed until now to pay back Farnsworth for some laboratory expenses. This reimbursement came just in time to provide the family with enough cash to live for at least the next two or three months.

In March 1932, Phil and Pem were hit by a tragedy far worse than losing all their money. Eighteen-month-old Kenny developed a serious throat infection. Without the benefit of modern-day antibiotics, all the doctors could do to stop it from spreading was to perform a complete tracheotomy, which meant Kenny would never talk again. Phil and Pem were at the hospital day and night, watching their son in agony. The doctor suggested they get some rest in a nearby empty room, leaving an intern to watch the child. Phil returned just an hour later to find the intern asleep and the boy turning blue. Phil called the doctor and got Pem, but it was too late. "We had to stand helplessly by," Pem wrote, "and watch his precious life slip away."

The executives at Philco were concerned only with meeting their business objectives. When Farnsworth said he was taking the train back to Provo, Utah, to bury his son, they wouldn't permit him the time off. Everson and McCargar had to talk him out of quitting and splitting with Philco then and there. Farnsworth agreed to stay at work in Philadelphia, while Pem traveled alone. "It's hard to relate the agonizing loneliness and grief I suffered during those four seemingly endless days crossing the continent, knowing my baby lay cold and alone in a coffin in the baggage car ahead."

A wall of silence went up between Phil and Pem. He was so blinded by achieving his own objective that he failed to realize the ramifications of his decision. They were in terrible pain, and both felt so guilty and responsible that they each thought the other blamed them for the loss of Kenny. Actually, Pem was most deeply troubled by the fact that Phil chose to continue obsessing over his invention when she needed him the most. Emotions were contained on opposite sides of the wall, and the lack of communication deadened their relationship. They were still sharing the same home, keeping up pretenses, but they were united only by their remaining son, Philo III. No longer living like husband and wife, relations grew even colder as the months went by, and they came to behave like strangers.

The personal tragedy exacerbated the constant pressure from the television battle. Farnsworth was sinking into a depression as deep as the country's. He developed sharp stomach pains that were diagnosed as an ulcer, and he began drinking to diminish the pain. Still, his drive to perfect television continued, and he remained capable of bursts of manic productivity at his laboratory. When he came home, he said little or nothing to Pem. He would do little else but work and pour glasses of whiskey down his throat, taking advantage of the widespread talk of a repeal of Prohibition. His brainstorms were so constant that he lived on little or no sleep. Farnsworth's younger brothers and sisters headed east to be with their ailing, grieving brother. When they arrived in Philadelphia, however, they were all amazed at Farnsworth's ability to shut out the rest of the world and his personal problems while focusing on television.

RCA was not spared pain during the economic decline. In 1931, the corporation had posted its first annual loss, of more than $1 million, and deficits continued to mount. With radio sales suddenly dropping off and with phonograph and record sales plummeting by 90 percent within a span of three years, Sarnoff was forced to lay off several hundred workers on the RCA production line in Camden. He slashed his own salary, from $80,000 to $50,000, but of course the lower paychecks were able to buy much more because of the terrific price deflation in the economy. During the downturn, he still was able to send his three sons to elite private schools, and he took his wife on a Caribbean cruise with the Goulds and the Vanderbilts. Asked whether the constant pressure from running such a big enterprise during such tough times ever gave him stomach acid, Sarnoff replied, "I don't *get* ulcers; I *give* them."

He kept his headquarters staff lean, with only seven employees, included Otto Schairer, head of the patent department. Schairer saw to it that all of Zworykin's engineers in Camden were continually fed with all the latest patent information, especially when it came to the patent activities of Philo T. Farnsworth. Schairer even issued a special booklet describing all of the Farnsworth applications as well as the expiration dates of the patents that were already issued, and any time a chance arose to strengthen RCA's position, Sarnoff and Schairer snatched it.

One particular opportunity concerned Charles Francis Jenkins. As Sarnoff had expected, the public completely lost interest in mechanical television and the false hype spewed by the Jenkins Television Company. The firm declared bankruptcy and was sold to the Lee De Forest Company, which also went bankrupt shortly thereafter. RCA swooped in to acquire the patents of both, if only to retire the mechanical approach and make sure no one distracted the American public in the same way again. Less than two years later, Jenkins himself was dead, reportedly dying penniless and brokenhearted over his failure.

Some rivals were more difficult to dispense with. One that would continually challenge Sarnoff's supremacy was a crafty entrepreneur named William S. Paley. Born in Chicago, the son of Russian Jewish immigrants, Bill Paley entered the family's cigar business at a young age. Slim, dark, and handsome, Paley was a bon vivant, a playboy, and an Ivy League graduate. One of the only things he and Sarnoff had in common was the ambition to make it big in broadcasting.

The Paley family had already built a successful public company, based in Philadelphia, when an interesting opportunity arose. The

Columbia Phonograph Company bought the operating rights for a chain of radio stations in 1927 in order to get its musical recordings heard on the radio and to offer an alternative to the NBC stations, which were mainly playing RCA Victor recordings. Bill's father, Sam, marketed their La Palina brand of cigars on the new Columbia network, sponsoring a singer who plugged the smokes between tunes. Sales of the cigars doubled virtually overnight. By 1928, the Paleys had sold their cigar business and parlayed the resulting fortune into control of the radio network itself, then relocated to New York as the underdog to Sarnoff's NBC.

At age twenty-seven, Bill Paley found himself the president of the fledgling Columbia Broadcasting System, where he invented a clever new business model. Whereas NBC *charged* its affiliates for use of its programs, CBS *paid* affiliates to air its programs. Paley covered those costs entirely by selling advertising time, becoming the first to clear national time slots for sponsored soap operas, comedies, and jazz bands, the kind of programming shunned by the stodgy Sarnoff. Unaffiliated stations flocked to the CBS network, and David Sarnoff now found himself fighting yet another battle on yet another front.

As far as television was concerned, Bill Paley wasn't interested. He let a small cadre of employees run experiments with mechanical setups, but he personally didn't see a need for television, especially now that his corner of the radio business was booming. The public wasn't buying many new radio sets, but that didn't hurt CBS. Paley's company wasn't in the manufacturing business. Audiences were, however, spending more and more time listening to all the free programming on their old sets, yielding a bonanza for CBS and its advertisers. Paley had no incentive to promote the idea of television, and he derisively called Sarnoff "the televisionary" whenever his rival made public pronouncements on the subject.

Sarnoff, of course, didn't take that as an insult. Besides, a rivalry with CBS was good for business. He knew from the start that NBC could never monopolize programming. The public had to at least believe they had freedom of choice as far as news and entertainment was concerned. The best he could hope for was for NBC to be a member of an oligopoly of a few national networks.

What was really distracting Sarnoff from his focus on television was the antitrust suit. The Justice Department had built up a strong case against RCA, and a full-blown trial was set for November 15, 1932. The very date itself presented Sarnoff with an escape hatch. It was becoming obvious that Herbert Hoover was yesterday's man, and Democrat Franklin D. Roosevelt was bound to become the next president. There would be one week between Election Day and the opening of a trial against a lame-duck administration.

Taking advantage of the circumstance, Sarnoff devised a plan. Knowing that most of the charges against him were true, he worried what the determination of the court would be to remedy his monopolistic practices. Sarnoff came up with a punishment that he privately favored, and then let it leak to the press that he was afraid that the government would take that very same action. The remedy he had in mind was to split RCA from the rest of the radio combine, to force GE and Westinghouse to sell all RCA stock and sever ties between the companies once and for all. To run his own private empire unfettered by the bureaucracy was one of his long-standing desires.

After meetings with the top GE and Westinghouse executives, wherein he negotiated the terms of a breakup, he handed the carefully framed list of "concessions" to the Justice Department—just three days after Roosevelt's landslide victory. As he expected, the defeated Hoover administration suggested only minor modifications. The trial was canceled, and a landmark consent decree was signed by all parties on November 21, 1932. Sarnoff's rivals rejoiced over what they perceived as RCA's defeat, but Sarnoff considered it his independence day. "The government handed me a lemon," Sarnoff bragged to his associates. "And I made lemonade."

Publicly, Sarnoff appeared impervious to the antitrust investigation, and it didn't impede his preparations to move his corporate headquarters to a newly constructed seventy-story tower in midtown Manhattan. The RCA Building was the first of twenty-two properties in Rockefeller Center, a mammoth urban-renewal project conceived by John D. Rockefeller Jr. before the market plunge.

In June of 1933, the newly liberated RCA made its move. Sarnoff called his section of the art deco complex Radio City, and he presided over the new domain like a nineteenth-century czar. Sarnoff hung portraits of Lincoln and Marconi on the oak-paneled walls of his office on the fifty-third floor, a subdued and uncluttered space that "conveyed a sense of aloof power under perfect control," according to Sarnoff's official biographer. His desk was built onto a raised platform, designed to compensate for his stocky frame and to intimidate visitors.

At its eastern entrance, the limestone RCA Building faced an open-air courtyard, Rockefeller Plaza, where a commissioned sculpture of a golden Prometheus overlooked the fountains. According to myth, Prometheus was the great benefactor of humankind, as he was the Greek god who stole fire from Zeus and gave it to the people of the Earth. The imagery appealed to Sarnoff, the self-styled prophet of the electronic age. RCA's majestic new headquarters and its adjoining NBC studios became instant symbols not only of the new status of the twentieth-century corporation but of America's leadership in technology. At age forty-two, David Sarnoff was now firmly in his seat of power.

The summer of 1933 was an ominous time for humanity. By July, Hitler's Nazi Party was suddenly the only political party in Germany. Suffering from 30 percent unemployment, the German people traded democracy and human rights for the prospect of a better economy.

Albert Einstein left Berlin in disgust. "Two things are infinite," proclaimed Einstein, "the universe and human stupidity; and I'm not so sure about the universe." The world's most famous physicist soon settled in Princeton, New Jersey, just a few doors down from Vladimir Zworykin, who could often be seen out walking his dog Rex. At RCA Laboratories, according to one engineer, "they used to say that Zworykin's dog must be a very intelligent dog because it ran around with Einstein's dog."

It was also at this time that Philco severed its ties with Farnsworth. The end run had failed. Farnsworth later learned that when Sarnoff found out about the Philo-Philco plan to commercialize television, he threatened to rescind the Philadelphia company's license to produce radios under RCA's patents, which would effectively put Philco out of business. There is no formal documentation proving such an ultimatum was issued, but Sarnoff obviously wouldn't want to leave a trail of evidence that could be handed over to FDR's Justice Department in Washington and have investigations begin all over again. Perhaps even more so than price-fixing, collusion, and restraint of trade, using one monopoly (in this case radio) as leverage to form another monopoly (television) is an especially insidious yet difficult-to-prove violation of antitrust law. Such threats most likely happened in telephone conversations.

There were other reasons for the split up as well. After all they put him through, Farnsworth wasn't exactly in love with the top brass at Philco. The two companies also had completely different goals. Philco was a low-margin manufacturer that mass-produced boxes. It had little stomach for expensive, long-term research and development, and the depression made the short-term prospects look grim. Farnsworth, meanwhile, was almost solely concerned with his research and his efforts to continue building up a broad patent structure over television. During his two years working with Philco, he filed applications for six additional patents, including an improved and more sensitive Image Dissector. While the breakup meant that Philco's television manufacturing effort was on indefinite hold, Philco still maintained its patent license from Farnsworth.

After the split, Pem expressed her preference to go back home to San Francisco. Even McCargar wanted to retreat to the Green Street lab. Farnsworth, however, was determined to stay on the East Coast. That's where the action in broadcasting is, he said. He knew he couldn't afford to keep much of a staff, so he had to lay off Arch Brolly once again and to say good-bye to Russell Varian for good. He persuaded the others to support his move to a new laboratory near his home in Chestnut Hill.

Along with Cliff and a loyal engineer named Tobe Rutherford, he boxed up his equipment and books and secured space in a low-rent suburban office complex at 127 East Mermaid Lane in suburban Philadelphia. He applied to the Federal Radio Commission for his own license to operate an experimental TV station, while George Everson, optimistic about an upward bump in the stock market, took up residence at the Plaza Hotel in New York, working full-time to sell stock in the renamed Farnsworth Television for cash to meet salaries and lab expenses.

With his plan for an end run quashed, there was now only one way to meet his objective. Philo T. Farnsworth would have to face RCA head on, attempting a rush right up the middle.

Farnsworth (right) next to mobile transmitter at one of the first outdoor experimental all-electronic telecasts, in Philadelphia, 1934.
(SPECIAL COLLECTIONS, J. WILLARD MARRIOTT LIBRARY, UNIVERSITY OF UTAH)

CHAPTER TEN

Who Owns What?

No matter how hard Philo T. Farnsworth worked at his suburban Philadelphia laboratory, he wasn't making progress in advancing television to a commercial stage. According to the party line laid down by David Sarnoff, it was RCA that was developing true commercial television, and when it was ready, RCA's own pending patents based on the work of Zworykin's team would be available to manufacturers for license. RCA notified all the potential licensees of Farnsworth's patents that the Patent Office must have made a serious mistake. This calculated and clandestine campaign of misinformation and threats cut off Farnsworth's ability to license his patents, which he had counted on as his main source of potential revenue.

Meanwhile, RCA went into a state of silence about the technical details of its own television work, offering no public demonstrations of Zworykin's apparatus during the years 1932 through 1935. Indeed, Sarnoff was so obsessed with controlling all information on

television personally that he sent out an internal memo with a subject line that read "public statements and publicity on television."

> In view of the many angles involved in the above subject and
> the likelihood of misunderstanding, either by the public, the
> press, our stockholders, or prospective investors, or all of them,
> it is essential that no statements be made on the subject of tele-
> vision except those approved by RCA. . . . I have asked Mr. Mullen
> [head of the RCA Department of Information] to take up with
> me for my approval in each instance any statement which any-
> one in the organization may feel it necessary to make in the
> future on the subject of television, and I will personally approve,
> recommend changes, or disapprove such statements.

By contrast, information about Farnsworth's progress always
seemed to find its way to his competitors. Whenever Farnsworth
would give public talks, the front row of the audience would be
lined with engineers snapping photographs of his slides. Some of
those ideas would find their way into rival patent applications, from
both RCA and other companies.

Finally, Farnsworth decided he had had enough of RCA's espionage, delays, and propaganda. He needed the Patent Office to clar-
ify the situation once and for all. With the help of Donald Lippincott,
his trusted patent attorney, Farnsworth filed suit against RCA. This
legal action became known as Patent Interference Number 64,027.
At issue was nothing less than the big question: who invented electronic television? While Sarnoff was content to let this question
linger as long as possible, in order to buy time for Zworykin, Farnsworth knew that the dispute had to be resolved before he could
move ahead.

The legal wrangle between Farnsworth and RCA went to the very
heart of what made the U.S. patent system a great engine of economic

growth. In the words of Abraham Lincoln (the only U.S. president ever to hold a patent), "the patent system added the fuel of interest to the fire of invention." In Lincoln's estimation, the introduction of the U.S. patent laws was one of "the three most important events in the world's history," along with the advent of printing and the discovery of America itself. The patent system that had given rise to so many new industries was now being called to arbitrate the birth of television.

In room number 3714 at the U.S. Patent Office, the examiner of interferences and his board members officially opened the case of Philo T. Farnsworth versus Vladimir K. Zworykin. Under the direction of David Sarnoff and patent chief Otto Schairer, the RCA team consisted of five attorneys, headed by Samuel B. Smith. Farnsworth's three-lawyer team was led by Donald Lippincott. Patent Interference Number 64,027 was ready to begin, and the winner of the case would be granted controlling rights to the invention of television.

The issue at hand was extremely specific, although it was also enormously far-reaching. The trial was focused on a single claim— claim number 15—in Farnsworth's original "television system" patent, filed in 1927 and issued in 1930. The nut of the dispute came down to one seminal sentence, which described Farnsworth's

apparatus for television which comprises a means for forming an electrical image, and means for scanning each elementary area of the electrical image, and means for producing a train of electrical energy in accordance with the intensity of the elementary area of the electrical image being scanned.

In his opening statement, Lippincott admitted that Farnsworth's claim was "very broad," but added that "all of the terms used in the count, with the single exception of the term *electrical image*, have meaning which were well understood in the art at the time." And so the definition of this new term would form the crux of the case. In a clever stroke, Lippincott submitted Zworykin's own words from the pretrial deposition as to what an electrical image is.

> By electrical image, I mean an arrangement in space of a measurable electrical quantity such as current, charge, or potential being proportional in magnitude in every point to the distribution of light intensity of the optical image to which this electrical image corresponds.

Since Zworykin's previously stated definition was essentially the same as Farnsworth's definition, it seemed to offer RCA little wiggle room. "It would therefore appear that Zworykin should be bound by his own definition," argued Lippincott. "This materially simplifies the issue." Lippincott then went on to establish that Farnsworth's apparatus performed what was described in his issued patent in accordance with this definition, and he argued that Zworykin's original 1923 patent application did not describe the ability to form an electrical image, but rather, in Lippincott's words, a "substantially uniform potential," essentially an unrecognizable array of light, which would "result in distortion of the received signal and failure of the device to achieve its primary purpose."

Finally, Lippincott cited Zworykin's own statement that, according to his own definition, Zworykin previously admitted that his own device would be *inoperative.* In short, the Farnsworth team presented quite a strong opening.

In the RCA opening statement, attorney Samuel Smith shifted the focus away from what the invention in question actually was to the issue of who conceived their invention first. Zworykin claimed that his conception took place in 1917, while he was still in Russia, and he claimed that he introduced it in the United States in 1919, showed it to a colleague in 1921, and fully disclosed its operation—

so-called reduction to practice—in his December 29, 1923, application. By contrast, RCA pointed out, Farnsworth was claiming conception in 1922 and reduction of the idea to practice on January 7, 1927.

The trial thus began on an awkward note, with the Farnsworth side focusing on who invented electronic television according to a mutually acceptable definition—and with the RCA side focusing on who first came up with the idea. The RCA strategy was an attempt to divert the court to Zworykin's 1923 concept, with the hope that the examining board might not understand the subtleties of what it means to scan, transmit, and reproduce an electrical image, something Zworykin didn't actually achieve until 1931, according to Farnsworth.

Now it was time to present the evidence. RCA began by describing its system, but instead of submitting to the court a design based on the 1923 application, Samuel Smith described what seemed to be a new and improved system. This was a most perplexing development, as this was RCA's golden chance to show a television system based on that 1923 design, or at least show documentary evidence that such a system once existed. In failing to do so, the attorneys either were choosing for some reason to hide it from public view or were concealing the fact that the original Zworykin device was never built or never worked in the first place.

Lippincott objected to RCA's submission of the modified description, pointing out specific inconsistencies that would cause the new Zworykin system to work as advertised whereas the older one would not. "Under the theory of operation now advanced for the first time," Lippincott protested, "the operation of the Zworykin transmitter is quite different."

For their part, RCA's lawyers took no issue with the description of the Farnsworth apparatus.

The RCA lawyers did make quite a big point of criticizing Farnsworth's expert witnesses, especially MIT-trained Arch Brolly, who

Samuel Smith said was "not competent" and "did not understand" the operation of the Zworykin device. Poking holes in the depositions of the Farnsworth witnesses, the RCA lawyer at one point concluded that "it is nothing short of preposterous for [Brolly] to pose as an expert" and that "his testimony is of no value." It was true that Brolly had been a Farnsworth employee and therefore probably biased, but it was also true that Farnsworth was handicapped in finding so-called experts in the art because there were few, if any, true experts in electronic television outside RCA and Farnsworth's own company.

To establish their chronology of events, the RCA team called as a witness one Joseph Tykociner. Born in Poland, Tykociner was a Westinghouse engineer and a distinguished inventor who joined the University of Illinois faculty in 1921. That was the year he testi-fied that Zworykin disclosed his invention to him, and all their communication occurred in the Russian language. The credibility of this oral testimony was crucial—first, because there was no writ-ten evidence to back it up, and two, because it went to the heart of RCA's case that Zworykin was the first to conceive.

"Have you ever seen a device constructed as disclosed by the Zworykin application?" RCA's counsel asked.

"Yes," Professor Tykociner replied. "I have seen a device."

"Did it operate?"

"It did operate."

"Could you sketch for me the device which you saw operate?"

"Yes," he replied, and the witness drew the sketch.

In their cross-examination of this testimony, the Farnsworth lawyers contended that neither Tykociner nor Zworykin himself established that the Zworykin device formed an electrical image, as defined and required. Nor did they establish exactly where or when the witness actually saw the device, or whether the demonstration the witness referred to was the same as the one RCA was now describing in the patent court.

While RCA's lawyers maintained that the earlier device and the current description were "substantially identical," Lippincott pointed out that Tykociner's recollected sketch was so *exactly identical* to Zworykin's sketches in his patent application that it defied credibility. The Farnsworth lawyer noted that Zworykin and his principal witness had been in continual contact over the past fifteen years. Thus, Lippincott asserted, those two had ample opportunity to revisit, revise, and even agree to distort. "The exact correspondence of the sketches of the various witnesses, and of their description of the mode of operation, after so long a period, is the strongest kind of indication that their memories have been strongly colored by later events."

When it came to establishing the Farnsworth chronology, Lippincott and his team faced a big problem. Upon conceiving his idea, Farnsworth only disclosed it to two people: to his father, now deceased, and to his high school science teacher, Justin Tolman, who had since left Rigby, Idaho. Farnsworth hadn't been in touch with Tolman since moving away from Rigby, and he had no idea as to his whereabouts or whether the teacher remembered much about the matter in question.

Lippincott, in a special trip to Utah, finally located Mr. Tolman on a sunny day in Salt Lake City, where Tolman was living in retirement. The old teacher was out working in his rose garden.

"Excuse me, sir," Lippincott asked. "Are you Justin Tolman?"

"Yes," he replied, "I am."

"Do you remember a student in Rigby, Idaho, by the name of Philo Farnsworth?"

"I surely do. Brightest student I ever had."

"My name is Donald Lippincott, and I'm a patent attorney representing Mr. Farnsworth. His camera tube, the Image Dissector, is in interference in the Patent Office. Do you remember him discussing it with you?"

"Yes, I do."

After that brief confirmation, Lippincott invited Tolman to testify in the trial. In his testimony, Tolman said that he not only remembered Farnsworth but did his best to make sure none of the students who came after ever forgot what happened in Rigby. He had regaled all of his subsequent classes with the story of the farm boy who conceived electronic television. The time period as to when Farnsworth disclosed his concept to his teacher could not be called into question, for the school records verified that Farnsworth was Tolman's student during and only during a four-month period in the spring of 1922.

Under examination as to what Tolman remembered about his student's blackboard drawing of the television system, Tolman was able to recall and sketch for the court only very basic details, but they matched key elements in Farnsworth's 1927 patent application. Asked whether he could show written evidence, Tolman reached into his breast pocket and produced a folded-up, well-worn sheet of notebook paper. When he unfolded it, Tolman revealed a shockingly simple sketch of the Image Dissector. "This was made for me by Philo in early 1922," he said. The teacher had saved the drawing all these years.

Seeing that, the RCA team then took a different line of argument: that the whole situation was wildly implausible, as stated in the RCA brief prepared for the final hearing.

In March of 1922, when Farnsworth alleges that he made his invention, Farnsworth was a mere boy of fifteen years. He has endeavored to establish himself as a genius who foresaw great possibilities in television and poses as an individual who was able to conceive an invention . . . that great men of science and skill . . . had spent years in developing, although Farnsworth derived *his* knowledge of electricity only from such publica-

tions as *Electrical Experimenter* and *Radio News*. . . . The Patent
Office will readily agree that these publications could not possibly have served, in 1922, as a logical source of *fundamental
information* to develop a complicated television device. . . . He
had only a grade school education. He understood physics, electricity and chemistry because "we had a Delco electric lighting
system on our farm.". . .Obviously, the television idea was little
better than a dream on his part.

Obviously, the RCA team failed to understand Einstein's dictum
that "imagination is more important than knowledge." To dissolve
RCA's attack, the counsel for Farnsworth simply pointed out that
what happened five years later, in 1927, was also quite extraordinary and improbable.

If we are considering probabilities only, it is extremely improbable that a boy of twenty, whose formal education ceased with
the completion of his first year in college, should have filed
the application on the Farnsworth device and been granted a
patent. No other person out of one hundred and twenty million
in the country at the time did so, but in spite of this improba-
bility the fact remains that the patent was issued. In order that
this might be the case, it was necessary that the invention be
conceived.

The most sensational segment of the trial was saved for the
end, and this concerned the Zworykin visit to Farnsworth's Green
Street lab in April of 1930. Zworykin testified that he was invited
by Farnsworth to visit the laboratory, but Lippincott noted that
Zworykin's own documentation shows that the invitation, "if it
could be considered such, came from *the patent department of his
own company*."

One after another, four witnesses, associates in the Green Street lab that day, came forward for Farnsworth. All told of the time when Zworykin held the Image Dissector in his hands and said: "This is a beautiful instrument. I wish I had invented it myself."

Confronted with this testimony on the witness stand, Zworykin paused for several minutes. Instead of orally testifying his response, he painstakingly came up with a written explanation that he slowly read into the court record. He didn't deny making the 1930 statement, but in his carefully crafted use of words, Zworykin said his "exclamation" was just an attempt to be "polite." It didn't serve as proof of anything, he said. He really didn't think very highly of the Farnsworth apparatus, especially compared to his own work.

RCA's Smith said that it was "scarcely necessary to dignify the testimony of Farnsworth and his witnesses by commenting on this statement at length. The statement, if made at all, was made out of politeness to his host, as Zworykin has testified, perhaps colored by the very human and natural wish that he also had invented Farnsworth's specific type of apparatus as well as his own. It is thoroughly inconsequential, however, and nothing more needs to be said."

Lippincott said that Zworykin's explanation was a "marvel of ingenuity." As for Zworykin characterizing his remark as an off-the-cuff "exclamation," Lippincott agreed wholeheartedly. "This is exactly what it was—an exclamation of surprise and honest admiration for the work of a fellow scientist." In the years since Zworykin had made his exclamation, the attorney continued, "Zworykin's *wish* that he had been the inventor has fathered the belief that he actually *was* the inventor."

If the statement was indeed inconsequential, then what happened next was "inexplicable," according to the Farnsworth counsel.

He stopped at the Westinghouse factory on his way back to Camden and had Dr. Wilson [a fellow engineer] duplicate the tubes of the Farnsworth type. Zworykin states he advised his company against acquiring the Farnsworth patents. In spite of this, Dr. Zworykin's employers sent a technical expert and a patent attorney to San Francisco and to these men the entire application files of Farnsworth and his associates were thrown open.

Lawyers for RCA refused to respond to this. Instead, they kept objecting in the harshest terms to the introduction of such charges and evidence into the court record.

In closing, counsel for Farnsworth summed up the ample evidence, including detailed lab journals, sketches, photographs, corroborating witnesses, and a fully issued patent, proving that Farnsworth conceived and demonstrated exactly what he claimed in that patent. "The evidence shows that Zworykin did not conceive an operative device until after Farnsworth's filing date," Lippincott concluded. "For these reasons an award of priority to the party Farnsworth is respectively requested."

Samuel B. Smith closed RCA's case by summing up the assertion that Zworykin was the "first to conceive and reduce to practice the invention described by the interference count," and that "Farnsworth has been unable to corroborate his alleged conception in March 1922."

"Wherefore," he concluded, "priority should be awarded to Zworykin."

This was not the kind of case in which a decision could be issued on the spot. The gritty details were highly technical, and the examiners needed ample time to go through the volumes of evidence, the testimony, and the final briefs. The judgment wouldn't be rendered until many months after the arguments were concluded in April 1934.

Meanwhile, television seemed to be on ice. Hugo Gernsback halted the publication of *Television News* due to the lack of news about television. Mechanical television was no longer alive in America, and the trial seemed to put its electronic counterpart on hold. So Gernsback folded coverage of any developments into his other broadcasting magazine, *Radio Craft*. In Washington, D.C., the Roosevelt administration worked with Congress to create a more active regulatory body to replace the Federal Radio Commission. The new Federal Communications Commission now had explicit authority over television station licensing, but it remained steadfast in its opposition to changing television's status from experimental to commercial.

RCA maintained its public silence about television matters— and it could well afford to do so. The radio business was now staging an unexpected recovery, as it seemed to be one of the few industries to benefit from the depression. Cheap ten-dollar portables were all the rage, and millions of families now owned more than one set. The movie business also proved resilient, and RCA's RKO Pictures venture suddenly scored big at the box office, with the release of *King Kong* and a series of films that paired Fred Astaire with Ginger Rogers. As a result, RCA turned a $4.2-million net profit on revenue of $79 million in 1934, and it had plenty of cash in the bank and no debt.

Certainly, FDR's Fireside Chats had a lot to do with RCA's prosperity during those tough times. The president was taking some drastic actions: closing the banks in order to restructure the entire system, severing the U.S. dollar from the gold standard in order to halt deflation, and proposing a raft of radical New Deal legislation. All of this needed careful, calm explaining, and his regular radio addresses, spoken informally to people sitting in their living rooms, seemed to soothe the nation.

RCA salesmen were coming back with some amazing tales. People were skipping meals and selling their refrigerators and even their blankets and pillows to pay the rent, but they wouldn't go without their radios. No longer a novelty or a luxury item, the radio was becoming perhaps the most necessary household appliance of all. When Roosevelt took office in 1933, about 50 percent of U.S. households owned a radio. By the end of his second term, the number would jump to nearly 90 percent. Radio achieved similar success in many other countries, and RCA had been licensing its patents worldwide.

Behind the scenes, television research at RCA accelerated. The corporation sunk more than $5 million into lab work in Camden, erected a giant television transmission antenna on top of the Empire State Building, and opened an experimental TV studio at the NBC complex in Radio City. Zworykin's original budget had become a joke inside RCA. Zworykin was "the greatest salesman in history," Sarnoff said. "He put a price tag of $100,000 on television, and I bought it." Neither Sarnoff, nor his board, nor the shareholders seemed angry at the additional cost, however, because the radio monopoly kept replenishing the corporate coffers. In fact, RCA had so much money that it soon started paying its first dividends to shareholders.

In his ongoing effort to make RCA the preeminent corporation in the United States, Sarnoff made a series of job offers to Albert Einstein. The prestige of having Einstein on the RCA payroll would be incalculable, if only because Sarnoff would be able to say, "Albert Einstein works for me." More specifically, it seems that Sarnoff wanted Einstein to contribute to RCA's television efforts.

What did this deeply theoretical physicist know about practical invention? Quite a bit, as it turns out. Einstein's first regular job, as a young man, was his seven-year, full-time position at the Swiss Patent Office in Bern. During those years, he moonlighted as a scientist, writing his breakthrough papers on the photoelectric effect and relativity. But by day, he was slogging through patent applications, deciding which inventions were unique and original, and which were not. "Einstein's intuition for seeing the strengths and weaknesses of a good idea, developed in the Patent Office thirty years earlier, had not left him," wrote Einstein's biographer Ronald Clark.

The case of Farnsworth versus Zworykin was still awaiting a decision when Sarnoff and Einstein met face-to-face at 30 Rockefeller Plaza in June of 1935. The two had had a brief encounter once before. During Einstein's 1921 visit to America, he toured RCA's transatlantic station in New Brunswick, New Jersey, and conferred with Charles Steinmetz, GE's resident genius. Sarnoff managed to get himself there and pose in a group photo, which shows the young Sarnoff leaning over at an odd angle to increase his chance of appearing in the picture with Einstein at its center. Einstein, of course, wouldn't have had much reason to remember that David Sarnoff.

Now perched behind his immense raised desk in his plush office, *this* David Sarnoff gazed down at his wild-haired, owl-eyed prey. He wasn't asking the professor to leave his position at Princeton's Institute for Advanced Study, only to act as a part-time "scientific consultant," perhaps lecturing to the engineers and discussing their inventions, perhaps contributing new ideas and approaches, and of course, making it known to the outside world of his affiliation with RCA. The pay would be generous, perhaps even more than the $16,000 annual salary Einstein was earning at Princeton.

It was a complicated matter, and not just because of the awkward point of how much money should be paid to Einstein, under what terms, and what his exact role would be. During this time, Einstein was summering at a seaside cottage in Watch Hill, Rhode Island, as the guest of Dr. Gustav Bucky, an old friend who was not only a physician but an inventor. The two men would sail together and work on various ideas. They even filed for a patent on a camera improvement. It was Dr. Bucky who really wanted to work with RCA, and Einstein seemed to suggest that Sarnoff needed to engage the services of both of them. Further complicating matters was that Dr. Bucky was treating Einstein's wife, Elsa, who was gravely ill. The whole thing led to a series of misunderstandings, as alluded to in a letter to from Elsa Einstein to Sarnoff, which is translated from German:

> The business affair that was under consideration by you and my husband did not reach a fortunate conclusion at the time. I may say to you that this has been a matter of deep regret, both to my husband and myself. The situation then was an unfortunate one. You came to us under other assumptions, and thus everything that could have worked out so well came to naught. Isn't that a shame? My husband deplores it, and I hope you feel the same way. Could we not wait a month or two and then take up the matter again? My husband believes it is possible. It would be a great pleasure to him to act as scientific consultant for your Corporation. . . . My husband has such great joy in solving technical problems. . . . As soon as I am well again, I cordially invite you, together with your good wife, to come to us in Princeton for a Sunday.

The dance between Einstein and Sarnoff went on for almost an entire year. Hanging in the balance, of course, was what this would all mean for Philo T. Farnsworth. How would Farnsworth react at this difficult time if he found out that his ultimate hero and his worst enemy were collaborating?

It was also at this time that Sarnoff's old friend Joe Kennedy got himself an unlikely job. Under his stated theory that "it takes a thief to catch a thief," President Roosevelt appointed Kennedy, in the summer of 1934, to be the first chairman of the new Securities and

Exchange Commission, set up to stamp out the type of fraud and stock manipulation that had helped precipitate Black Tuesday, bring on the Great Depression, and, not incidentally, build up the great Kennedy fortune. Old Joe was quite adept at this job, as it was said that he could sniff out an illegal stock pool by just looking at the ticker stream.

Under Kennedy's leadership, the SEC investigated about 2,300 cases of possible securities fraud. He didn't go after any major members of the New York Stock Exchange. Rather, almost all of the cases involved the manipulation of small-time, over-the-counter stocks. At this point, Farnsworth Television was one such creature. Faced with a whopping $30,000 legal bill from the trial and $5,000 per month in salaries and lab costs, Everson and McCargar were living on company expenses in New York, selling as much stock as they could to pay these bills. This coincided with a run-up in the price of company shares, which was fortunate. But such activity could also smell fishy to Sarnoff's friend at the new SEC.

The danger was real. "The company difficulties stemmed largely from McCargar's under the table dealings," Pem wrote years later in a note she placed in the Farnsworth Papers, a special archive of documents housed at the University of Utah. "Phil was warned against McCargar by the other Crocker Bank officials, but his alternative was to sell out and go to RCA, which he refused to do. And George Everson persuaded him to go along with McCargar."

All of this conspired to make the tension greater as Farnsworth awaited the all-important Patent Office verdict. As always, though, he had the incredible loyalty of his small group of employees. In fact, one new employee came from the ranks of the company's shareholders. Seymour "Skee" Turner, the son of a San Francisco clothing store owner, was deep into Farnsworth Television stock and was so enamored by the prospect of commercialization that he came to Philadelphia to see whether he could help. Farnsworth told him that he had no funds for a salary but offered him a spare bedroom in the house instead. Another colorful character, Bill Eddy, was a mostly deaf, former U.S. Navy officer who showed up one day at the Chestnut Hill lab looking for a new career in this thing called television. With little money for food, Turner and Eddy would chip in for bags of week-old bread for lunch. For dinner, Eddy raised rabbits in his backyard.

On a personal level, Phil's relationship with Pem had hit bottom. They were hardly speaking to each other but still kept up outward appearances, and one of their ongoing activities was attending dances with a group of friends at a local music hall every Saturday night. Each week, Phil was dancing more and more often with a pretty young woman named Kay, and less and less with Pem. Pretty soon, Kay's husband, Hank, asked Pem to dance. Hank was not only a great dancer but tall, blonde, and handsome.

"I decided to show Phil that two could play this game," Pem recalled. "It went on for weeks, with Phil outwardly unconcerned. I was actually thinking about running off to Reno for a divorce so I could marry Hank."

One Saturday, Donald Lippincott and his wife, Ruth, arrived for a visit. Not only had he done a brilliant job leading the patent fight against RCA, but he was also a great friend of Farnsworth. They all went to the dance together that night, and talking about old times seemed to ease the tension a bit. At one point, the band began to play "Always," the Irving Berlin ballad that Phil and Pem considered their song.

"I think this is our dance," said Phil.

"At first, it was like dancing with a stranger," Pem recalled, "because I was not at all sure we still loved each other."

"What's the matter with us?" said Phil. "We must be crazy. We need to talk. Let's get out of here."

The wall between them came tumbling down that night, as they each revealed the guilt they felt over the loss of Kenny. They were not blaming each other, as they had each thought. Rather, each blamed themselves. "From that night, we gradually rebuilt our relationship," wrote Pem, "this time with such a close bond that nothing ever again threatened us." They soon conceived another child, Russell Seymour Farnsworth, nicknamed Skeezix, after a popular cartoon character.

Instead of just sitting around and waiting for the patent decision, Farnsworth decided to do some showing off. After all, his staff had fashioned a fully mobile television camera that scooted around on a tripod with wheels. And they were building TV sets displaying crisp, 343-line pictures at thirty frames per second on screens that measured ten inches on the diagonal. Farnsworth was still way ahead of RCA, although Sarnoff's secrecy prevented him from knowing this for sure.

One day in the newspaper, Farnsworth spotted an article about Mary Pickford appearing in a play in New York. This was his chance to redeem himself after the disaster at Green Street four years earlier. He sent an invitation to her, and she agreed to swing by the laboratory the following Sunday afternoon. To greet her, Farnsworth asked Cliff and Tobe Rutherford to come in on their day off and set up the demonstration.

Pickford arrived in a chauffeured limousine and was surprisingly polite and accommodating to the neighborhood kids who crowded around her as she emerged from the car. She even paused to sign autographs and shake some rather grimy hands. Inside, she witnessed the transmission of a film loop from *The Taming of the Shrew*, the one in which Pickford is combing her long hair. She seemed quite taken with the sharpness of the picture, but if she was wondering whether TV would put the movies out of business, she didn't say so. She agreed to sit under the bright arc lamps to be televised live, but that lasted only a few minutes before she started to bake. "Whew!" she exclaimed, remarking that the lamps were hotter than those used for making color movies.

The success of the Pickford visit emboldened Farnsworth to get out and give more talks about his recent advances. In the summer of 1934, he spoke at the Franklin Institute in downtown Philadelphia, after which one of the directors invited him to set up a television demonstration lasting ten days. One of the country's oldest science museums, the Franklin Institute not only was prestigious but also was aiming to become one of the city's biggest tourist attractions. The museum's directors believed that Farnsworth's demonstration would be a huge draw for people who came to town to see the Liberty Bell.

As soon as Farnsworth agreed, he realized he had a problem on his hands: what would he televise for ten whole days? The folks at the institute invited the mayor to appear on TV and officially kick off the event. Skee Turner hurried to the offices of local booking agents, telling them that their clients would benefit from all the hoopla and publicity.

When the exhibit opened, Farnsworth staged a surprise at the main entrance. He pointed a mobile camera at the incoming stream of visitors, while a receiver just inside the door televised their faces, allowing people to watch their friends and family members. This created quite a commotion, which attracted more and more people off the street. Tickets cost seventy-five cents per person for a twenty-minute presentation, and with the theater inside able to hold only a couple hundred seats, lines began forming right away. Inside, the audience sat to view the live show as Farnsworth's lab staff operated the cameras, which relayed the images to TV monitors set up in front of the seats.

The entertainment program got off to a shaky start, as a professor from Swarthmore played his cello, only to break a string when hitting a high note. He kept playing, but another string broke, and then the hot lights started blistering the varnish on the instrument. Seeing this, Skee Turner motioned to the line of chorus girls waiting in the wings. As they bounced out kicking to jaunty music, the crowd rose to its feet. An entire row of newsmen starting jotting down notes and snapping photographs. Things took off from there, and the next edition of the *Philadelphia Ledger* carried photos from the event and a headline that read: "Epochal Television Set Invented Here. New Device Shown at Franklin Institute Hailed as Most Sensitive Devised."

The show went on day after day, with the lines outside getting longer and longer. Acts included puppet shows, ventriloquists, dog tricks, dancing bears, and a trained monkey that at one point escaped from its cage, slipped out a back door, and began romping down a city street trailed by Pem and several policemen. Skee Turner, an avid tennis player, invited members of the Davis Cup team to swing their rackets and bounce some balls before the camera, which prompted the newspaper to report that "they're televising tennis." Farnsworth even took a camera outside to televise impromptu football scrimmages, and then up to the roof of the building, to shoot nearby landmarks and buildings in plain sunlight.

The shot that received the most attention from the media came at night, when Farnsworth trained his Image Dissector on the moon. The press celebrated this as the television debut of the man in the moon. "First recorded use of television in astronomy was announced yesterday in Philadelphia by Philo T. Farnsworth," declared a wire report carried in papers across the country.

While the Franklin Institute event was a great source of publicity, it didn't do much for Farnsworth financially, as the museum kept all of the ticket revenue, and it was a huge emotional drain on the company, as the telethon-like event left everyone associated with it completely exhausted.

Farnsworth aimed to build on all the attention by opening a new production studio in the Philadelphia suburb of Wyndmoor, where he launched a schedule of sporadic television programming. The experimental station was called W3XPF, and Farnsworth Television began transmitting from a seventy-foot broadcasting tower that pointed to the sky outside the studio. As for the biggest stars from these early broadcasts, studio audiences loved the dancing and singing kids, especially Baby Dolores, age four, and "Smiles" Blum, age eleven, also known as "Little Miss Television." But only a handful of people, mainly Farnsworth staff and some friends, had television sets installed in their homes to receive the broadcasts.

One hot summer's day at the end of July 1935, a deliveryman appeared at Farnsworth's laboratory with a stack of documents. He was dropping off copies of a forty-eight-page ruling from the examiner of interferences at the U.S. Patent Office. The arrival of the documents caused all work to stop dead, as Farnsworth and his staff crowded around to read the decision.

When Farnsworth started scanning the document, his heart must have sunk. "Farnsworth only has oral testimony prior to 1923," the ruling stated, "from him and from witness Justin Tolman." The patent examiners wanted hard evidence, and they clearly had considered the undated, unnotarized notebook drawing that Tolman produced as inadmissible. "The original [diagrams of the TV system] were drawn on a high school blackboard and erased. Since there is no other evidence of record tending to corroborate a conception by Farnsworth prior to Zworykin's filing date, except the oral testimony of the inventor, it follows that Farnsworth has not satisfied the burden upon him as junior party of proving conception prior to this date."

Still, the ruling also took issue with Zworykin's claims. Mainly, it said that a machine built according to his 1923 design would produce largely meaningless shades of darkness and light.

The Zworykin application, as filed, does not disclose a device
for producing an electrical image which is scanned to produce
television signals as required. It is admitted in the Zworykin
brief that the device produces at most a graded or shaded image.
Thus the charge pattern on the cathode at any instant does not
represent the true optical image, either as sent or as received,
but represents a graded or shaded version of it with at least a
small portion entirely missing.

The examiners were not swayed by the testimony of Zworykin
or that of his principal witnesses, especially not Professor Tykociner. "This testimony is not convincing," the ruling stated. "It
is entirely oral and is given some ten to fourteen years after the
alleged events . . . and appears to be influenced by subsequent
knowledge. . . . Zworykin's answers clearly suggest that his testimony is influenced by the present controversy."

Just as Lippincott had argued, the court was agreeing that the
device described in Zworykin's patent application was "an entirely
different invention" from the one described by the RCA witnesses.
This made it highly likely that RCA's described "mode of operation
was not realized at that [prior] time."

This sounded extremely encouraging from Farnsworth's point
of view, but since the document went on and on, with long passages
of highly technical and legal language, Farnsworth and his staff
jumped ahead to the final page, where the verdict was written in
black and white. "Zworykin has no right to make the count," the
ruling concluded. "Priority of invention is awarded to Philo T.
Farnsworth."

The court had affirmed his controlling patent. At age twenty-
nine, Philo T. Farnsworth was held to be the undisputed inventor of
television as the world would come to know it.

"Everyone went into raptures," recalled Bill Eddy.

Farnsworth was rejuvenated. With this clear victory over RCA in hand, no one would be able to doubt him again. Radio makers could now start producing commercial television equipment under license from him. A new industry was ready to be born. Once again, Farnsworth was ready to take on the world. Of course, the world was perfectly ready, willing, and able to fight right back.

Philo T. Farnsworth at his suburban Philadelphia laboratory. (CORBIS)

CHAPTER ELEVEN

Narrow Escape

To celebrate his tenth wedding anniversary in proper style, Philo T. Farnsworth decided to treat his wife to a trip to Europe. In November of 1936, Europe was approaching a state of turmoil, but Americans seemed to have little concept of the sort of trouble brewing over there. Of course, Phil was not exactly planning on simply seeing the sights and lounging around resorts. As Pem suspected, this was to be mostly a business trip, but it sounded too exciting to pass up. Pem arranged to leave their two boys in the care of Phil's mother, and off they went on the train to New York, where they boarded a luxury cruise liner bound for London. Phil had plenty of time to explain his business plans to Pem on their nine-day journey across the Atlantic.

Farnsworth had been to the British capital two years earlier to meet with John Logie Baird, the world's first and only remaining practitioner of mechanical television. Baird had achieved some financial success with his 200-employee company, mainly because the BBC had agreed to use his equipment in its television research and testing. Then a London firm called EMI, for Electric and Musical Industries, entered into a licensing partnership with RCA to develop electronic television in the United Kingdom, and that put Baird's inferior system on the outs. When Baird learned about Farnsworth through press reports on the Franklin Institute event, he invited the American to demonstrate his electronic system to the BBC. It was a big success, resulting in Baird wiring to Farnsworth the sum of $50,000 for an exclusive license to produce Farnsworth-style TV sets and cameras in England. Along with stock sales, this massive cash infusion helped pay for Farnsworth's lab expenses and outstanding legal fees. But now Baird was having major trouble building his own all-electronic system, and he had called Farnsworth for urgent help.

Upon their arrival, Pem and Phil checked into the luxurious Grosvenor House Hotel, where they reveled in their well-appointed room overlooking Hyde Park. During the day, they parted company, with Pem touring the city, shopping at Piccadilly, and marveling at a magnificent parade in honor of the lord mayor, while Farnsworth labored at the studios of the Baird Television Company, which were housed at the Crystal Palace. An improbably shaped Victorian edifice of steel and glass sitting on Sydenham Hill in south London, the Crystal Palace was so gigantic that it acted as London's all-purpose exposition center, museum, conference venue, social hall, and office complex.

In the evenings, the couple reunited for lavish dinners, often with newfound British friends. One night they went dancing in tux and gown at the Hotel Savoy only to find that their type of fast-paced, American steps were met with scorn by this regal crowd.

For the Farnsworths, all the pretense and pageantry of London was intensified when King Edward VIII created a royal scandal by relinquishing the throne smack in the middle of their stay, the only voluntary abdication in the history of the empire. Lacking official consent to marry American divorcee Wallis Simpson, Edward chose the lady over the crown and handed his royal hat to his brother, who became King George VI. Although it was considered very poor taste to mention the name of this woman in polite society, the Farnsworths heard whispers about Wally wherever they went, and the tabloids were exuberant at being given such a gift. Within a month, Wally Simpson landed on the cover of *Time* magazine as its first female "Person of the Year."

After Farnsworth succeeded in getting Baird's system up and running, Pem insisted that it was really time to relax and stop thinking of work. They took a boat across the English Channel and then boarded a train to the French Riviera, only to be woken at night by a commotion after a stop in Monte Carlo. It was like something from an Agatha Christie novel; there had been a murder in the car next to theirs. The victim was the hostess of a tearoom in Nice, where Edward and Wally had carried on their secret affair, and the case remained an unsolved mystery thereafter. Once on the Riviera, attempting to get away from it all, Phil and Pem were surprised to find that Edward and Wally had the same idea, and so a pack of rabid reporters and photographers rampaged through the seaside village that the Farnsworths were touring.

Phil and Pem planned to stay on the Riviera through Christmas and New Year's, but their attempt to fully unwind was broken up by an urgent telegram from Baird in London. The Crystal Palace was on fire, and Farnsworth was needed back in London for an emergency salvage mission. The *Times* of London carried this report:

> The greater part of the Crystal Palace at Sydenham and nearly all that was in it perished in flames last night. The fire was still

burning at a late hour this morning, and even after 2 A.M. crowds were still arriving to watch the spectacle. The flames roared up the entire height, perhaps 150 feet. Masses of glass dropped continually, and section by section the huge skeleton of iron-work visibly bent and twisted and fell with heavy crashes and in immense showers of sparks. The glare shone on the faces of thousands of people ranked along the railway line below. Hundreds of birds from the aviary within the central arch were released from their cages before the collapse of the roof. Except for a gaunt framework of brown glass and smol-dering beams at the north end, there was nothing left. The two main features of the fire, which chiefly mystified the public, have been its origin and the speed with which the flames tore through the building. Although the building was, by virtue of its construction, a natural flue for any flame, three previous fires had been extinguished with little difficulty. This time the high wind blowing over Sydenham was strong enough to carry large pieces of glass to the shore of the lake 150 yards away. Apart from floors, chairs, tables and the like, there was wood in the walls and roof, which had not been replaced by steel. . . . Blackened but unbroken retorts [canisters for heat-ing chemicals] were littered in the storeroom of the television laboratory, while two of John Logie Baird's workmen were looking hopefully for their bag of tools near a barely recogniz-able lathe.

By the time he arrived at the scene, all of Farnsworth's work in London had gone up in smoke. The system that he and Baird had constructed was now a charred ruin, and any hopes for suc-cess on the British television scene were now on indefinite hold. Indeed, this disaster was the beginning of the end for Baird, as the BBC would soon choose the RCA/EMI system for its official television development. Farnsworth's hopes for conquering the British Empire were extinguished by this mysterious, ferocious fire.

The business portion of their European vacation resumed when the Farnsworths arrived at the Berlin airport at the beginning of January 1937. They claimed their luggage and waited in a long line at the customs gates. Officials in brown uniforms searched their baggage and ordered the Americans to hand over all cash and traveler's checks. In return for their confiscated money, they were handed just enough German marks to pay for their expenses during their stay.

The customs officials then escorted the couple to a pair of men who said they were to be their "courtesy drivers." Dressed in dark suits and caps, they kept a close watch over everything the two said and did, whispering to each other and scribbling notes on a small pad. They were agents of the Gestapo.

The drivers took the couple to the offices of their German host Paul Goerz, the president of Fernseh, the company that manufactured Farnsworth televisions under an international licensing agreement similar to the one Farnsworth had with Baird. Competing against Fernseh in Germany was Telefunken, which was under license from RCA.

Using the Farnsworth technology, Fernseh had vaulted ahead of its rival when it successfully broadcast the 1936 Olympic Games in Berlin the previous summer. These were the legendary games in which Jesse Owens led the U.S. team in its march past a scornful Chancellor Hitler at the opening ceremony. The black track star undermined the dictator's myth of Aryan supremacy when he captured four gold medals, shattering world records as Hitler watched in disgust. Nevertheless, the Nazi Ministry of Propaganda aimed to use the event to springboard Germany into the world's leadership position in television, and it succeeded on that score. Twenty-five television receivers were rigged to project to screens in theaters around the city, and 160,000 viewers watched the games for free, the largest television audience yet.

Farnsworth was visiting Goerz to congratulate him in person and, more important, to collect overdue patent royalties. Tall, bald, and dressed in a high-collared suit, Goerz said he despised the Nazis, but he informed Farnsworth that he was going to have trouble paying Farnsworth any of those royalties. Asked why, Goerz explained in hushed tones that he was appointed against his will to be director of television for the German government, and that all the revenue and expenditures of the company now went through the Nazi Party. In fact, it was now illegal for any money to leave the country at all. Farnsworth had arrived in Berlin with the intention of freeing up those desperately needed payments, and it now was clear that coming here was a huge mistake.

As if any further explanation was needed, Goerz pointed out the window. On the streets below was a procession of tanks, long-range cannon, other heavy artillery, and lines of uniformed soldiers marching in lockstep. Everything was draped in giant red banners with black swastikas. Pem later remarked that she could smell war blowing in the breeze.

Goerz escorted the Farnsworths on a tour of the Fernseh factory. The halls were dark and gray, and they encountered many closed doors with the sign VERBOTEN. Goerz opened one of the doors and started to show the two inside. They were met by a soldier who thrust his rifle across the entrance.

"It's okay," Goerz said in German, "they are making his tube in there."

The soldiers let them enter.

Goerz also took Farnsworth on a long drive to Stuttgart to visit the factory of the Zeiss-Ikon Optical Company, a parent company of

Fernseh. There they met a Jewish executive, introduced as Herr Wild, who rode his bicycle to work every day. He optimistically claimed he didn't mind because it kept him in shape for skiing, but the truth was that the Nazis had confiscated his car. When he got a minute alone with Farnsworth, Wild told of his dark fear for his son, Rudolph, a law student. If you could offer my son a job in the United States, Herr Wild pleaded, perhaps he could escape the catastrophe that was no doubt coming. Farnsworth said he would see what he could do.

The next day, back at the Fernseh office, Farnsworth told Goerz that years earlier a German government official had paid a visit to his laboratory in Philadelphia, and Farnsworth gladly showed him a television demonstration. Farnsworth promised the man that he would visit the next time he came to Berlin, and he now told Goerz he'd like to do so.

When Goerz heard the name of this visitor, he became "quite agitated," according to Pem. Goerz then began whispering. He told Farnsworth that this man had since risen quite high in the Nazi Party, and that his office was now located one or two doors away from the office of the führer himself. Goerz suggested that a visit to Berlin's Nazi Party headquarters would not be a wise idea, but Farnsworth insisted that it was the polite thing to do.

Goerz said he would escort Farnsworth to the building and wait with Pem nearby, but he would not go inside with him. He had once been a member of a military wing that Hitler saw as disloyal; many of the members of the unit had been executed. Goerz was spared only because of his useful technical knowledge. He didn't want to serve as reminder of the führer's special kindness. Yet Goerz was as good as his word, and he took Farnsworth to the Nazi headquarters the next day.

When Farnsworth emerged from the building after a short time inside, he was white as a ghost, and he and Pem quickly retreated to the hotel. Pem never knew the name of this German official and said that Phil rarely spoke of the visit.

At the time, Hitler's notorious communications ministry director, Joseph Goebbels, had already established radio as central to the Nazi propaganda machine. The Nazis made sure every home had a radio, even if they had to give them away. Since they completely controlled the airwaves, the Nazis made it a top priority to broadcast their justifications and their scapegoating into the brains of virtually every German citizen, with proper breaks for symphonic music of German composers, of course. Goebbels certainly saw Farnsworth's invention as an even more powerful propaganda tool, and the 1936 games were only the start of his grand plan for television. Farnsworth's mysterious contact person was most likely someone working for Goebbels.

Just as FDR's men would later agree, Hitler's men deemed technology as the key to victory. Many top German scientists and engineers, such as Einstein, had already fled the country. The Nazis were detaining important scientists and engineers to assist in their war preparations, and broadcasting was of chief importance in those efforts. The ones who stayed and refused to cooperate with the Nazis were often not seen again.

Can we go home now? Pem asked back in the hotel room. Phil said he too had seen enough of the Nazis and would arrange passage.

He called Goerz to tell him that they wanted to leave at once, but the latter informed them that their exit visas had been canceled. Farnsworth threatened to go to the American consulate. Goerz said that wouldn't help, but he promised he would try to do what he could.

That night at 11 P.M., at the Eden Hotel in downtown Berlin, there was a knock at the door of the Farnsworths' room. With trepidation, Phil went to open it while Pem sat on the bed quivering.

Farnsworth saw through the eyehole Paul Goerz with a group of seven other men.

As he opened the door a crack, the men said that they were "friends."

Several of the other men worked with Goerz at Fernseh. They were accompanied by a few of Baird's top scientists, who said they had slipped quietly into Berlin from London out of concern for Farnsworth's safety. Pack your bags, one of the men said, we need to go now.

Where are we going? Farnsworth asked.

To the boat train, one of the men said. It's the only way.

Pem and Phil had already packed their bags. They threw on their coats and headed down five flights of stairs and out the back door into the cold January night. The group walked briskly, avoiding the main avenues for unlit alleyways and narrow streets. Once they reached the train, their escorts carried their luggage on board and crowded as much of the group as they could into a private cabin. One engineer popped open a bottle of champagne, began pouring it in glasses, and proposed a toast to their safe departure. Goerz gave Pem a box of German chocolates as a parting gift. Someone else explained that the boat train would take them to the port of Hamburg.

As a spontaneous way to commemorate the moment, Pem had each of the men in the cabin sign their names to the wrapper on the chocolate box. "Greetings to all the staff of Farnsworth Television Inc.," the salutation read. "Prosit!" In the upper corner of the wrapper one of the men drew a stamp with a comic rendering of a Hitler face, complete with little mustache. The date, "14 Jan 1937," was written below the signatures of the scientists, who stayed with the Farnsworths for just a few more minutes, until it was time for the train to leave.

The trip to Hamburg took about two hours. When they arrived at the port station, Phil and Pem waited huddled on a bench for the rest of the evening. Finally, they caught an early-morning ship, the SS *Europa*, into the North Sea through the English Channel and back across the Atlantic. Four days later, they steamed into New York Harbor.

When she saw the Statue of Liberty, Pem said, "I could have kissed her."

Soon after they were safely home, Farnsworth offered a job in his company to Rudolph Wild and arranged for him to escape from Germany to America, where he became a valuable addition to the staff. Rudolph's family later perished in the Holocaust.

At his desk in Princeton, Albert Einstein finally wrote up a brief proposal upon which he felt that he and David Sarnoff might agree. In a May 1936 letter to Sarnoff, which like his wife's earlier note had to be translated from German, Einstein relayed the news that "my relations with Dr. Bucky have become so diminished with regard to technical matters that I would be able to enter into closer association with a technical enterprise without him and with no hard feelings whatsoever. Therefore, I should be glad if you would again revert to your proposal made on our prior occasion."

But once again, Einstein threw something unexpected into the plans. This time, instead of urging RCA to hire his friend, he was asking Sarnoff to pay the salaries of two research associates.

Accordingly, I would accept no fee for myself, but would propose that the proper compensation, to be suitably increased from time to time, be paid to the young theorists designated by me. It would be a great help for my scientific work, because no longer would I have to lose considerable time in always changing my assistants; instead I could work with really endowed and zealous people for years at a time. It would be of value if this could come to pass soon, as otherwise, I must lose my excellent young colleague—a Russian Jew, born in America—to his and my own regret. He has the opportunity to accept a position in Russia. Yours, A. Einstein.

David Sarnoff was quite clearly insulted by Einstein's proposal. He wanted the man himself, not the dubious distinction of paying Einstein's interns. Einstein, meanwhile, obviously had no understanding that an appeal to Sarnoff's Russian Jewish roots was futile. After reading this letter, Sarnoff had had it with Einstein. In a terse note addressed to the scientist's home at 112 Mercer Street, in Princeton, New Jersey, Sarnoff wrote, "I am leaving for Washington today, and will be back the early part of next week, and I will then give your suggestion careful consideration and you will hear from me shortly."

After receiving these corporate code words for putting something on the back burner indefinitely, Einstein was probably relieved. It seems as if Einstein never really wanted to expend any effort on RCA's behalf. Those that knew him best often said that he had no great use for money and that he cherished more than anything else his time to think on his own, free of outside obligations.

Unable to enlist the world's top scientific mind in his television crusade, David Sarnoff reverted to legal maneuvers. Under the terms of the U.S. Patent Office decision that favored Philo T. Farnsworth, RCA had been granted one month to file an appeal, which it promptly did. The U.S. Patent Office's Board of Appeals had rapidly rendered a new decision, written in March of 1936. The judgment took up only six pages and was mostly a summation of the prior case. On the final page, the Board of Appeals had concluded that "the Examiner of Interferences properly held that the party Zworykin's disclosure does not support the count in view of the definition given in the party Farnsworth's application. For the reasons above stated, the decision of the Examiner of Interferences is affirmed in awarding priority to the party Farnsworth."

Once again, Farnsworth had won his status as the inventor of electronic television.

However, the new verdict, in a legalistic footnote, left the door open a tiny crack for RCA. The party Zworykin had appealed the original decision not on the merits of the case or on the procedure of the arguments or on the evidence itself, but rather on the belief that using Farnsworth's *electronic image* term as the controlling definition of electronic television was not the proper thing to do. The RCA team argued that it was too specific. In its appeal, RCA had called for a broader term, that of an *optical image*, essentially defining a device that simply projects something, regardless as to whether the result corresponds dot by dot to the original subject that was scanned.

The court was throwing up its hands as to this matter, saying that "it is our judgment that the question of priority as to this count is *res adjudicata*," a term for a matter that cannot be reopened and relitigated by that legal body. In other words, the Patent Office could not go back on its own precedent. It could not alter the very definition that is supported by an entire body of its own patents and case law.

In making this statement, the Patent Office was recognizing that it was not the only authority in the country. If the party Zworykin wanted to file his case in another court, one outside the Patent System, that court could very well decide that Zworykin's patent application had merit and therefore should be granted by the Patent Office. Such a move would not reverse the Patent Office's decisions; nor would it establish priority over the Farnsworth invention. It would simply mean that Zworykin had indeed invented *something*. That something might not be in line with the established definition of electronic television, but Zworykin might be entitled to a patent on his something. The Patent Office was saying that the English language is not precise enough to come up with a definition agreeable to everybody, so who are we to deny someone else from using a different definition?

For nearly two years, RCA searched high and low for a court somewhere that would be amenable to deciding that Zworykin's *something* should be eligible for a patent. Eventually it found a forum in Delaware. It was a lay court; it had no pretense of having any scientific expertise.

By now, Zworykin's patent problems were a convoluted jumble. He had been issued a separate patent on his Kinescope receiver, yet he wouldn't give up on his more crucial 1923 complete television system application, which not only had been defeated by Farnsworth but had also been challenged by three other inventors: an independent inventor in Chicago, an AT&T engineer, and a former RCA engineer. Zworykin won the first two of those other challenges, and the Delaware court also found that Zworykin's design should be awarded priority over the third one as well. Therefore, patent number 2,141,059 was issued to inventor Vladimir K. Zworykin on December 20, 1938, an incredible fifteen years after the original filing date.

This particular "Television System" patent didn't meet the Farnsworth definition and therefore had no technical or legal effect on Farnsworth's 1930 patent. It existed purely in a parallel reality defined by RCA. Nevertheless, this patent was better, mathematically speaking, than the one Farnsworth held. Zworykin's 1938 issue date meant that his would remain in effect for eight years after Farnsworth's expiration date. Those would turn out to be eight crucial years.

During the time RCA's lawyers were out searching for an agreeable court, David Sarnoff lifted the shroud of secrecy surrounding

Zworykin's work. Sarnoff sent out invitations to all major licensees of RCA's radio patents, executives from more than seventy U.S. manufacturing companies, including Philco and Zenith. The unveiling took place on a beautiful day in July of 1936 at the top of Radio City, and the event was followed by a complimentary banquet in the ballroom of the new Waldorf-Astoria Hotel, a meal that became known as the first TV dinner.

The demonstration began with the transmission of RCA talking heads sitting at their desks, first RCA chairman Harbord, followed by patent chief Schairer, then President Sarnoff. The gathered throng watched Sarnoff explain that "television was too great in its promise for all mankind to be the exclusive preserve of any one company, and RCA was preparing to share the fruits of its pioneering with all others, including foreign licensees." He told of the progress that EMI in England and Telefunken in Germany were already making, but he cautioned that it was still too early to design commercial television sets for the United States. This demonstration was only to prepare everybody for the future.

After Sarnoff spoke, the invited men watched a live telecast of a parade of long-legged Bonwit Teller models showing off the latest summer fashions. Then an actor delivering a monologue gave way to comics doing some shtick, followed by televised films of trains and army maneuvers. Continuing in the amnesiac tradition of the press to announce a "first," only to be followed by a similar "first" and then another, the *New York Times* headline read that "Television Stages First Real 'Show'," above a story that completely ignored its own earlier reports of the Farnsworth demonstration at the Franklin Institute, never mentioning that RCA's five-by-seven-inch TV screens were not as big or as sharp as the Farnsworth picture demonstrated two years earlier.

In any case, the RCA demonstration served as a wake-up call to the entire radio industry. At CBS, Bill Paley hired a brilliant Hun-

garian engineer named Peter Goldmark to head up its television
efforts. Paley hadn't yet changed his mind about keeping radio his
top priority; he was mainly motivated by his will to beat Sarnoff.
"Sarnoff at RCA had his wary eye glued to the television future,"
Goldmark said. "Paley was keeping his eye on Sarnoff."

One of Goldmark's first moves was to lead a CBS field trip to
Farnsworth's studios near Philadelphia. "Dr. Goldmark and Phil
developed a high regard for each other's professional attainments
and were most congenial in their discussion of television problems," wrote George Everson. CBS purchased Farnsworth cameras
and receiving tubes on a regular basis in order to set up its own
experimental studio, then invited Everson and McCargar to see it.
"It appeared to us by far the best television we had seen yet," Everson wrote. By 1937, CBS had set up a larger studio in Grand Central
Station and constructed a transmitter on top of the Chrysler Building. Paley's sole concern was that it be "bigger and better than
RCA's."

Guglielmo Marconi died at age sixty-three on July 19, 1937.
Throughout the years, Sarnoff and Marconi had kept up close relations, with Sarnoff paying Marconi a generous consulting salary.
They visited each other, traded advice, and appeared at events
together, each using his own brand of prestige to bolster the other's
image.

Marconi was respected as a great inventor in America. But in
his native Italy, he was a full-blown national icon who was swept
up into the politics of the time. He became a senator and then a
member of the Italian Grand Council of Fascism, a radical group
led by Benito Mussolini, who rose to be dictator. Marconi's death
occurred only a few months before the tyrant of Italy entered into
his notorious alliance with the tyrant of Germany. If Marconi
had lived longer, Sarnoff would have been forced to make a tough

choice: either sever his close ties to a man who would have been aligned with Hitler's cause, or keep his connection to a father figure he revered above all others. Now Sarnoff could simply eulogize his mentor without messy politics getting in the way.

Sarnoff orchestrated a special tribute program on the NBC radio network, and he personally took to the microphone. "The world has lost a great man," Sarnoff said. "Science has lost a great genius. I have lost a great friend."

Marconi's death and the subsequent outpouring of homage also went a long way toward solidifying Sarnoff's preferred creation myth for radio. In any objective reality, Marconi invented the wireless telegraph, while the inventions of Lee De Forest and Edwin Howard Armstrong led to the construction of the modern radio. The U.S. Supreme Court even went so far as to invalidate Marconi's basic U.S. patents for radio, the very foundation upon which RCA was built, awarding priority to Nikola Tesla instead, but the decision came after both Marconi and Tesla were quite dead. Sarnoff, of course, preferred that these lesser names just fade away in favor of the view that Marconi invented radio and that Sarnoff was the Prometheus who had delivered it to humankind.

The creation myth of television was of even greater importance to Sarnoff, and he had a huge advantage in shaping this new reality. Whereas the story of radio had to be edited after the fact, the story of television could be shaped in real time, as it unfolded in the present.

On April Fool's Day in 1937, not long after his narrow escape from Germany, Philo T. Farnsworth was working at his Chestnut Hill laboratory when Jesse McCargar stormed into Farnsworth's office.

"You go out there and fire all of those men," said the president of Farnsworth Television.

McCargar, of course, had tried to pull this same stunt before, but this had to be McCargar's idea of a practical joke, Farnsworth thought. Apart from the towering inferno in London and being chased out of Germany by Nazis, things were going fairly well. Why would McCargar do this now? Farnsworth made an attempt at acknowledging McCargar's twisted sense of humor, but it turned out that McCargar wasn't kidding. With royalties from the European partners cut off, and with commercial television in the United States still not on the immediate horizon, McCargar was of the clear opinion that the company could no longer go on the way it was.

"No, Jess, I won't do it," Farnsworth objected. "I've spent too much time training them. They're too important. Each one of them contributes his share."

"Either you go out there and fire them," McCargar insisted, "or I will!"

"I think you better calm down and consider the consequences. I'm certainly not going to fire my men."

"Well, then, I'll do it." With that, he marched out to the lab floor and shouted, "You're all fired! Pack up your stuff and leave!"

The men froze, unable to believe what they were hearing.

Something drastic must have been happening with the company, something that Farnsworth had missed while he was away in Europe. It was quite possible that McCargar's wheeling and dealing of company stock might have been detected by the authorities at the SEC. But Sarnoff's friend, Joe Kennedy, had since grown bored with the top job there and left his chairmanship, accepting a position as head of the Maritime Commission in the second FDR administration, so the heat should have been off by now. And besides, Everson would have told him if this was the case.

"Go on!" insisted McCargar, as the men scowled at him. "Get out!"

At this point, Farnsworth couldn't do anything about it. Most of the staff had grown so sick and tired of McCargar that they were almost relieved to leave. Arch Brolly, Bill Eddy, and Tobe Rutherford all told Farnsworth that as long as McCargar was with the company, they would never return. Eddy soon ended up working at RCA. Cliff was the only one who came back to work after McCargar's flare-up, and that was out of a loyalty that nothing could shatter.

The next day, George Everson came in from New York to try and smooth things. He told Farnsworth that McCargar was going through a rough patch right now because his second wife was divorcing him.

"I'm not surprised," Farnsworth said. "Jesse is just plain mean. I don't see how anyone could live with him."

This time, Everson's charms weren't working. Farnsworth said that he could no longer be associated with McCargar after what had just happened. A short time later, Farnsworth came up with an idea to reorganize the company so completely that it would not only rid them of McCargar but also send the enterprise in a completely new direction.

Farnsworth now controlled an impressive array of more than twenty-five patents, plus at least seventy-five pending applications. He had largely achieved his goal of building up a formidable patent structure around the art of electronic television. Licensing revenue was bound to pick up at some point, but now was the time to shift gears from research to development and become a full-fledged manufacturing company.

Everson thought it was a great idea. Of course, the new plan would require an enormous amount of capital. Fortunately, the stock market had recovered to a seven-year high, and Everson had excellent contacts at a good investment banking house in New York that could probably float a large block of Farnsworth shares on the market, enough to buy out the remaining interests of the Crocker Bank officials, including Jesse McCargar. Since time was of the essence, Everson suggested that the investment firm could also help acquire an existing manufacturing plant, instead of building one from scratch. The whole plan sounded entirely reasonable. What could go wrong?

As this plan was being hatched, an omen appeared in the sky and on the radio, in the first coast-to-coast breaking news bulletin ever broadcast. At dusk on May 6, 1937, the only aircraft emblazoned with the Nazi swastika that was ever permitted to enter U.S. airspace was coming in for a landing at the Naval Air Station in Lakehurst, New Jersey. The hydrogen-filled dirigible named after Paul von Hindenburg, the late German president who was forced to nominate Hitler as chancellor, had floated effortlessly over Boston and then New York. But as the mighty zeppelin was approaching the mooring, a spontaneous fireball engulfed the tail and shot forward, consuming the entire 800-foot-long, ten-stories-high airship within thirty-four seconds. The technological pride of the Third Reich killed thirteen passengers, twenty-two crewmen, and one civilian on the ground, as radio announcer Herb Morrisson immortalized the disaster with his cry of "Oh, the humanity!"

To many, the Hindenburg explosion was the result of the extremely volatile mixture of arrogance and technological know-how that was at the core of the Nazi regime. For Farnsworth, who had already seen this danger up close, it was one more sign that war was coming. "Phil expected a war, and didn't think it would be a short one," Pem said. "He felt that his patents would start to expire before the war was over." His most important patents, issued in 1930, were set to expire in 1947. All this made executing the company's reorganization plan even more urgent in Farnsworth's eyes.

One of the first items of business was to get the company's licensing agreements in order. A "supplemental agreement" between Farnsworth and Fernseh stated that if the German company could not deliver royalties, the earlier agreement would be terminated. With that, the Nazis kept whatever technology they had stolen from Farnsworth, and Farnsworth's German foray was over.

The most significant patent-licensing agreement in the company's history was signed in the summer of 1937. This agreement, with AT&T, immediately gave Farnsworth Television the prestige it had long sought. This cross-licensing pact granted Farnsworth the rights to use some key AT&T transmitter patents for free as well as rights to send television signals over AT&T's inter-city cables. The contract also granted AT&T the rights to deploy all Farnsworth patents, which would let the phone giant produce televisions and perhaps even revive its idea of a picturephone. AT&T would pay royalties to Farnsworth for those rights. "The agreement constitutes a recognition of our patents by the greatest corporation in the world," stated a letter sent out to all Farnsworth Television investors.

With the help of their investment banking firm, Kuhn, Loeb & Company, the Farnsworth team targeted for takeover an outfit called the Capehart Company of Fort Wayne, Indiana, a maker of high-end, high-quality radios and phonograph systems. If the deal went through, Farnsworth, his family, and his remaining staff would be saying good-bye to Philadelphia and moving. To generate revenue and garner production experience ahead of the expected TV boom, the combined company would be producing radios and record players until the FCC gave television the green light.

The Farnsworth team first needed a green light at the SEC for their public offering plan, but in the SEC's regulatory tar pit, all they were getting was month after month of red tape. "The position taken by the Commission seemed to be that you were guilty until you proved your innocence," remarked Everson. "In our case, the attitude seemed to be one of daring us to prove that we were not all a pack of dishonest rogues." The fees for the accountants, lawyers, and bankers, not to mention expensive trips to Washington, D.C., were quickly mounting into the six-figure range, enough to bankrupt the company if the deal didn't materialize, and the whole thing was dependent on a stable stock market. But when Hitler's army took Austria in March 1938 with virtually no opposition from anyone, the resulting tremors sent the market plunging to its fifth worst annual performance of the century.

Stuck in Philadelphia with barely any funds to run the lab or the studio, Farnsworth in the spring of 1938 was growing depressed and his drinking was increasing. He had to get away. Along with Pem, Cliff, and Lola, he drove off on vacation to northern Maine, where the foursome went backpacking and camping near Mount Katahdin, the highest point in the state. Farnsworth loved the land up there because it reminded him of his boyhood in the western wilderness. On the way home, approaching the New Hampshire border, he wanted to stop and see a property in Brownfield owned by Everson's friend George Haley, who had invited the group to stay there whenever they wanted. So they pulled over to ask a local farmer for directions.

"Ta Haley fom?" said the farmer. "Weall jus ga ta rud dan a piece ta the next lef tun. Go in theah a piece on hits ta fust place on ta lef. Kinda run down 'tis, be'en umpty nigh onta fifteen yeaws naow. Doahs an windas been stole th'ave. Shame's what 'tis."

Somehow, Farnsworth understood every word. When they arrived, they saw a wreck of an old house overrun with small animals. The place was straight out of the previous century, complete with a wood-burning stove and a gigantic fireplace suited for cooking soup and beans in cast-iron kettles. The woodwork throughout the house was impressive. Outside, there were giant trees in every direction, and a clear stream flowed nearby. Later, when they did a bit of research at the town hall, they discovered that the house was more than a century old and that the original deed had been handwritten by Daniel

Webster, who had been working in the office while attending Frye-burg Academy down the road.

Farnsworth declared that he wanted to buy the place, and nothing would change his mind. In short order, he purchased the house along with sixty acres of surrounding woodlands. It was almost as if Farnsworth was yearning to revert back to an earlier time.

When he decided to build a dam to turn his section of the creek into a trout pond, everyone thought he was nuts. Then it started to dawn on Pem that her husband would never be able to truly relax. At least this project would get his mind off the company's troubles and provide him with some of the physical exercise that he was missing while working so hard on television.

The work lasted all summer and through the fall of 1938. Along with Cliff and some local men that he hired, he would begin the workday at 7 A.M. They constructed a massive concrete foundation, loaded giant boulders onto a wagon pulled by horses, cemented them in place, then finished the top with sand and gravel. They would quit around 4:30 each afternoon. Pem's visiting father fixed up the house by installing new windows, and they scoured the place from top to bottom, all while Pem made sure her two boys didn't get lost roving the woods. In the evenings, they all sat around the fire telling stories. The Farnsworths didn't arrive back in Philadelphia until after Thanksgiving.

Now drawing a salary of $100,000 and living in Manhattan's East Seventies in a newly purchased, six-story, thirty-room town house with servants quarters and a private elevator, David Sarnoff was also worried about the coming of war. He too aimed to launch commercial television before the situation in Europe got out of hand. He wanted to make good on his title of "televisionary," so he switched his tactics abruptly. Instead of urging the FCC to delay commercial approval, he became the principal pusher of a standard broadcasting format.

As the complex technical standards were being hashed out at the FCC, Sarnoff embarked on a two-month tour of RCA's European affiliates. Unlike Farnsworth on his 1936 visit to Europe, Sarnoff, two years later, would not be able to obtain a visa to Germany even if he wanted one. Instead, he traveled to France and Switzerland, but spent most of his time in England, where he could visit his old friend Joe Kennedy and get the inside scoop on the worsening political situation.

After his two short stints running bureaucracies for FDR, Kennedy had conveyed to the president that he deserved a reward. The reward he requested was the ambassadorship to England. He relished the idea of being the first Irishman to hold the post and was also impressed that five previous men in that job later became president themselves. When he heard the suggestion, Roosevelt reportedly laughed so hard that he almost fell out of his wheelchair. Then he reconsidered. In light of Kennedy's well-demonstrated amorality and the rumors that he was pondering a run for president in 1940, FDR decided that Kennedy was so politically dangerous that perhaps shipping him out of the country would be a grand idea.

By the time Sarnoff arrived in England, Kennedy had been in his post for six months. Along with Rose and the seven youngest Kennedy children (Joe Jr. and Jack were attending Harvard), Kennedy was living it up, attended by two dozen house servants at the thirty-six-room ambassador's residence at Prince's Gate, a mansion given as a gift to the United States by J. P. Morgan. As a housewarming gift, Sarnoff had sent the Kennedy's a set of RCA Victor recordings of Arturo Toscanini, who then conducted the NBC Symphony Orchestra. Before Kennedy moved to England, he and Sarnoff often brought their families to Toscanini's rehearsals and studio broadcasts, so the present was warmly received.

Sarnoff was visiting his friend at a time of unprecedented stress. Prime Minister Neville Chamberlain was determined to avert war, and his appeasement of Hitler after the Austria takeover had only emboldened the dictator to cast his eye toward Czechoslovakia. Joe Kennedy had supported Chamberlain all along, and some of Kennedy's careless statements about keeping the peace and remaining neutral as well as his bad-mouthing of Roosevelt caused a major rift with the administration in Washington. In mid-September of 1938, at the same time Sarnoff was visiting England, the international crisis came to a head when Chamberlain went to Munich to cede a third of Czechoslovakia to Germany in return for Hitler's promise to remain friendly, an accord that treated Hitler like a world leader rather than a megalomaniac dictator.

"I believe it is peace for our time," Chamberlain stated. "Peace with honor." The Chamberlain action was soon understood as one of the biggest diplomatic debacles in history.

Remarkably, Kennedy continued to speak out as one of the biggest boosters of Chamberlain's appeasement policy even after it had proven to be bankrupt, thus embarrassing FDR and perhaps encouraging Hitler. In a high-profile speech after the Munich agreement, Kennedy said it was "unproductive" for dictatorships and democracies "to widen the division now existing between them by emphasizing their differences." In Washington, D.C., Felix Frankfurter, who was about to be appointed by FDR to the Supreme Court, said, "I wonder if Joe Kennedy understands the implications of public talk by an American ambassador. Such public approval of dictatorships, in part even, plays into their hands."

Sarnoff returned to New York shaken and confused by the actions of his friend and by the overall turmoil in Europe. For perhaps the first time, Sarnoff felt the full weight of the world on his shoulders. He was now responsible for 20,000 employees and to 250,000 shareholders, plus the millions upon millions of people who relied on NBC radio for their news and views of the events of the world. In this respect, it could be argued that Sarnoff was even more powerful than the president. FDR's actions were still hamstrung by opinion polls showing that the United States continued to be isolationist and wanted to remain at peace; by contrast, Sarnoff, through the tool of broadcasting, had the power to influence and alter that opinion. But how would he exercise that power?

Sarnoff called for an all-hands conference of RCA's top 320 executives, including the 150 most important employees at NBC, and he prepared a speech with his reaction to the events in Europe. The evening was billed as the "RCA Family Dinner," and it was held at the Hotel Astor on October 14. The title of Sarnoff's address was "Cooperation."

> During the past two months, while I was visiting England, France and Switzerland, I watched the world, especially the old world, in great convulsion. I saw new pages of history being written. I saw the clock of civilization being moved backward. What happened a fortnight ago in Munich established a new direction for the world. Its true significance cannot yet be measured or even envisioned. But one thing is certain—that the world on this side of the Atlantic and the world on the other side are now two different worlds, and fortunate is he who by birth or circumstance or luck finds himself on this side.

Here we have a David Sarnoff who is for the first time careful not to predict or read too much into the future. There was no doubt that he was appalled at what he saw in Europe, as he spoke of seeing "people spending their weekends digging trenches" and that "gas

masks were being fitted for men, women and children" and of the
"delivering of sand bags to be put on the rooftops." But he admitted, "I am unable to see in Europe a solution to the problems facing
the people there without very radical change—change that may bring
in its wake war or revolution or chaos."

His main point in calling the dinner was his appeal for everyone
in the RCA family to cooperate and treat one another with respect,
so as to stem the tide of anti-Semitism and hatred. "We might perhaps draw a useful lesson," he said, "that once you make hate the
motivating force to guide humanity, solutions are no longer within
the power of civilized people."

The most significant part of Sarnoff's speech came when he
articulated his view of how NBC should cover the conflict, a view
that shaped the standard of objectivity in broadcast journalism for
generations.

It might have been smarter in this instance to have editorial-
ized all those news bulletins. Some other stations did so, and
gained applause. The NBC followed its policy of sticking to the
facts without bringing heat into the situation. We could easily
have edited and interpreted instead of merely reporting the
news. But suppose the Munich effort had resulted in war instead
of peace. Then immediately you would have had a demand for
government control of broadcasting in this country, inspired
by fear of the editorializing of news bulletins. Government
people might have said that broadcasting in this country was
no longer a purveyor of news; it had assumed the role of a
maker of opinion. And anything that would interfere with our
neutrality might lead us into war. The French government has
issued a decree forbidding any station to transmit news without
first submitting the items to the government for approval.
Already freedom of speech over the air is buried there, and

THE LAST LONE INVENTOR 249

not even a funeral march! Even in England, the Hyde Park of
Europe, the news bulletins of the BBC were carefully censored.
Not a single station in England broadcast the speech made by
Chancellor Hitler at Nuremberg. But you heard it here, over the
networks.

Finally, Sarnoff addressed the topic of television. "Regardless
of all the difficulties of the moment, regardless of all the unsolved
problems that television possesses today, I am just as sure that
television will be here and that it will exceed sound broadcasting
in importance as I am of the fact that I now stand before you." After
all the tentative talk of the crisis in Europe, Sarnoff was back on
solid ground. Here was a topic he could handle with unqualified
certainty.

So far, television had mystified and confused all others who
tried to predict its arrival. In the current issue of Hugo Gernsback's
latest magazine, *Radio and Television*, the editor essentially threw up
his hands. "The chief trouble with television is that it has been
over-publicized by irresponsible writers and others who made the
public believe that television was here, when indeed it was not,"
wrote Gernsback, implicitly exempting himself from those who
should be deemed irresponsible. "This naturally created a great
deal of disappointment. . . . There is nothing revolutionary in sight
in television today. So unless something of a revolutionary nature
in television comes along, no one in his right senses should put up
a penny in buying television stock."

Once again, Gernsback was predicting blindly. In fact, there was
something of a revolutionary nature on the immediate horizon. As
Sarnoff stood before his top executives, he was formulating a plan
to induce the birth of commercial television once and for all by
staging an event that he hoped would serve as the catalyst, something akin to the Jack Dempsey fight that sparked the sudden radio

boom in 1921. Historians would treat this coming event as the beginning of the television era. But the plan wasn't widely known as of yet, and Sarnoff revealed the details only to his top lieutenants.

One of those lieutenants posed a threat to the plan. Sitting in the RCA Family Dinner audience that evening, somewhere among the top RCA names such as Zworykin, Harbord, Nally, Jolliffe, and Schairer, was a rising and aggressive young executive named Edwin A. Nicholas. "Nick" to his friends, he was head of RCA's licensing division, charged with negotiating rights to RCA's patent portfolio with outside firms. Sarnoff didn't yet know it, but Nick Nicholas at this time was being interviewed by Philo T. Farnsworth's company to become its new president. He was planning to leave RCA to accept the position if and when the pending public offering of Farnsworth stock was accomplished. More than any other sin, David Sarnoff despised disloyalty to the family.

In January of 1939, the Congress of the United States summoned Philo T. Farnsworth as the star witness for an important hearing. The hearing was part of a probe of such wide scope and enormous magnitude that Farnsworth couldn't possibly have known the full dimensions of what he was stepping into. In the press, the matter was simply called "the Monopoly Investigation." The official language of the joint resolution that opened up the affair called for a "full and complete study and investigation with respect to the concentration of economic power in, and financial control over, the production and distribution of goods and services."

The whole thing started with President Roosevelt. He received wide credit when his New Deal initiatives seemed to spark an economic revival, but beginning in 1937 the employment rolls began to contract once again, and the Great Depression was starting to seem more like a permanent way of life rather than a temporary crisis. At this point, FDR began searching for structural problems within the

economy that were preventing a robust rebound. He came up with
a root cause he deemed so insidious as to be analogous to the anti-
democratic forces at work in Germany, Italy, and Japan. These are
the words the president chose in proposing his monopoly study:

> The liberty of a democracy is not safe if the people tolerate the
> growth of private power to a point where it becomes stronger
> than the democratic state itself. That in its essence is fascism:
> ownership of government by an individual, by a group or any
> controlling private power. . . . I am calling for a thorough study
> of the concentration of economic power in American indus-
> try and the effect of that concentration upon the decline of
> competition.

Taking up the cause in Congress was the senior senator from
Wyoming, a rabble-rousing Democrat named Joseph O'Mahoney.
"I yield to no member on this floor in my devotion to the interests
of the wage earners," O'Mahoney declared as he proposed FDR's
monopoly investigation. "I yield to no member of the Congress in
my desire and effort to achieve social justice for the workers of the
country." By virtue of this new crusade, the press began calling him
Senator O'Monopoly, or simply Monopoly Joe.

Members of the minority party were outraged from the get-go.
"If any member of the House thinks this resolution will bring about
a bona fide investigation into the economic situation in the United
States, he is guileless, credulous, and simple-minded," said Clarence
Hancock, a Republican representative from New York.

Consisting of members of the House, the Senate, and various
executive branch departments, the officially named Temporary
National Economic Committee had begun its investigation in the
summer of 1938. Their mission was to scrutinize industries ranging
from insurance to banking, from finance to manufacturing, looking

for instances of systematic anticompetitive behavior harmful to workers and consumers, then coming up with legislation to address antitrust loopholes. By its very nature, the probe became a fishing expedition. Since there was no way the monopoly committee could fully hear all sides of such a broad range of issues, specific anecdotes about malfeasance were at a high premium.

The centerpiece of the hearings, taking place over five days in mid-January of 1939, was the probe into patents. Since patents by definition grant the holder a limited monopoly over an invention, there were great hopes among committee members that there were smoking guns buried in this subject. Some of the biggest industrial behemoths in the country drew much of their power from pools of patents. Foremost among these companies were General Electric, AT&T, and RCA, which was known in Washington simply as "the Radio Monopoly."

With opinion polls showing that the public feared corporate trusts like these just as much as they feared foreign dictators, the entire matter put David Sarnoff and RCA on the defensive. "I have tried myself not to function as a dictator," Sarnoff told executives at the RCA Family Dinner, "regardless of the powers which may be conferred upon the President in the Corporation's by-laws."

By the time Farnsworth arrived in Washington, the stage was set for the struggling inventor to provide the committee with the red meat it sought. First, the committee heard from establishment leaders such as Vannevar Bush, the president of the Carnegie Institution and the nation's foremost authority on research and development.

"I judge from what you have said that the patent system as it now operates tends to restrict the opportunity of the individual," Chairman O'Mahoney stated.

"I feel that it does," said Bush, "and of the small group, and incidentally, also of all those who use the patent system."

Although Bush was recommending only minor, evenhanded changes in the patent system, the senator was able to elicit responses that—if taken out of context—seemed to suggest that the whole system needed to be rejiggered so that it was no longer dominated by corporations with vast capital resources.

Appearing next was William Coolidge, director of GE's Research Laboratory, the nation's first and largest corporate lab, a place nicknamed the House of Magic for the constant stream of innovations it was producing. His testimony provided little more than a noncontroversial view of how a large research operation works.

A smoking gun seemed to be uncovered in the testimony of Frank B. Jewett, president of AT&T's Bell Labs. Jewett said that his lab's $10-million annual budget was justified because it yielded great cost-saving devices, such as a special vacuum tube that could last for 50,000 hours, as opposed to ordinary tubes, which last for 1,000 hours. One member of the committee asked if this long-life tube was available to the general public. Jewett said the tube was not widely available, which left the obvious impression that this great invention was being suppressed and withheld from the world by a monopoly. The committee members implicated RCA in this industrial plot because it had a cross-licensing agreement with AT&T for that device. By the following morning, major newspapers had blown the story up out of all proportion.

While Farnsworth was at the Patent Office preparing for his testimony, three lawyers from RCA burst in with samples of tubes and documents that seemed to show that tubes that lasted 10,000 hours were available, and that those were sufficient to meet current consumer demands. The RCA men then asked Farnsworth for a favor: could he submit this evidence to the committee and clear up the negative implications surrounding AT&T and RCA? In an amazing twist, Farnsworth found himself being asked to absolve his adversary of wrongdoing.

At 10:30 A.M. on January 19, 1939, in the Caucus Room of the U.S. Senate Building, Chairman O'Mahoney sat at the center of a gigantic dais, flanked by committee members, each behind his own microphone. Philo T. Farnsworth took his seat opposite them, at a much smaller witness table. He was accompanied by George Everson, who recalled that Farnsworth suffered from "a bit of stage fright" and exhibited "great diffidence." Hordes of reporters and spectators lined the gallery.

Here was Farnsworth's big chance to get back at RCA. None of the top executives from the radio monopoly were invited to appear at the hearing, and they were clearly distraught over the fact that Farnsworth could launch into specific monopoly charges. Farnsworth could have described the constant harassment from RCA and its many attempts to interfere with his patent applications. He could have recounted how Vladimir Zworykin appeared at his laboratory under false pretenses, then reported back to David Sarnoff with what he learned. He could have told how RCA was spreading misinformation about the validity of his patents, and how he had to endure years of expensive litigation to clear it up. He could have exposed Sarnoff's unfair relationships with radio manufacturers who were contemplating getting into television. He could have told how RCA had intimidated Philco during the time Farnsworth was its partner. He could have complained about how RCA had been influencing the FCC to delay television until it had come up with its own quality system. Any one of these complaints could have been served up as a five-course meal for Monopoly Joe and his cohorts.

RCA was so worried about Farnsworth's testimony that patent chief Otto Schairer set up a public speech for the same day in New York, a preemptive statement about "the patent problem" that seemed to be designed to be entered into the *Congressional Record* as an immediate response to Farnsworth. In his address to the National Industrial Conference Board, Schairer advocated patent system reforms that curtailed some of the very same abuses that RCA was guilty of in its efforts against Farnsworth. Abolish appeals of interference claims, so as not to tie up inventors in court for years, Schairer said. Place a strict time limit on the number of years an unapproved application can remain pending. That reform would have effectively slashed most of the life, and perhaps even killed, Vladimir Zworykin's 1923 application.

RCA's fears about Farnsworth were unfounded, however. Instead of attacking RCA, Farnsworth acted as if he had just come straight off the potato farm. "My first technical training came from having charge of a farm lighting system at the age of twelve," Farnsworth began, adding that he "studied electrical physics through popular magazines."

"Well," quipped Chairman O'Mahoney, "let's chalk one down for the popular magazines."

Farnsworth continued to unfold for the committee his life's story, complete with technical details about obscure scientific matters such the principles of electron multiplication. Things began to get interesting when a committee member asked why television usage was at a more advanced stage in England and Germany than in the United States. Farnsworth offered a vague explanation of how the governments in those countries were footing much of the cost of programming. In addition, he said, the FCC has been slow in its effort to adopt a unified broadcasting standard for the United States. Then he switched to his optimistic view that television "will be in the American home before very long."

At one point, Senator O'Mahoney cut to the chase. "You see," he said, "there is a concept that we are still living in the era of the rugged individualist, to use a phrase that has been in common parlance for some time. But stories such as you are telling us this morning clearly demonstrate that era is receding rapidly into the past."

"Yes," responded Farnsworth. But the inconclusive comments that he and the senator traded after that made it clear that Farnsworth was not about to offer up suggestions as to what to do about the corporate takeover of invention. An exasperated O'Mahoney eventually gave up on that line of questioning.

Finally, the committee got down to the matter of the long-life tube and whether AT&T and RCA were keeping it from the public. "I don't believe there is any market for a 50,000-hour tube," Farnsworth said, "because nobody wants a tube that will last 50 years in a radio. Sets become obsolete after perhaps 10,000 hours, and if people want a tube which will last 10,000 hours they can get them. They are on the market now."

That did it. With his testimony, Farnsworth not only got AT&T off the hook, but he also exonerated his enemy, RCA, just as the RCA lawyers wanted him to do. He offered virtually no unkind words for the patent process in general, mainly because he truly believed the U.S. system was excellent and deserved to be the envy of the world. RCA's anticompetitive business tactics that had haunted Farnsworth for a decade were left unexamined, in part because the committee members didn't know exactly what to ask about.

There were several reasons Farnsworth failed to speak up when he had the chance. He was certainly naive as to how the game of business and politics really worked, but the idea of seeking assistance from the government also went against his self-image as a self-reliant individual. What's more, he felt that things were going pretty well and that television was close to becoming a commercial reality. He didn't know that he'd be proven wrong by events in the immediate future.

If Philo T. Farnsworth wouldn't offer compelling evidence against industrial monopolies, then who would? No further witnesses were called to address the corporate control over patents, and the radio monopoly and other bastions of corporate power made a narrow

escape from the clutches of the once formidable antimonopoly movement. The Monopoly Investigation continued to generate headlines
for much of the year, but the entire effort to diffuse the concentration of wealth and economic power soon lost its steam, and the committee was finally disbanded in 1941. Senator O'Mahoney's rhetoric
resulted in no significant legislation, and FDR's designs on taking
on corporate fascists were overtaken by the coming war against real
fascists.

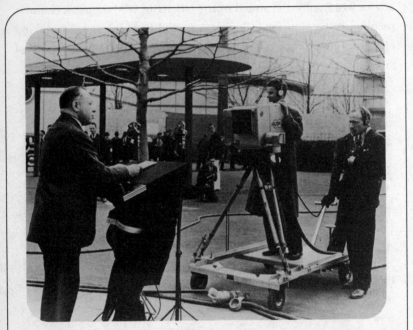

*On April 20, 1939, David Sarnoff introduced television to the public
from a makeshift podium at the site of the World's Fair in Flushing
Meadows, New York. His speech was broadcast over network radio and
transmitted to television sets placed in windows and showrooms of New York
City department stores.* (DAVID SARNOFF LIBRARY)

CHAPTER TWELVE

All's Fair, World's Fair

In March of 1939, after more than a year and a half of red tape and delays, the Securities and Exchange Commission granted the go-ahead for Philo T. Farnsworth's initial public offering. The newly organized Farnsworth Television & Radio Corporation could now sell stock to general investors. The offering of 600,000 shares at six dollars each was large enough to require the services of nine brokerage houses, and it was an unqualified success, as investors optimistic about the future of television gobbled up all the available equity in the company.

The timing was critical; the very day following the stock sale, Hitler's army marched into Prague and seized Czechoslovakia. Stock exchanges around the world took a sudden deep dive, and the investment bankers involved in the Farnsworth deal agreed that the offering would have been canceled if they had been forced to wait any longer. After about $600,000 in commissions, legal fees, accounting and administration bills, the corporation received $3 million, enough capital for the newly energized company to move ahead with its manufacturing plan and land an experienced executive as its new president.

Edwin "Nick" Nicholas officially signed on to lead the corporation, replacing Jesse McCargar, who remained on board as a largely powerless vice president, something Farnsworth could accept. "Mr. Nicholas was regarded as one of the most able and well-liked men in the entire radio industry," Everson noted. "He was young and aggressive and had courage and imagination. That he was willing to leave his splendid association with RCA and take his chances with us was added proof of the soundness and value of the Farnsworth developments."

Nicholas immediately went to work negotiating with his former employer, trying to sweep away years of bitter history. Donald Lippincott had spent an entire decade trying to get RCA to take out a license for Farnsworth's patents. He was told again and again by RCA patent chief Otto Schairer that this would go against corporate policy. RCA owns patents and collects royalties. It doesn't license outsider patents and pay royalties, and it certainly never licenses someone else's patents without the right to be the exclusive company that could grant sublicenses to everyone else. RCA was determined to be the one-stop shop for all television patents, just as it was with radio. It wasn't about to share control of the industry with anyone.

Being an insider, however, Nicholas knew RCA's fundamental weakness as far as television was concerned. Not only had RCA lost to Farnsworth in the 1934 patent suit, but it also had lost to Farnsworth on another interference, in 1938, over RCA's Image Orthicon camera tube, which surpassed Zworykin's Iconoscope in quality. RCA was able to keep using that name, which it had trademarked, but the Patent Office ruled that this television camera was really a Farnsworth invention too. Nicholas recognized that RCA needed to pay Farnsworth for a license if it wanted to go into commercial television. The only question was whether RCA would keep stalling until Farnsworth's patents expired. Sure enough, when Nicholas first approached Schairer and Sarnoff with a proposal, the RCA men put it off. They didn't reject it outright; they just said they needed to consider it carefully. Perhaps the RCA leaders were angry and hurt that Nicholas had had the audacity to leave the family. Whatever the reason, it looked as if RCA was simply going to let the clock run out.

David Sarnoff shrewdly exploited this stretch of time. The World's Fair of 1939 was approaching. The exposition at the edge of Queens, on more than 1,200 acres in New York City's Flushing Meadows, was simply the "greatest show of all time," stated *Time*. According to the magazine, the 1939 World's Fair was "the biggest, costliest, most ambitious undertaking ever attempted in the history of international expositions."

The theme of the fair was "Building the World of Tomorrow." The whole production was dedicated to the gleaming, bright, technological future in which we would all live. The most popular pavilion was the Futurama, the General Motors showcase that sat just off the Grand Central Parkway. Long lines of people stood for hours to ride on a train of comfortable, moving "sound chairs" with piped-in music and narration that explained exhibits showcasing life in the far-off year of 1960. Across a virtual United States, visitors rode as if flying, cruising along newfangled "superhighways" that connected cities and countrysides of the future, complete with shiny new cars pulling into long driveways and parked in garages next to lush lawns. The ride ended with the perfectly utopian admonition, "All eyes to the future!"

The symbols of the fair were the pair of striking structures sitting side by side on the fairgrounds, erected especially for the two-year-long event. The Trylon was a tall, thin pinnacle, pointier, and, at 610 feet, taller than the Washington Monument, Next to it was the Perisphere, a perfectly round, hollow building eighteen stories high and 180 feet in diameter, with an indoor space twice the size of RCA's Radio City Music Hall, then the world's largest enclosed theater. From the outside, these two massive geometric objects were so brilliantly white that to glance at them on a sunny afternoon would hurt your eyes.

Inside the Perisphere, visitors gazed from a suspended walkway at a scale model of an entire metropolis, dubbed Democracity, which included the outlying suburbs where all the people actually lived. As they contemplated the future of American civilization, circa 2039, vistors heard the theme song of the fair, with the lyrics:

> We're the rising tide,
> Coming from far and wide,
> Marching side by side on our way,
> For a brave new world,
> Tomorrow's world,
> That we shall build today!

The 1939 World's Fair opened within that narrow shaft of time between the two darkest events of the century. The Great Depression had just ended, and the economy was growing once again. Yet World War II would break out in Europe while the fair was still welcoming visitors. Opinion polls showed that keeping America out of the conflict was the top priority of the public, and the World's Fair was perfectly timed to become the manifestation of optimism itself, projecting the hope that all would be well. Americans yearned to believe, if just for one fleeting moment, that the future was a sunny, safe place. If only you could get to the fair, you could forget all about the world's problems. Once you saw that future right before your eyes, everything would be okay.

Sixty nations participated in the fair, many with large pavilions that presented traditional foods, clothing, and scenery from their homelands. Japan and Italy had pavilions, but not Germany. For some countries, their pavilion seemed to be all that was left. "This pavilion appears under the flag of the independent Czecho-Slovak republic," noted the fair's official program, "such as existed prior to the events of last September and March." By the end of the year, another pavilion would be completely stranded. "The Poland Pavilion's staff did not go home that winter," writes David Gelernter, author of *1939: The Lost World of the Fair.* "Home was no longer on the map. They opened a Polish restaurant on 57th Street." By the following June, fair goers would be dining in the luxurious French pavilion at the same moment that the Nazis would take Paris.

The publicity leading up to the opening of the fair reinforced the stature of RCA. *Life* magazine pictured RCA executives huddled around their newest model television, which was to debut at the fair, not mentioning of course that it had been built illegally, infringing the patents of someone else. The cover of a special World's Fair edition of the *New York Times Magazine* featured a commissioned George Washington statue in front of the Trylon and Perisphere. In the centerfold of the issue was an instructive RCA advertisement. The table of contents displayed titles such as "World of Tomorrow," by H. G. Wells; "The City of Tomorrow," by Robert Moses; "Machines as Ministers to Man," by Henry Ford; "Wheels, Keels and Wings," by GM research chief Charles Kettering; "World of Undying Hope," by *Times* writer Anne O'Hare McCormick; and "Might of the Speeding Word," by David Sarnoff, who wrote:

Mail was sent by stagecoach a hundred years ago, and it is only ninety-five years since the first hesitant telegraph line was opened between Washington and Baltimore. The telegraph did not displace the pony express courier system in the West until

1861. And Bell's telephone was only a curious gadget as recently as 1876. Practical radio is a child of the twentieth century, and broadcasting is less than twenty years old. Yet today we live in a world where instantaneous communication is taken for granted. . . . Just before us is a new era which brings television out of the laboratory. . . . Facsimile will bring a system of transmitting such material as printed matter and pictures and record it at some distant point. If we go a step further we may visualize motorists in separate cars talking to each other by radio. . . . The means are at hand. . . . One cannot know the possibilities ahead without believing that the promise of the future is still greater than all the glories of the past.

David Sarnoff knew instinctively that television had to debut at the fair. At a cost of millions of dollars, RCA paid for the construction and operation of a 9,000-square-foot pavilion near the Perisphere, where it would showcase its latest television cameras, receiving sets, and programming. Shaped like a colossal radio tube, the immense yellow structure was branded with bright red RCA logos.

As visitors entered, they walked past the TV cameras, which entitled them to an "I was televised" wallet card with spaces for printing their name and the date. Inside the glass atrium entryway, a giant statue of Nipper the Dog greeted visitors from his pedestal. The "Radio Living Room of Tomorrow" exhibit featured an immense wall unit that housed a combined radio, record player, television, music recorder, film projector, and facsimile machine.

On display were RCA's first commercial TV sets, housed in cabinets that projected straight up through a lens that magnified and reflected the image to be viewed indirectly on a mirror built into the unit's lid. To avoid the appearance of visual trickery, RCA designed transparent Lucite plastic cabinets for these sets, which exposed the innards of the apparatus.

RCA's plant in Camden produced thousands of TRK-12 cabinet TV sets, similar to the mirrored units at the fair. The corporate sales force stocked all the major stores in the New York City area with enough inventory to respond to the expected demand. Promotional dollars ensured that RCA televisions were placed in street-level store windows at all of the city's famous department stores, including Macy's, Bloomingdale's, and Wanamaker's. The sets carried luxurious $600 price tags, although less expensive models as low as $150 were soon added to the line.

Ten days before the opening of the fair, on April 20, David Sarnoff staged a press conference. The buds on the trees were beginning to open, filling the air with a sense of hope, promise, and boundless optimism. This was to be the defining moment in David Sarnoff's career. At age forty-eight, firmly in command of an awesome global enterprise and in control of the country's most prestigious broadcasting network, the portly president of RCA was surrounded by reporters, photographers, and radio microphones. He exuded authority as he stepped up in his dark suit to a makeshift podium in front of the RCA Television pavilion. A mobile television camera, operated by a man on a wheeled platform, zoomed in for a close-up of a round, earnest face. The occasion called for a grand rhetorical flourish, and Sarnoff delivered the goods.

It is with a feeling of humbleness that I come to this moment of announcing the birth in this country of a new art so important in its implications that it is bound to affect all society. Television is an art which shines like a torch of hope to a troubled world. It is a creative force which we must learn to utilize for the benefit of mankind. . . . Now, ladies and gentlemen, we add sight to sound!

With that, he cued his men to lift the veils, exposing shiny new television sets displaying fluid pictures of the very event that was taking place right then and there, mirroring reality and pseudo-reality back and forth infinitely. By putting the moment squarely in the present tense—"Now . . . we add sight to sound"—Sarnoff paved over television's messy past and plucked it from the far-off future. Television was finally in the here and now, where it would remain.

Sarnoff announced that NBC would also begin operating as a television network too. Starting with the opening ceremonies of the World's Fair itself, NBC was launching the first schedule of regular television broadcasts—including movies, sports, news, and live entertainment programs from studio 3-H in Radio City. In his proclamation, Sarnoff made no mention of Farnsworth, of course, but he also failed to acknowledge Vladimir Zworykin. The spotlight was reserved only for Sarnoff himself.

In doing all this, Sarnoff not only was violating Farnsworth's patents but also was bypassing the sovereignty of the FCC. "Without FCC adoption of commercial standards, Sarnoff was gambling that public enthusiasm would stampede the industry and the commission behind the RCA system," wrote RCA's Kenneth Bilby. While Philco and Zenith did object loudly, "the FCC remained indecisive, neither condoning nor condemning Sarnoff's plan." Technically, Sarnoff may have been breaching various rules and laws, but at this special moment, he was able to manufacture a little bit of extra authority to do so with impunity.

The resulting ballyhoo in the national media turned Sarnoff's stunt into an official, historic event. The gathered throngs of reporters ate it up and propagated the message far and wide. Radio covered it live, and virtually every major newspaper and even the most sophisticated magazines relayed and analyzed the story. "Last week, of course, witnessed the official birth of television," began the *New Yorker.*

The gates to the fair opened to the public on a sunny Sunday morning at eleven o'clock, April 30, 1939. A parade of 30,000 people, led by uniformed soldiers, marched down Constitution Mall, the fair's main thoroughfare, as visitors paying seventy-five cents each streamed onto the fairgrounds. Shortly after 3 P.M., standing in front of the Trylon and Perisphere, before a gallery of executives, dignitaries, and political leaders dressed in top hats and tails, David Sarnoff yielded the podium to the leader of the free world. In dedicating what he called the "world's fai-yah," Franklin D. Roosevelt became the first president of the United States to be televised. With his booming voice, the paraplegic president used his head to motion emphasis of his words as he held himself up with special handles built into the lectern.

The ceremonies climaxed that evening when Albert Einstein switched on the lights and appealed to the crowd in his thick German accent that "science must enter into the consciousness of the people." Unfortunately, the string of spots that were to illuminate the Trylon sputtered and malfunctioned, but the embarrassing moment was immediately eclipsed by a spectacular fireworks display over the lagoon.

Through it all, the broadcast signals were relayed to RCA's tower atop the Empire State Building and radiated throughout the New York City region. While only about 2,000 sets existed to view the festivities, the overall message was received clearly across the entire country: RCA's David Sarnoff was responsible for bringing us television. This was the reality that the public perceived.

Philo T. Farnsworth was in New York City at the time. He was there to attend board meetings of the Farnsworth Television & Radio Corporation. Dragging on day after day, even through the weekend, the meetings were called to resolve the complex issues facing the company. When could Farnsworth move with his men out to Fort Wayne, Indiana? That was the site of the Capehart radio plant that the company had purchased with its newly raised funds, and the executives needed to set a budget and a timetable for its operations. When could the manufacturing of televisions begin? What broadcasting standard was the FCC likely to select? Could the company make enough money producing radios and phonographs if television were to be delayed?

Perhaps the biggest item of contention was what to do about RCA. In response to Sarnoff's performance at the World's Fair, would it be prudent to sue RCA for patent infringement? Nick Nicholas made a strong and convincing appeal for patience. He was confident RCA would come to the negotiating table soon enough. He was optimistic that a deal beneficial to all parties could be reached. Lippincott, Everson, and even Farnsworth went along with that view. The meetings themselves, however, put Farnsworth into a funk. So far, he disliked corporate life. Three million dollars certainly solved some problems, but it created brand-new ones, and Farnsworth enjoyed the process of inventing, not corporate planning.

During his stay in the city, Farnsworth refused to attend the World's Fair. He knew about the RCA television pavilion, and he figured that seeing it would make him deeply depressed. He wanted to demonstrate his brand of television at the fair, too, but such a promotion would clearly be way too expensive for his fledgling company. Farnsworth did give permission for his ten-year-old son, Philo III, to attend the fair with a friend. Yet he would never ask his son about the experience.

On the afternoon of April 30, Farnsworth was walking back to his hotel from that day's board meeting. When he saw RCA televisions projecting the opening ceremony in a department store window, he stopped cold in his tracks. David Sarnoff was on the air, yielding the podium to President Roosevelt. Farnsworth stepped closer to the window and listened to the sounds that were being piped out to the streets. Other pedestrians were stopping to watch and listen too. Sarnoff was clearly taking credit for the invention in a way that Farnsworth knew he could never match, creating an impression that could never be erased. Sarnoff was doing this through the very power of television itself.

Farnsworth's entire existence seemed to be annulled in this moment. The dreams of a farm boy, the eureka moment in a potato field, the confession to a teacher, the confidence in him shown by businessmen and bankers and investors, the breakthroughs in the laboratory, all the years of work, the decisions of the official patent examiners, those hard-fought victories, all of those demonstrations that had come and gone, the entire vision of the future. All of it was being negated by Sarnoff's performance at the World's Fair. Would the public ever know the truth?

Sarnoff was the man in charge of the corporation, the man with the authority, the one making the speech. He was the one who owned the microphones. He was the one who designed the pavilion. He was the one surrounded by the cameras and the recorders of history. He was the one who was directing the camera to turn from himself to the face of our nation's leader. His vision of the future was the one being perceived. Was this the impression that would endure?

Farnsworth couldn't believe what he was seeing. The agony of it set off sharp pains in his stomach. All along, television was supposed to bring pictures of reality to the people. It never occurred to him that his invention would be used to subvert reality, to manufacture impressions that were not true. He really had created a monster, just as that patent attorney in Hollywood had presumed long ago. No one paid attention to the distraught man grieving in the middle of the day on a street crowded with happy people. They detoured around him without a second glance, so they could stand in the lines, mesmerized by the rows and rows of televisions flickering and calling to them from behind the glass.

During World War II, workers at the Farnsworth Corporation plant in Fort Wayne, Indiana, produced electronics for the U.S. military. Philo T. Farnsworth himself was recuperating at his cabin in Maine.

CHAPTER THIRTEEN

Breakdown, Breakout

W ITH HIS INTRODUCTION OF TELEVISION AT THE WORLD'S FAIR, David Sarnoff had left RCA exposed to a patent-infringement lawsuit from Philo T. Farnsworth. RCA would have likely lost such a battle given the fact that it had lost all its previous patent fights against Farnsworth. With RCA television sets for sale in department stores and with NBC broadcasting an extensive schedule of baseball, boxing, Broadway shows, and live dramas from Radio City, the risk of an embarrassing and expensive lawsuit was now too high for Sarnoff to endure. Faced with no alternative, he agreed in May 1939 to open serious negotiations to license the Farnsworth intellectual property his engineers were already incorporating into RCA's products.

The two sides met in a conference room high up in the RCA Building at 30 Rockefeller Plaza. Talks between RCA patent chief Otto Schairer and Farnsworth president Nick Nicholas got off to a shaky start, and discussions dragged on for months. "At first, they seemed so far apart that it looked utterly hopeless," noted George

Everson. "Only the clear underlying fact that neither company could get along without the other kept the discussions alive." In September of 1939, full-blown war broke out in Europe, thus increasing the pressure on both sides to popularize television before the United States was drawn into a global conflict. By the end of the month, they came to terms: RCA would pay Farnsworth Television & Radio Corporation a fee of $1 million, plus ongoing royalties for every television set it sold.

This was a great victory for Farnsworth. He had refused to sell his television patents outright to RCA, and now he got the type of nonexclusive deal he wanted all along; he was free to license his patents to all other manufacturers as well. For RCA, the deal was unprecedented. Never before had the corporation agreed to pay royalties to anyone. As he signed the contract at RCA headquarters in the presence of executives from both parties, Schairer had tears in his eyes as he reminded the assembled group how unusual this agreement was. At least that is how the Farnsworth executives remembered it. RCA forever denied that one of its corporate officers shed a tear on this occasion.

The licensing pact put Sarnoff and Farnsworth in an odd position. For the first time, they were on the same side, with the same interest in pushing television forward to their mutual benefit. If any other company wanted to enter the television business, they now needed two licenses, to make use of the patents of both. The meaning was clear: Philo T. Farnsworth had denied David Sarnoff the television monopoly he had coveted, but now that their battle was over, they needed to find a way to cooperate.

When the U.S. Senate held hearings on the television standards process in April of 1940, David Sarnoff went on the record with this tribute: "It is only fair that I should mention this," he said. "An American inventor who I think has contributed—outside RCA itself—more to television than anybody else in the United States, is Mr. Farnsworth, of the Farnsworth Television System. I believe the industry will require the license under the Farnsworth patents as well as the RCA patents if they are to go ahead."

In the summer of 1940, the Federal Communications Commission took up the issues raised in the Senate, aimed at putting an end to the technical squabbling among rival television manufacturers. All the companies that wanted to produce televisions, or were making them already, had to come together to try and hammer out a standard broadcasting format. Television makers had to agree on a specific frequency for each channel on the dial, the FCC said, and they needed to settle on a specific number of image lines to be displayed on the viewing screen. If the public couldn't be guaranteed that today's television sets would be able to receive tomorrow's programming—no matter who was broadcasting—they would never buy televisions en masse.

The urgency was obvious to David Sarnoff. With the World's Fair introduction, he had expected to ignite a sudden firestorm of interest in television. Internal projections were for RCA to sell upward of 40,000 sets within the first year, but when the public purchased only a few hundred sets in the first six months, Sarnoff could see that his plan wasn't working. He blamed Zenith and Philco for the failure, as they were publicly lambasting him for trying to flood the market with televisions before a standard was set. "Philco and Zenith were more interested in getting me than in creating a television industry," Sarnoff said. "I've had plenty of cats and dogs thrown at me, but never like that."

At the behest of the FCC, the standards effort was coordinated by the Radio Manufacturers Association (RMA), a private trade group that included all the major players. The messy proceedings persisted for months. RCA was pushing for a standard with 441 lines of resolution, while upstart Allen B. DuMont Laboratories showed it could produce sets displaying more than 600 lines. Philco at one point backed out, then jumped back in, while Zenith's representatives were always enraged at RCA over something. In the middle of it all, CBS caused an uproar when it began demonstrating a low-resolution *color* system. Although it sported a mere three-inch screen and was based on a spinning, mechanical disk setup that was incompatible with electronic systems and thought to be obsolete, the color setup worked. Most everyone else voted down the CBS system, but it did result in further delays. Philo T. Farnsworth got so frustrated with the fighting that he disengaged himself and assigned another representative to do his company's bidding.

Finally, the RMA's National Television Standards Committee (NTSC) appointed an independent electrical engineering expert named Donald Glenn Fink to sort through and evaluate all the rival monochrome broadcasting formats. Fink settled on a standard he deemed an optimal balance in light of what the industry could produce and what was pleasing to the viewer. All televisions, Fink said, should display images with 525 lines of resolution at a rate of thirty frames per second. In April of 1941, this recommendation was accepted by the RMA and officially approved by the FCC, which then assigned channels two through thirteen to the very high frequency (VHF) band and set aside a portion of the ultrahigh frequency (UHF) band for channels operating above 300 megahertz. Channel one was reserved for police and fire department radio. With this, commercial television could begin at last.

The FCC-approved format has turned out to be incredibly resilient, enduring wave after wave of technological change, most notably the introduction of electronic color image scanning and transmission in the 1950s, as well as the advent of cable, videotape, big-screen TVs, and DVDs. The NTSC standard has staved off demand for so-called high-definition television for decades and remains today the most pervasive media format ever devised.

Yet it didn't have a chance to catch on right away. Just seven months after the FCC approved commercial television, the Japanese bombed Pearl Harbor. Soon after, the U.S. government officially

banned the production of consumer electronics altogether, divert-
ing all parts, labor, and manufacturing capacity to the effort to win
World War II. Most commercial television broadcasting was also
suspended during the war.

With television now on hold, David Sarnoff became as determined
to win the war as he was determined to win the television battle. He
saw his military involvement as an honor of the highest degree and
as tangible proof that he was an American patriot who had shed his
immigrant heritage. In the early 1920s, he had joined the U.S.
Army Reserves as a member of the Signal Corps, and RCA chairman
James Harbord used his own military connections to win for Sarnoff the rank of lieutenant colonel, even though Sarnoff lacked the
required experience. On weekends, Sarnoff would attend army sem-
inars and functions. "No one," said Harbord, "ever wore the uniform
more proudly." By the time the United States entered the war, Sarnoff was fifty years old and had been promoted to a full colonel.

On December 7, 1941, Sarnoff dispatched a telegram to President
Roosevelt: "ALL OUR FACILITIES ARE READY AND AT YOUR INSTANT SERVICE.
WE AWAIT YOUR COMMANDS." Thereafter, Sarnoff converted RCA into a
military contractor, producing everything from radar tubes, sonar
systems, and radio transmitters for the Allied communications effort.
At its newly opened campus in Princeton, New Jersey, RCA Laboratories became devoted almost exclusively to wartime research and
development, with a staff of 1,300 scientists and engineers.

In March of 1944, Sarnoff was summoned for an active-duty
assignment, and was told to report directly to General Dwight D.
Eisenhower in London. Without revealing the full details of the secret
plan to storm the beaches of Normandy and free Europe from the
Nazis, Eisenhower told Sarnoff to construct a powerful broadcasting
station that could centralize all electronic communications in one
place and relay information across the entire continent, an assignment that also brought Sarnoff into personal meetings with Prime

Minister Winston Churchill. On D-day, June 6, 1944, the Allied Forces Network that Sarnoff put in place worked as planned; Allied generals used the network to coordinate history's most massive military operation, and military journalists reported the news of the invasion to the rest of the world with unprecedented quickness. After France was liberated, Sarnoff played a key role in reconstructing war-torn French Radio, linking Paris once again with London and New York.

Upon his return to the States, Sarnoff spent several weeks in Washington, D.C., attending military briefings and pushing for a reward for his services. On December 7, 1944, Sarnoff received his desired prize when FDR appointed him an honorary brigadier general of the U.S. Army. Back in New York, he let the word spread through RCA that he was no longer Mr. Sarnoff; he was now to be called General Sarnoff, or simply General.

Shortly after the war ended, RCA chairman Harbord resigned and died, and Sarnoff added RCA chairman to a list of titles that still included RCA president and NBC chairman. Sarnoff packed his board of directors with former military officials and moved to boost his reputation even further when he made a job offer to Eisenhower himself after the triumphant five-star general received his ticker-tape parade in Manhattan. Under the terms of the offer, Eisenhower would be paid a generous salary to become the figurehead president of RCA. Eisenhower declined and accepted a less controversial job as the head of Columbia University, but the fact that the offer was taken seriously spoke volumes about General Sarnoff. His already lofty stature as a commanding authority figure of national importance had been increased tenfold.

Philo T. Farnsworth was only thirty-three years old when he achieved his patent-licensing victory over RCA. It was around this time that he was selected, along with Bill Paley of CBS, the actor Spencer Tracy, Nobel laureate Ernest Lawrence, and Yankee first-baseman

Lou Gehrig, as one of the "Outstanding Young Men of 1939," an annual list of prominent men in their thirties, created by the biographer Durward Howes, that was always reported far and wide in the press. For a short time, this list made the name Philo T. Farnsworth known across the United States.

The drawn-out standards process at the FCC along with the coming of the war convinced Farnsworth that his controlling patents would expire before his vision of television would be realized. This sent him into a deeply depressive state at a time when depression wasn't treated like the disease it is. He began drinking not just at night but during the day. After Pem insisted that he go get medical help, he saw a doctor who suggested that Farnsworth take up smoking cigarettes to calm his nerves, and so he did.

The Farnsworth Television & Radio Corporation had already been relocated to Fort Wayne, Indiana, and was profitably making high-quality radios and phonographs as well as broadcasting programs via radio and an experimental television station. Phil and Pem finally moved out there in November of 1939, but this only made Phil even more depressed. "He found it difficult to adapt to the new environment," wrote Pem, "where the priorities revolved around manufacturing instead of invention, where the principal objective was making money instead of progress."

One day in early 1940, Farnsworth came home looking terribly ill, and he informed his wife that he just couldn't keep on living this way. His mind was still actively conjuring inventions all the time, while his body always felt tired and worn. "It's come to the point," he told Pem, "of choosing whether I want to be a drunk or go crazy." He was having a severe nervous breakdown yet refused to go see a doctor, relenting only when Pem threatened to pack up, take the kids, and leave him. The doctor prescribed some sort of liquid medication, which seemed to brighten Farnsworth's spirits and ease his pain for a few days, but pretty soon he was just staying in bed, sleeping, and refusing food.

Finally, Pem received a referral to see a renowned doctor at the Brigham Hospital in Boston. Now weighing just 100 pounds and seemingly near death, Farnsworth was carried like a sick child by a friend to the train. When Phil and Pem arrived at the hospital in Boston, the doctor identified the drug Farnsworth had been taking as chloral hydrate, a highly addictive sedative that did far more harm than good. Phil made steady progress toward normal health after three months of rest and treatment at the hospital, but he was still depressed about television, and he refused to talk about the subject or even mention the word.

Phil and Pem spent the war years at their place in the woods of Maine. As he regained his strength, Phil worked with his brother Carl on building extensive additions to the house, including a large study, a new wing of bedrooms, a second floor, extra bathrooms, and closets, and they installed oil-fueled furnaces and an indoor swimming pool. After selling a large chunk of his company stock, which was now listed on the New York Stock Exchange, Farnsworth used the proceeds to buy eighty additional acres of adjacent land. He assembled a crew to build a farm for raising animals for food, and he supervised the construction of a small laboratory, where he, Cliff Gardner, and two other men resumed their television research.

Farnsworth received two important visitors during the early part of the war. One was Donald Lippincott, who was now serving as a colonel in charge of patents for the Army Signal Corps. Lippincott suggested that the military be allowed free use of Farnsworth's patents in its effort to create advanced radar tubes, and Farnsworth agreed wholeheartedly. Lippincott then met with David Sarnoff in New York and got him to agree to the same.

The other visitor was David L. Webster. The head of the physics department at Stanford University, Webster had hired former Farnsworth employee Russell Varian, who developed at Stanford his pioneering radar tube. Webster asked Farnsworth to join a secret research project, which was based at the University of Chicago and led by Enrico Fermi. From what he could glean of the sketchy details, Farnsworth suspected that the military was developing an atomic weapon. In his ominous 1939 letter to FDR, Albert Einstein had initiated what later became known as the Manhattan Project by warning of a German effort to build the bomb, but Einstein himself refused to be personally involved in creating a weapon of mass destruction. Like Einstein, Farnsworth also refused to take part in the secret project.

Farnsworth's company, however, was totally consumed by wartime production. Staffed by hundreds of men and women, its factories in Fort Wayne fulfilled millions of dollars of electronics contracts for the Pentagon.

Shortly before the war ended, Phil and Pem received some amazing news: their son Philo III scored so well on college preperatory exams that he was admitted to MIT at the age of fifteen. After the war ended, however, the family was struck by a spell of tragedy. Phil's brothers Lincoln and Carl crashed while flying a private airplane. Lincoln survived, but Carl died. Not long after that, a raging forest fire swept through western Maine and consumed the entire town of Brownfield, including Farnsworth's house, laboratory, and farmlands, just days before a scheduled appointment to properly insure their property. Phil and Pem were able to escape with little more than their lives, the clothing on their backs, and the original lab journals from Green Street.

Finally, in 1947, the day Farnsworth had been dreading arrived. His seventeen-year patents on the television camera and television receiver expired. Farnsworth still held more than 100 other television-related patents, some of which were quite valuable, and many had up to ten years of life remaining, but the two golden ones had now lapsed into the public domain, and all promises of royalty payments for them ceased, just weeks before the sudden breakout of a nationwide television obsession that seemed at first like a fad but grew only more intense over time.

David Sarnoff with President Dwight D. Eisenhower at the opening of a color broadcasting studio in Washington, 1958. Between them is Sarnoff's son, Robert, an NBC executive. (DAVID SARNOFF LIBRARY)

CHAPTER FOURTEEN

Post War

As the war was coming to an end, General David Sarnoff called an all-hands meeting of RCA's top officers. "Gentlemen," he said, "the RCA has one priority: television. Whatever resources are needed will be provided. This time we're going to get the job done. There's a vast market out there, and we're going to capture it before anyone else."

As soon as the war was over, Sarnoff went on the road to convince all NBC radio affiliates to upgrade their equipment and air NBC television programs. By then, the FCC, concerned about a stranglehold on competition, had forced RCA to divest half of its broadcast holdings, so Sarnoff had chosen to keep the NBC Red network and to sell for $8 million the NBC Blue network, which was soon renamed the American Broadcasting Company, or ABC.

By the end of 1946, RCA's production lines were stamping out sets with a ten-inch viewing screen and a retail price of $385. Creative programming began cropping up around the country. In Chicago, the former Farnsworth and RCA employee Bill Eddy hired Arch Brolly, another Farnsworth alum, and began operating WBKB-TV. Eddy produced a puppet show he called *Kukla, Fran & Ollie,* got a zookeeper named Marlin Perkins to show off his animals, hired young news-casters named Hugh Downs and Mike Wallace, and made a two-year deal with Phil Wrigley to televise Cubs games at no cost.

Starting in the fall of 1947, television caught on even more fero-ciously than radio did a quarter century earlier. American consumers bought 1 million sets within two years, with 80 percent of the market controlled by RCA. In 1948, Milton Berle's *Texaco Star Theater* debuted on NBC, and CBS responded with a variety hour hosted by Ed Sullivan. The average television family was now watching for more than three hours each day, and early TV owners often had to set up numerous chairs in their living rooms to share their viewing with their neigh-bors. Restaurants, nightclubs, and movie theaters in major metro areas experienced a sharp drop in business. When an NBC drama series called *Kraft Television Theater* plugged a new product called Cheez Whiz, Americans bought tons of Cheez Whiz, and the mean-ing was clear: if television could sell Cheez Whiz, it could sell any-thing. Advertising dollars quickly shot past the $100-million mark, and RCA's total television investment to date was rapidly recouped many times over.

On the evening of January 7, 1949, NBC aired "Television's Twenty Fifth Anniversary Special," a milestone that must have seemed odd to the lion's share of viewers who had their televisions only for a year or two at most. The date was selected to commemorate the December 29, 1923, filing of Vladimir Zworykin's patent applica-tion. On the program, David Sarnoff spoke from his office in Rocke-feller Center, telling the viewing public his story of how television was invented and how it works. By his side was Zworykin, intro-duced as the "inventor of television." That broadcast probably reached a greater number of people in a half hour than all the peo-

ple who had ever heard or read the name Philo T. Farnsworth over a
lifetime.

The following year, Sarnoff lobbied the Radio and Television
Manufacturers Association to bestow on him the title "Father of
Television." His effort was successful, and RCA memos informed all
employees that these designations were official: only David Sarnoff
was to be called the Father of Television, and only Vladimir Zworykin
was to be called the Inventor of Television. No one disputed it.

In January of 1948, Phil and Pem flew to Fort Wayne, and Farnsworth
received a hero's welcome from the Farnsworth Corporation's
employees, all of whom wanted to shake his hand. But there was bad
news from the company's president, Nick Nicholas. As Farnsworth
already knew, the company had designed a complete line of television sets, from portable tabletop models to handsome console sets
for living rooms. It had even acquired a furniture company to produce the wooden cabinets. Samples were ready in late 1946, and the
corporation then spent $500,000 advertising them in glossy maga-
zines. But the incredible demand for television sets had surged past
available supplies of crucial parts, and some of those parts were
radio devices only available from RCA. There were now seventy-
five manufacturers of television sets in the United States, and RCA
had always managed to put the Farnsworth Corporation at the very
bottom of its priority list for those parts. Nicholas had some more
bad news. The manufacturing delay was now exacerbated by the fact
that the banks were calling in the loans that the company had taken
out to retool its plants during the war.

Fired up by the challenge, a reinvigorated Farnsworth went to
work while Pem set up a new home in Fort Wayne. Pretty soon, Farnsworth had television sets rolling off the assembly lines, and Nicholas
got the banks to give them a one-year reprieve. To promote sales to
high-end customers, Farnsworth Television signed on as the sponsor

for ABC's Metropolitan Opera program, shown in sixty-two cities on Sunday afternoons. In September of 1948, Pem gave birth to their fourth son, Kent, and it seemed as if Philo T. Farnsworth had embarked on a new beginning.

But it was really the end of his television efforts, as this final burst of activity came too late. When the one-year bank deadline was up, the company was in even deeper trouble. As a last-ditch effort to cover the loans, Nicholas offered to sell perpetual usage of all the remaining Farnsworth patents to RCA, GE, and Zenith for onetime royalty payments. All three firms accepted the offer, yielding a total of about $3 million, which put the Farnsworth Corporation just short of paying off its debt. With no more options, Nicholas moved to put the company up for sale, and since Farnsworth now owned only a sliver of shares, he was forced to go along.

In the spring of 1949, the New York–based industrial conglomerate International Telephone and Telegraph Corporation (ITT) swooped in to buy the remaining assets for $1.4 million in stock, a fire-sale price that included the provision that Farnsworth himself stay on as vice president of research. ITT never intended to remain in the television business, and that was made clear when it phased out production by the mid-1950s. What the ITT executives had really purchased was the brain of Philo T. Farnsworth.

ITT dubbed its new Fort Wayne division the Farnsworth Electronics Company, and the bosses put its namesake to work designing various electronics components for scientific, commercial, and military use. But at home at night, Farnsworth began to focus on a new invention, and this was the quest that would occupy him for the rest of his life.

At one point during his television work, Farnsworth had seen a strange and unexplained blue glow in one of his Multipactor tubes, and he had wondered ever since whether it was a spontaneous emission of energy. He came to believe strongly that there must be a totally safe way to harness the atom for peacetime purposes, and around the time he had refused to join the Manhattan Project, he had begun to devote more and more time to thinking about nuclear fusion.

Whereas the atomic bomb employed the process of nuclear *fission*, in which the atom is *split* by bombarding radioactive nuclei with extra neutrons, *fusion* is the opposite process, that of *combining*, or fusing, atoms together. Both fission and fusion reactions throw off excess energy—in an amount described by Einstein's equation $E = mc^2$—but whereas fission also yields hazardous radioactive waste by-products, fusion yields safe by-products such as helium. Both fission and fusion produce energy with astonishing efficiency, but the radioactive fuel required for fission—uranium, for instance—is extremely scarce, whereas the fuel required for fusion is plentiful; the hydrogen atoms that are needed can be extracted from seawater.

Achieving fusion is difficult because any two hydrogen atoms have the same electrical charge and thus repel each other. To overcome that force of repulsion, the atoms need to be heated to fantastic temperatures. The sun is fueled by fusion, and the hydrogen bomb achieves fusion only because it is combined with a fission bomb which is triggered first. Farnsworth wanted to find a low-temperature or perhaps a split-second way to achieve fusion safely. That would render the current nuclear reactors on the drawing boards obsolete, because they employed the potentially hazardous fission process. In short, Farnsworth was dreaming of the ultimate invention, devising a completely safe way to generate an endless supply of virtually cost-free energy. He was after one of the holy grails of modern science.

One day in the late 1940s, while Farnsworth was in New York for a corporate meeting, he and Pem paid a visit to a friend named Frank Rieber, whom they had met through patent attorney Donald Lippincott. Rieber was a wealthy geological scientist who lived in a luxurious town house on the Upper West Side, and hanging on his wall was a portrait of Albert Einstein, painted by Rieber's mother, an accomplished artist and friend of Einstein's. Farnsworth remarked how much he admired the work, and Rieber said he believed it to be the only time Einstein ever sat for a painted portrait.

Farnsworth also mentioned how much he admired Einstein himself and that he longed to see what Einstein thought of his latest invention idea. "Why wait?" Rieber asked, offering to telephone Einstein right away. Farnsworth was stunned by this development and gave his quick approval. Rieber went to the phone in his bedroom and reached Einstein at his home on Mercer Street in Princeton. When he emerged from the bedroom, Rieber explained that Einstein already knew of Farnsworth and his reputation as a brilliant inventor. "I've got Einstein on the phone," Rieber said, "and he'd be delighted to talk to you."

Farnsworth again was surprised, but perhaps he shouldn't have been. "Einstein's explanation of the photoelectric effect," wrote biographer Ronald Clark, "had already helped to prod forward television from experiment to reality," so it made sense that Einstein would have been tracking the progress of electronic television from afar, and that he knew of Farnsworth's work.

Farnsworth entered the bedroom and picked up the phone, while Rieber closed the door on his way out. The telephone conversation between Philo T. Farnsworth and Albert Einstein lasted nearly an hour. When Farnsworth broached the subject of fusion, Einstein expressed his reservations on the subject, indicating that he himself was headed down the same path of research until the events of August 1945. The detonation of the atomic bomb over Hiroshima and then Nagasaki had left Einstein deeply troubled and guilt-ridden over the fact that he had played a key role in the events leading to the bomb's development. Afterward, he abandoned all thoughts of atomic energy because he feared it would lead to further disaster, instead opting to dedicate himself to the so-called unified field theory of the universe.

Still, Einstein said that his own reservations were personal, and that he saw no reason why Farnsworth shouldn't pursue the idea. Einstein listened to Farnsworth's mathematical approach to creating the necessary nuclear equations, and he encouraged Farnsworth to publish his ideas and pursue the invention of a controlled fusion reactor.

When Farnsworth emerged from the bedroom, his face radiated a positive glow, according to Pem. This was the shot in the arm that he needed. With some of the same old zeal that he had summoned for his television work, Farnsworth from that point on plunged deeply into fusion, immersing himself in the science and math of the problem. No one else at ITT understood Farnsworth's concept of isolating a fusion reaction inside a cloud of electrons, so the company was reluctant to fund the work, but the executives relented and authorized a small budget when they saw how determined Farnsworth was.

As Farnsworth turned toward fusion, David Sarnoff intensified his television efforts, marshaling the combat for color broadcasting. CBS said its color system was ready, and that buying black-and-white sets was a waste of money, but in January 1947 Sarnoff won an FCC decision to prevent CBS from broadcasting in color on the grounds that it would disrupt the market for monochrome television. CBS brought up charges of foul play when six months later a key FCC commissioner accepted a job as an NBC vice president. In 1950, the FCC reversed its decision and ruled that CBS had every right to proceed. Sarnoff appealed all the way to the U.S. Supreme Court, which in 1951 affirmed the rights of CBS.

By drawing out the fight, though, Sarnoff bought a crucial block time, a ploy that had worked for him in the past. "We've lost a battle," he said, "but not the war." At RCA Laboratories in Princeton, Sarnoff had launched a crusade to devise a system for color that was even better than CBS's, in order to control the all-important standard for transmission. Sarnoff demanded that all engineers were to work sixteen-hour days, and all other projects were to be shelved. In the end, RCA would pour $130 million into what was until that time the largest and most costly electronics development project ever. The CBS format employed a spinning disk to separate red, green, and blue hues; Sarnoff mandated that RCA's color cameras be all-electronic, with no moving parts, adhering to the same total faith in the electron that Farnsworth and Zworykin had always evangelized.

As the color war was being waged, RCA was seeding the market with millions upon millions of its black-and-white sets. At every turn, Sarnoff repeated his "compatibility" argument. Only RCA color broadcasts could be viewed on the RCA monochrome sets that people were buying. "Every set we get out there makes it that much tougher on CBS," he said. If viewers wanted to watch CBS color broadcasts on their black-and-white sets, they had to buy a special adapter for $100.

Sarnoff took a harsh beating in the press for his tactics, and his actions led to yet another major investigation from the U.S. Justice Department, this time under Eisenhower. Once again, a president whom Sarnoff supported and befriended had turned against him. There was even a report that a particularly zealous government attorney wanted to put Sarnoff in jail for the abusive way he was using his black-and-white television monopoly to trample competitors and hold back rival color technology.

Yet Sarnoff emerged triumphant. When the FCC reversed itself once more and made RCA color the official transmission standard in December 1953, Sarnoff took out full-page newspaper ads declaring his "great victory." Initially, RCA's pricey color TV sets were a flop, but Sarnoff was adamant about keeping at it until the marketplace came around. In 1958, RCA entered into a landmark consent decree with the Justice Department, agreeing to license its color TV patents to any American set maker at no cost.

David Sarnoff's victories over CBS were mostly confined to the technology arena. When it came to the art of programming, Sarnoff was often blindsided by the hidden dimensions of the new medium. In the late 1940s, Bill Paley conducted a well-publicized talent raid of NBC stars, making lucrative deals to lure Jack Benny, Groucho Marx, Edgar Bergen, Al Jolson, Red Skelton, George Burns and Gracie Allen, and the *Amos 'n' Andy Show* over to CBS. Paley also signed Frank Sinatra, Bing Crosby, and later, Jackie Gleason. The biggest TV sensation of the decade, *I Love Lucy*, was also carried by CBS. Sarnoff never appreciated—indeed, he resented—the immense star-making power of broadcasting. The supremacy of talent remained Sarnoff's blind spot for the rest of his career. Insisting that it was beneath his dignity, he simply refused to cater to the whims of mere entertainers, while Paley enjoyed nothing more. CBS vaulted ahead in the new audience measurement system called the Nielsen ratings and stayed number one for the rest of Sarnoff's life.

One thing Sarnoff seemed to understand was the political ramifications of the new medium. When General Eisenhower announced his run for the presidency of the United States in 1952, General Sarnoff signed on as his unofficial broadcasting strategy consultant. The first national political ads to appear on U.S. television networks were twenty-second spots for Ike. When Democratic candidate Adlai Stevenson countered by buying a half hour of prime time to broadcast a long-winded speech, he was bombarded with hate mail for interfering with an episode of *I Love Lucy*. Eisenhower beat Stevenson not once but twice.

Yet Sarnoff failed to act when his leadership was needed most. Television conquered the country in an era of caution and timidity, at a time when Senator Joseph McCarthy was spouting demagoguery, and the resulting anti-Communist hysteria terrorized not only

ordinary citizens but the rich and powerful as well. The lunacy went on
for years until CBS finally summoned the courage to act. Only when
Edward R. Murrow aired a special edition of his *See It Now* program
in 1954 that featured McCarthy hanging himself with his own absurd
statements was McCarthyism finally chased from the national stage.

Politically, Sarnoff simply wanted to cozy up to the winners in
order to preserve his own self-interest. In 1960, he backed Richard
Nixon for president, based in part on how smooth Nixon had been
alone in front of the TV camera in his successful Checkers speech
and how well Nixon had handled the stiff Soviet premier Nikita
Khrushchev in their historic televised matchup. When Nixon was
faced with the tough choice of whether to take part in what would be
the first televised presidential debate, Sarnoff was the last person
to speak to Nixon before the Republican announced his decision to
do it. By now, television had suddenly found its way into 90 percent
of American homes, so the stakes were enormous.

> It was the day that changed politics [wrote author David Halber-
> stam]. John Kennedy had gone in, if not exactly an unknown,
> certainly the underdog, and he had come out looking a winner,
> while Richard Nixon had in one brief appearance squandered
> the advantage of eight years of the vice-presidency, and had come
> out looking a loser. The effect was so great that it was sixteen
> years before two presidential nominees again debated, though
> the entire nation wanted more debates. There was simply too
> much to lose. The big winner that night in 1960, of course, had
> been television, more specifically the networks. Television was
> legitimized as the main instrument of political discourse.

Afterward, when virtually every Republican in the country was
lamenting the profound stupidity of putting Nixon on television
next to Kennedy, there were reports that Sarnoff had put him up to

it. "I'm not the son of a bitch," Sarnoff protested. "If he asked me whether to debate, I'd have said debate, but it didn't come up." In any case, Sarnoff didn't exactly ingratiate himself with the eventual winner. Sarnoff's move to support Nixon so enraged the Democratic candidate's father, Sarnoff's old friend Joe Kennedy, that he refused to forgive this betrayal, and the two men never spoke to each other again.

Philo T. Farnsworth crossed paths once again with David Sarnoff in 1953, when both men had their signatures engraved, along with those of other technology luminaries, on a three-foot-high, silver trophy presented at a conference in Chicago to the father of science fiction, Hugo Gernsback, in honor of Gernsback's fifty years of service to the electronics industry. It was also that year that the annual awards bestowed for the best science fiction writing were named the Hugo Awards.

Farnsworth never had an award named after him, but his invention did. When former Farnsworth employee Harry Lubcke became president of the Academy of Television Arts and Sciences, he was fishing around for a name for the awards given for the best work in the field. He decided to name the awards the "Immy" after the ubiquitous Image Orthicon camera, which was based largely on Farnsworth's patents but built by RCA. After the trophy was designed, that nickname was modified to "Emmy" to refer to the statue's female figure holding an atom.

By the mid-1950s, Farnsworth had disengaged himself from television to such an extent that he had eight television sets in his house yet none of them worked. One day, his son Kent came home from school crying, telling his parents that no one in school would believe his father invented television because he was the only one who didn't watch. So Farnsworth hooked up a set for his son and then turned into one of TV's earliest critics.

"Like any father of an eight-year-old, he thinks there are too many darned cowboy movies at the dinner hour," noted a story in the local newspaper, the Fort Wayne *News Sentinel.* "At the Farnsworth house, young Kent occasionally talks his parents into a TV dinner in the living room . . . and Dr. Farnsworth has just as much trouble as you or I in guarding against TV becoming a monster, devouring all of the time that should be set aside for reading and conversation."

In 1957, Farnsworth accepted an invitation to appear as the mystery guest on a CBS game show called *I've Got a Secret.* It was the only time Farnsworth would appear on national television during his lifetime, and footage of the broadcast shows a gaunt, withdrawn man who looked older than his fifty years. After the studio audience was let in on the "secret" that the guest invented electronic television when he was fourteen years old, a panel of celebrities began asking Farnsworth questions to figure out who he was. In recognition of an honorary doctorate he received, Farnsworth was identified to the panel only as "Dr. X," which threw the celebrities off track, as they assumed his contribution was to the medical field. "Does what you do cause pain?" asked actress Jayne Meadows. "Sometimes it does, yes," replied Farnsworth, stringing out the joke for the audience.

When host Garry Moore finally revealed Farnsworth's identity, the panelists honed in on the irony. "Now tell me, truthfully," asked comic Henry Morgan, "are you sorry you did it?" Farnsworth said he was proud of the accomplishment, and "generally speaking," he said television was a blessing to humankind. As his prize for stumping the panel, Farnsworth collected a carton of Winstons, a check for eighty dollars, and Moore's undying thanks: "We'd all be out of work if it weren't for you."

As hinted by Henry Morgan's question, these years were a time of great national ambivalence toward television. The quiz show scandals of the late 1950s unleashed a tidal wave of cynicism over television programming, and when Edward R. Murrow spoke at an industry convention in 1958, he attacked television for its "decadence, escapism, and insulation from the realities of the world," then offered up a challenge: "This instrument can teach, it can illuminate, it can even inspire," Murrow said, "but it can do so only to the extent that humans are determined to use it to those ends. Otherwise, it is merely wires and lights in a box." Pretty soon, Paley forced Murrow out of his job. By 1961, FCC chairman Newton Minow denounced television as "a vast wasteland," and Murrow joined Minow as a member of the Kennedy administration.

Even Vladimir Zworykin became disillusioned by how the invention was being put into use. Asked in an interview what specifically about television was he most proud of, Zworykin replied in his thick Russian accent.

"Da switch," he said.

"Excuse me?" said the interviewer.

"Da switch," repeated Zworykin, "so I can turn the damn theenk off!"

Despite Zworykin's disillusionment, despite Farnsworth's alienation, and even despite Sarnoff's own privately expressed disappointment about the overcommercialization of the new medium, television became an unqualified financial success, and it certainly wouldn't be the last time marketing and image would trump engineering and science. On the strength of color broadcasting and color television sales, RCA's stock took off on a trajectory it hadn't seen since the Roaring Twenties. Profits swelled, and RCA vaulted to number twenty-six on the Fortune 500 list of industrial giants. At the annual shareholders meeting in 1965, Sarnoff paused to take a brief look back, and he declared, "This is the year of fulfillment of our long struggle."

*Farnsworth with Pem in 1969, at their Salt Lake City home, at a morning plan-
ning session.* (SPECIAL COLLECTIONS, J. WILLARD MARRIOTT LIBRARY, UNIVERSITY OF UTAH)

Perceptions and Reality

ON THE MORNING OF JANUARY 4, 1961, READERS OF THE *New York Times* came across the face of Philo T. Farnsworth on the front page of their newspapers. "Encouraging promise of a low-cost nuclear fusion process was reported here yesterday by the International Telephone and Telegraph Company," the story announced. The Atomic Energy Commission (AEC) was also working on the problem, the story added, and it had spent $32 million on the project in 1960 alone. The government commission, however, was trying to control the the reaction using magnetic fields, whereas Farnsworth aimed to confine fusion using an electrostatic process. The news report sent ITT stock soaring, and Farnsworth was immediately given a big raise, a promotion, an upgraded lab facility, and an award of stock options.

In the context of the times, Farnsworth's goal wasn't that far-fetched. In his famous television speech of March 1961, President Kennedy took on the challenge of landing an American on the moon by the end of the decade. Which project was more fanciful—putting a man on the moon or controlling fusion? At the time, no one could really tell.

By the mid-1960s, Farnsworth was predicting that his invention, which he called the Fusor, was going to replace all known forms of energy. The Fusor would end pollution from the burning of fossil fuels, eliminate the hazards of nuclear waste, allow for the building of cars that wear out before their power packs run empty, and reduce electricity costs to the point that one could power New York City for a dollar per month. His ultimate dream was the fusion-powered spaceship that could fly to Mars with a palm-sized fuel container. His visions were beginning to echo Hugo Gernsback's long-ago predictions.

For Farnsworth, the fusion project was following a similar pattern to his early television efforts, the work of the gray old man mirroring that of the young rebel: he discovered an unconventional approach to a daunting problem, worked out a theory, built a machine, and pushed toward achieving a breakthrough. He filed for patents on his Fusor device, and two of them were issued. He even had a new adversary. In his view, the AEC had become the new RCA, ready to co-opt his idea when it proved viable. Yet this time, Farnsworth may have come up against a wall of impossibility, as a sustained reaction of this type has yet to be achieved. ITT cut off funding for the project in 1966 and put the ailing inventor on medical retirement at age sixty.

Yet he still wouldn't give it up. Phil and Pem sold their home in Fort Wayne and moved back to Utah. They were now living close to the spot where they had first met. They bought a ranch house near Salt Lake City, and Farnsworth kept up his fusion research. He set up a new lab not far from his home and hired old colleagues, but lack of progress only made Farnsworth deeply depressed once again, and the expense of running the lab had consumed all of his money and put the family deep into debt. His health went into free fall, and he seemed to lose the will to live any longer.

On July 20, 1969, Farnsworth's television legacy was brought into sharp relief. After the Apollo 11 came in for its landing on the moon, Neil Armstrong stepped out of the lunar module and unhitched a latch that released a television camera, a device based on a miniaturized version of a Farnsworth Image Dissector tube that ITT had provided to NASA. The entire project would not have been undertaken if television didn't exist, as the enormous cost could be justified only if the lunar landing was both a scientific mission *and* an experience that the rest of humanity could share. Along with 1 billion people worldwide, Philo T. Farnsworth watched in wonder as Armstrong and Buzz Aldrin became the first humans to take steps on soil beyond their own planet. As Farnsworth listened to Armstrong's famous "giant leap for mankind" declaration, tears welled up in his eyes. "This," he told Pem, "has made it all worthwhile."

Philo Taylor Farnsworth died on March 11, 1971, at the age of sixty-four, isolated from the business world and scientific community and all but totally forgotten. He was buried in Provo, Utah, at a small ceremony of family and friends.

Just nine months later, on December 12, 1971, David Sarnoff died in his sleep at the age of eighty. His wealth was modest by modern standards, with RCA stock worth about $8 million and other assets valued in the single-digit millions, but he was honored beyond compare, with twenty-seven honorary university degrees and more than 100 awards, medals, and citations, many of which he actively sought late in life. His passing was announced on NBC's *Meet the Press* the following morning, and a half-hour special program commemorating the network's founder aired in the afternoon. Three days later, at a funeral service inside New York's majestic Temple Emanu-El

that was attended by scores of luminaries, Governor Nelson Rockefeller eulogized David Sarnoff's "life of greatness."

Not long before his death, Sarnoff had turned control of the
corporation over to his son Robert, who had progressed through the
ranks as a capable leader of NBC. Bobby Sarnoff was widely blamed
for squandering the greatness of the parent company, turning the
electronics and communications leader into a conglomeration of
mismatched units by acquiring companies in businesses ranging
from car rentals to book publishing to frozen foods to real estate to
carpeting. The board fired Bobby Sarnoff, but it didn't stop the company's decline and loss of focus, as RCA then bought finance, insurance, and greeting card companies. By now, ultra-efficient Japanese
manufacturers had all but completely taken over the business of
making televisions.

In perhaps the most ironic corporate transaction of all time, the
General Electric Company purchased RCA in 1986, nearly fifty-five
years after it had been forced by the government to divest the radio
monopoly. Following completion of the $6.3-billion deal, GE pro-
ceeded to break apart David Sarnoff's old empire and auction off all
the pieces, save for NBC. Sarnoff's prized RCA Laboratories—since
renamed Sarnoff Corporation—had lost most of its luster by then,
and it was sold for the sum of one dollar to the nonprofit Stanford
Research Institute. Sarnoff would have fought the GE takeover from
the outset, said many of those who had known him, and he would
have been horrified by the dismemberment of the corporation.

As similar acquisitions followed—ABC was bought by the Walt
Disney Company, while CBS was acquired by Westinghouse, which
later sold itself to media conglomerate Viacom—television was
coming to be treated less like a technology and more like a corporate asset and a marketing machine. Television advertising has
mushroomed into a $50-billion industry in the United States alone,
surpassing newspapers as the nation's number one marketing

medium. According to Nielsen data, the average American watches more than four hours every day, with the rest of the world not far behind, making television humankind's dominant leisure "activity" and its window to a world that has become a house of mirrors. Yet there is no getting around the fact that television is also an invention, perhaps the single most successful technological creation in history when judged purely by the speed of its mass acceptance, and at its heart, it is still just a glass tube in which electrons paint images on a screen line by line, just as the teenage Philo T. Farnsworth had envisioned it while plowing a potato field all those years ago.

Recognition has been slow in coming Farnsworth's way. "As to who was the inventor of electronic television," said Donald Glenn Fink, the engineer who in 1941 devised the enduring NTSC format, "I think Farnsworth should clearly be given the credit, and I'm not sure that he does get it."

In 1973, the U.S. Patent and Trademark Office dedicated a National Inventors Hall of Fame, an institution now located in Akron, Ohio. Among the first inductees were Edison, Bell, Morse, Marconi, and the Wright brothers. Vladimir Kosma Zworykin was inducted in 1977, five years before his death. In 1984, after the U.S. Postal Service issued a set of stamps honoring forgotten inventors, including Farnsworth, Edwin Howard Armstrong and Nikola Tesla, the Hall of Fame finally inducted Philo T. Farnsworth as its seventy-seventh member. In 1981, the state of California named Farnsworth's Green Street laboratory an official historic landmark, commemorating the location with a special plaque.

As the fiftieth anniversary of David Sarnoff's introduction of television at the 1939 World's Fair approached, a group of elementary school students in Utah did some research into the history of television, and they grew determined to come up with a way to recognize

Farnsworth. They noticed that each state is entitled to be represented by statues of two figures in National Statuary Hall, in the U.S. Capitol. Utah at the time had only one: Brigham Young, who founded the state. The students successfully petitioned the U.S. Congress to install a statue of Farnsworth, and the sculpture was created and unveiled at a 1990 ceremony attended by Pem Farnsworth and her three sons. The bronze Philo T. Farnsworth stands there today, gazing down at a tube in his hands. Under his name on the figure's base are the words *Father of Television*.

ACKNOWLEDGMENTS

ODDLY ENOUGH, MY INTEREST IN PHILO T. FARNSWORTH AND HIS struggle to bring television into the world grew out of my work writing a pair of books about the Internet. In an attempt to grasp the ramifications of the World Wide Web explosion, I began researching how prior information technologies were viewed when they were new and how early predictions held up to reality over a long period of time. When my research led me to the story of the teenage farm boy who invented electronic television, I wanted to know more about how Farnsworth could possibly have accomplished all he did and what really happened to him. That his lack of widespread recognition was usually blamed on RCA mogul David Sarnoff seemed mysterious. Sarnoff's official biography didn't mention Philo T. Farnsworth at all.

When I heard that Farnsworth's widow was still alive, I was apprehensive about contacting her and asking her to revisit painful memories, but when I tracked down her telephone number and called, I was glad I did, and she seemed glad too. Elma G. "Pem" Farnsworth was about to turn ninety-two when I first met her in December 1999. I found her to be a remarkably generous woman, with an unforgettable spirit, a great sense of humor, and hardly an unkind word for anybody. As previously noted, this book wouldn't be the same if it weren't for her help, and I was pleased when she agreed to accept on behalf of the Farnsworth family a portion of my advance for this book, plus a portion of the book's future royalties, as recognition of the fact that sitting for interviews, recalling the details of long-ago events, and digging through documents is actually pretty hard work.

Immense thanks to Kent Farnsworth for sharing his recollections, observations, documents, and photographs of his father, and to Kent's wife, Linda, and the rest of the Farnsworth clan for welcoming me into their homes. Special thanks to Philo T. Farnsworth's eldest surviving son, Russell "Skee" Farnsworth, and to Rose Kaplin, for inviting me to a memorable lobster dinner and family reunion at the Farnsworth cabin deep in the woods of Brownfield, Maine. It's not often that one gets to meet so many Farnsworths at once, and it's not every day that you get to see a ninety-two-year-old woman handle a two-pound lobster so skillfully.

When it came to tracking down the "other side" of the story, I was fortunate to find Alexander Magoun, director of the David Sarnoff Library in Princeton, New Jersey. As previously noted, he was generous in providing his time as well as access to key archives, and I thank him for his honesty as well as his deep knowledge of Sarnoff, RCA, and the history of broadcasting. Although the materials included in the library were apparently cleansed long ago of virtually all references to Philo T. Farnsworth, the viewpoints I received from Alex Magoun helped add balance and perspective to the tale.

Additional research required trips to Washington, D.C. Special thanks to all the government workers who do a great job caring for the nation's records, especially to the helpful staff members at the National Archives, which houses the records of the old Federal Radio Commission, and to the staff at the Library of Congress's

Motion Picture, Broadcasting, and Recorded Sound Division, which hosts the extensive NBC collection of old radio broadcasts, television programs, and internal corporate memos from both NBC and RCA. Also fascinating are the library's transcripts of the U.S. Senate's "Monopoly Investigation" from the late 1930s. I conducted further research with the help of staff members at the Smithsonian Institute and the Library of American Broadcasting in College Park, Maryland.

The largest source of Farnsworth documents is maintained by the Special Collections Department of the J. Willard Marriott Library at the University of Utah in Salt Lake City. The Philo T. and Elma G. Farnsworth Papers and Photo Collection take up more than forty feet of shelf space, and the library provided me with three days of intensive dives into the life and times of the inventor of electronic television. Thanks to the staff members for guiding me through the collection and fulfilling copy and photo requests afterward.

I made an interesting side trip to the Snake River Valley, home to the Farnsworth Television and Pioneer Museum in Rigby, Idaho, the tiny town that the teenage Philo lived in when he came up with his idea. The museum is a low-budget operation, but the people there kindly took me on a tour of the Farnsworth tubes and artifacts that date back to his days in high school.

I found additional help, books, magazines, and resources at the San Francisco Airport Commission Aviation Library, the Museum of Radio and Television in New York, the New York Public Library, and the Boston Public Library.

Thanks to all the eBay members who consistently offer up a treasure trove of the old Hugo Gernsback magazines that inspired Farnsworth as a boy. I purchased a couple dozen issues of *Science and Invention*, *Radio News*, *Television News*, *Radio and Television*, and *Amazing Stories* spanning the years 1919 through 1941, and those articles, photos, as well as Gernsback's trademark editorials provide a vivid portrait of technological progress as it unfolded during the years in which this book takes place.

Thanks to the authors of the more than twenty different books that were instrumental in researching this one. A full account of those references, including Web links, and other sources for the information herein can be found in the Notes section and at this book's companion Web site, lastlone.com.

Special thanks to the following friends, relatives, and colleagues who read early versions of the manuscript and provided helpful feedback: Richard Albert, Jonathan Alsop, Amy Bolotin, John David Heinzmann, Marc Schumacher, Ralph Wahlert, and fellow Harper-Collins author Seth Shulman. It helps to have a couple of journalism professors as neighbors. Thanks to Jim Ross of Northeastern University and Doug Starr of Boston University for providing their comments and suggestions. Thanks to Rebecca Zacks, Bob Buderi, and John Benditt of *Technology Review* magazine, for editing and publishing my feature "Who Really Invented Television?" in their September 2000 issue.

I'm grateful to Regan Graves and Jennifer Wachtell at Miramax for their enthusiasm for this project. Tremendous thanks to Elyse Cheney, for sticking by me through my early ups and downs and for guiding my proposal to the perfect editor. Heaps of gratitude to the team at HarperCollins, especially to Leslie Engel and Jennifer Swihart, and to Marjorie Braman, for her vision and her careful, old-fashioned editing with multicolored markers.

To my parents, my family, and my friends: thank you for your love and support. Michaela and Lily, you may have been too young to remember our first visit to Green Street, but you are a daily source of inspiration. Finally, to Amy, for your constant love and patience ever since this crazy idea somehow hatched.

NOTES

PROLOGUE

1 "S.F. Man's Invention to Revolutionize Television," *San Francisco Chronicle*, 3 September 1928.

4–5 "Forging an Electronic Eye to Scan the World: David Sarnoff Pictures the Great Concentration of Effort Now Being Made to Achieve Television and Discusses the Future," *New York Times*, 18 November 1928, section XX, page 3; "Leaders Dispel Television Fears," *New York Times*, 16 December 1928, section XX, page 18.

6 Thomas Edison obituary, "Prospero Is Dead," *New York Times*, 18 October 1931, page 1.

CHAPTER ONE: FIELDS OF VISION

Facts and anecdotes from Philo T. Farnsworth's boyhood were drawn, in part, from my interviews in 1999, 2000, and 2001 with Elma G. "Pem" Farnsworth, and from her self-published memoir, *Distant Vision: Romance and Discovery on an Invisible Frontier*, and from my visit, in April 2001, to Rigby, Idaho, which is now the home of the Farnsworth Television and Pioneer Museum.

11–12 "Publisher's Announcement," by Hugo Gernsback, *Science and Invention*, July 1920, page 279; "Automobile Stunts" contest announced on page 276.

13 Genealogical data from FamilySearch Internet Genealogy Service (familysearch.org), the database maintained by the Church of Jesus Christ of Latter-Day Saints (the Mormon Church).

18 In the February 1922 issue of *Science and Invention*, the first prize of twenty-five dollars for the "Motor Hints" contest is awarded to P. T.

Farnsworth for his "Magnetic Thief-Proof Switch." The entry begins by
stating that "the illustration herewith shows a simple and easily made
secret ignition switch, which can be closed by means of a magnet carried
in the door pocket of the car, or in your pocket."

20 Hugo Gernsback's quote is from the July 1922 issue of *Science and Inven-
    tion,* but he had already been writing about the idea of television for years.
    In the May 1918 issue of *Electrical Experimenter,* he wrote: "There are some
    inventions which, although not yet existent, we may take for granted will
    be invented someday without any doubt whatsoever.... The subject of
    this article, *Television, or Seeing at a Distance,* is one of these inventions."

CHAPTER TWO: MAKING A GREAT MAN

Facts and anecdotes from David Sarnoff's boyhood and early career were pieced
together from documents I obtained on my visits in 2000 and 2001 to the David
Sarnoff Library in Princeton, New Jersey, as well as from the following books: *The
General: David Sarnoff and the Rise of the Communications Industry,* by RCA executive
Kenneth Bilby (Harper & Row, 1986); *David Sarnoff,* by Sarnoff's first cousin and
official biographer, Eugene Lyons (Harper & Row, 1966); *Empire of the Air: The Men
Who Made Radio,* by Tom Lewis (HarperCollins, 1991); and United States Early
Radio History, a Web site by Thomas H. White (www.ipass.net/~whitetho), which
makes a point of debunking several Sarnoff myths.

32–34 "July 2 Fight Described by Radiophone," *Wireless Age,* August 1921 issue,
       page 10. The Julius Hopp story is fleshed out in further detail at the U.S.
       Early Radio History site, in the article "The Battle of the Century."

34 On Sunday, July 3, 1921, the *New York Times* ran a full banner headline:
    "Dempsey Knocks Out Carpentier in the Fourth Round; Challenger
    Breaks His Thumb Against the Champion's Jaw; Record Crowd of
    90,000 Orderly and Well Handled." A small, boxed notice on the bottom
    of page 6 said, "Wireless Telephone Spreads Fight News Over 120,000
    Miles." In the last sentence, David Sarnoff's name is misspelled as
    "Saranoff."

38 Quote from Thomas Carlyle (1795–1881) referenced in the *Oxford Dic-
    tionary of Quotations,* third edition, page 131.

40–41 Official RCA version of *Titanic* events are quoted in an article titled
       "Radio," by David Sarnoff, as told to Mary Margaret McBride, in the *Sat-
       urday Evening Post,* issues dated August 7 and 14, 1926.

41–42 *Fortune* magazine profile on David Sarnoff, September 1932. Boston *Amer-
       ican,* April 16, 1912, page 4, reports that the person who "took charge" of
       receiving the faint signals about the *Titanic* by wireless was named Jack

Binns. It also noted that David Sarnoff managed the Wanamaker station but it didn't single him out as the only wireless operator there.

42–43 "Keep Your Mouth Shut; Big Money for You . . . ," New York *Herald*, April 21, 1912, page 1.

47 *Radio News* "Monkey Business" cover was published in July 1921.

CHAPTER THREE: COMMUNITY CHEST

Source material and quotes in this chapter were drawn primarily from George Everson's book *The Story of Television* (New York: W. W. Norton and Company, 1948), reprinted in 1974 by Arno Press and in 1998 by Ayer Company Publishers, North Stratford, N.H., from *Distant Vision: Romance and Discovery on an Invisible Frontier*, and from my interviews with Pem Farnsworth.

58–59 Permissions to quote lyrics granted by Hal Leonard Corporation, Milwaukee, Wis.

CHAPTER FOUR: PATENTLY BRILLIANT

Source material and anecdotes for this chapter were drawn in part from Kenneth Bilby's *The General: David Saranoff and the Rise of the Communications Industry* (New York: Harper & Row, 1986) from *Empire of the Air: The Men Who Made Radio*, by Tom Lewis (New York: HarperCollins, 1991), and from documents at the David Sarnoff Library.

65 Radio sales figures from page 162, *Empire of the Air*; advertisement from *Radio News*, inside cover, January 1925 issue.

66 Sarnoff quote from *The General*, page 65

71–72 The story of Bill Eddy (1902–1989) and the one-dollar patent checks is drawn from an interview Eddy gave to Jeff Kisseloff for the book *The Box: An Oral History of Television, 1920–1961* (New York: Viking, 1995), page 19. As noted in subsequent chapters, Eddy worked for Philo T. Farnsworth in the mid-1930s, before joining RCA.

73–77 The best source for the life of Edwin Howard Armstrong is *Man of High Fidelity*, by Lawrence Lessing, originally published in 1956, and reissued by Bantam in 1969. Also see *Empire of the Air*.

CHAPTER FIVE: GOING HOLLYWOOD

Stories and information in this chapter were drawn from documents housed at the Philo T. and Elma G. Farnsworth Papers, an extensive document archive at University of Utah's Marriott Library in Salt Lake City, from interviews with Pem Farnsworth, from *Distant Vision: Romance and Discovery on an Invisible Frontier*, and from George Everson's *The Story of Television* (New York: W. W. Norton & Co., 1948).

CHAPTER SIX: NETWORKING

Material in this chapter was drawn from documents at the David Sarnoff Library, interviews with Alex Magoun, the library's director, and from *The General: David Sarnoff and the Rise of the Communications Industry* (New York: Harper & Row, 1986).

94 Lyrics to the 1927 hit song, "The Varsity Drag," reprinted by permission of Hal Leonard Corporation.

97 Episode about Harry Warner happened in the mid-1920s, as told in Neal Gabler, *An Empire of Their Own: How the Jews Invented Hollywood* (New York: Crown Publishers, 1988), page 137.

98–104 AT&T started station WEAF in 1921, which broadcast the first paid commercials beginning in August 1922, which led to the Washington conference with Herbert Hoover later in the year. AT&T's stations were joined in the first radio network in 1923, the same year that the Federal Radio Commission was formed. The arbitration decision favoring RCA over AT&T was handed down in late 1924. The settlement between the two companies was reached in the fall of 1925. Sarnoff's promotion and raise happened around the same time as the official launch of NBC, on November 15, 1926.

103–104 The NBC inaugural program listings for the gala on November 15, 1926, was obtained from the Library of American Broadcasting, College Park, Maryland. Document number 12.

105 Thomas Edison quote from a 1926 issue of *Radio News*.

106–109 Joseph P. Kennedy background throughout the book attributed to *The Fitzgeralds and the Kennedys*, by Doris Kearns Goodwin, (New York: Simon and Schuster, 1987), and to *Sins of the Father: Joseph P. Kennedy and the Dynasty He Founded*, by Ronald Kessler (New York: Warner Books, 1997).

CHAPTER SEVEN: LIFE ON GREEN STREET

Stories and information in this chapter were drawn from interviews with Pem Farnsworth, from *Distant Vision: Romance and Discovery on an Invisible Frontier*, from George Everson's *The Story of Television* (New York: W. W. Norton & Co., 1948), from documents at the University of Utah Library, and from the laboratory journals kept at the Farnsworth family home and at the museum in Rigby, Idaho.

117–121 Albert Einstein background attributed to *Einstein: The Life and Times*, by Ronald W. Clark (New York: Avon, 1972, reissued in 1999 by Bard).

118–120 Photoelectric and electromagnetic physics background attributed to *College Physics*, fifth edition, by Francis W. Sears et al. (Reading, Mass.: Addison-Wesley, 1980).

122–123 All information and quotes from Farnsworth's patents are from the official patent document, as compiled on Jim Bieberich's Complete Philo T. Farnsworth U.S. Patent Collection, a CD-ROM available for order over the Internet.

123–124 U.S. patent laws have changed over the years. In Farnsworth's day, patents were granted for seventeen years from the date of issuance, a time limit since lengthened to twenty years, and pending patent applications can now be viewed by the public even earlier after the filing date.

128–134 General background on mechanical television attributed to *The Box: An Oral History of Television, 1920–1961* (New York: Viking, 1995) and *Tube: The Invention of Television,* by David E. Fisher and Marshall Jon Fisher (Washington, D.C.: Counterpoint, 1996), as well as issues of *Radio News.*

130 Story of John Logie Baird's gruesome experiment with an eyeball recounted in Baird's lab journal as quoted on page 25 of *Please Stand By: A Prehistory of Television,* by Michael Ritchie (New York: Overlook Press, 1995).

137–138 "S.F. Man's Invention to Revolutionize Television," by Earle Ennis, *San Francisco Chronicle,* 3 September 1928.

CHAPTER EIGHT: CONFRONTATION

Material from this chapter was drawn from interviews with Pem Farnsworth, from interviews with Alex Magoun, from the Utah Library documents, from the Sarnoff Library documents, from *The General: David Sarnoff and the Rise of the Communications Industry,* by Kenneth Bilby (New York: Harper & Row, 1986), from *Distant Vision: Romance and Discovery on an Invisible Frontier,* from *Tube: The Invention of Television,* by David E. Fisher and Marshall Jon Fisher (Washington, D.C.: Counterpoint, 1996), and from various issues of Hugo Gernsback's magazines.

145–146 "Radio News Publisher in Hands of Receiver," *New York Times,* 21 February 1929, page 32.

156–157 July 8, 1930, letter from A. F. Murray of RCA's Advance Development Division in Camden, New Jersey, to Philo T. Farnsworth at 202 Green Street, available at the Utah Library, as is the letter from the Crocker Bank executives to Farnsworth.

158 The profile of David Sarnoff when he became president of RCA appeared in the *New York Times,* on 12 January 1930, section IX, page 15.

161 The Get-Around-Farnsworth Department was the secret, unofficial name for this group at RCA, and Farnsworth himself found out about it only later, when he hired Sanford Essig, one of RCA's top television scientists, to work at the Farnsworth company. According to Pem Farnsworth,

Essig produced evidence that this department existed, although none of this direct evidence survives today.

162–164 "The Inventions of Reginald A. Fessenden," *Radio News*, January 1925, page 1140.

165–167 Background information about invention and famous lone inventors attributed to *American Science and Invention: A Pictoral History*, by Mitchell Wilson (New York: Bonanza Books, 1954).

166 Background information about the origins of corporate research and development laboratories attributed to *Engines of Tomorrow*, by Robert Buderi (Simon and Schuster, 2000).

168 Information about the aircraft Farnsworth took across country is from the San Francisco Airport Commission Aviation Library and from the Smithsonian's National Air and Space Museum. San Francisco's municipal airport, Mills Field, was dedicated on May 7, 1927.

169 "4,860,000 Listed as Out of Work," the Washington *Evening Star*, December 3, 1930, page 1. Cartoon also on front page.

169–172 Records of the Federal Radio Commission's meeting on 3 December 1930 were obtained in a search at the National Archives, record group 173, in College Park, Maryland.

172 Some of the background and description of Hugo Gernsback attributed to "Barnum of the Space Age: The Amazing Hugo Gernsback, Prophet of Science," by Paul O'Neil, *Life* 26 July 1963, page 62.

172–173 "The Future of the Inventor," by Hugo Gernsback, *Science and Invention*, July 1922, page 225; "Television Is Here, Inventor Claims," by Robert Mack, Washington *Evening Star*, 4 December 1930.

174 "A Radio Idea from the West: Farnsworth, Television Inventor from California, Explains His Image Receiver—He Believes Scenic Broadcasts Are Practical," *New York Times*, Sunday, 14 December 1930.

174–175 Albert Einstein quotations from the Clark biography of Einstein.

CHAPTER NINE: END RUN

Information for this chapter was drawn from Everson's book, from *Distant Vision: Romance and Discovery on an Invisible Frontier*, from interviews with Pem Farnsworth, from the Utah Library, from *Tube: The Invention of Television*, by David E. Fisher and Marshall Jon Fisher (Washington, D.C.: Counterpoint, 1996), from *The General: David Sarnoff and the Rise of the Communications Industry* (New York: Harper & Row, 1986) from the Lyons biography of Sarnoff, from the Sarnoff Library, from the Einstein biography, from *The Box: An Oral History of Television, 1920–1961* by Jeff Kisseloff (New York: Viking, 1995), and from various issues of Hugo Gernsback's magazines.

188–189 The *New York Times* ran a series of lengthy articles about Thomas Edison, beginning with a front-page obituary and tribute the morning of his death on October 18, 1931.

192–194 William S. Paley background attributed to *In All His Glory: The Life and Times of William S. Paley and the Birth of Modern Broadcasting*, by Sally Bedell Smith (New York: Simon and Schuster, 1990).

CHAPTER TEN: WHO OWNS WHAT?

Material was drawn from the same sources as the previous chapter, plus the memos and legal documents cited below.

200 The David Sarnoff memo quoted here is dated May 8, 1935, although the policy was clearly in effect well before that. Addressed to NBC president Merlin H. Aylesworth, this memo is one of many NBC documents housed at the NBC Collection at the Library of Congress in Washington, D.C.

201–209 The U.S. Patent Office trial between Farnsworth and RCA's Zworykin is described in detail in two lengthy documents, the seventy-six-page "Brief on Behalf of Philo T. Farnsworth" and the seventy-page "Brief on Behalf of Vladimir K. Zworykin." These documents contain dialogue from testimony, evidence presented, and supporting arguments for each side. They are available at the Utah Library.

213 The letter, dated October 29, 1935, from Albert Einstein's wife, Elsa, to David Sarnoff is available at the Sarnoff Library.

219–221 The forty-eight-page U.S. Patent Office court decision for Patent Interference No. 64,027 is dated July 22, 1935, and is available at the Utah Library.

CHAPTER ELEVEN: NARROW ESCAPE

Material was drawn from the same sources as the previous chapters, plus the additional ones below. Information on the events leading up to World War II attributed to *The Second World War*, by John Keegan (New York: Penguin, 1990).

225–227 The Crystal Palace fire of November 30, 1926, was reported in *The Times* of London on the following day. The cause of the fire remained a mystery; many believed it was the result of faulty wiring, while a few have made the case that it was the work of the Nazis in an effort to destroy England's lead in television technology.

231 The original, signed German wrapped box of chocolates is still available at the Utah Library.

232–233 May 1936 correspondence between Einstein to Sarnoff available at the Sarnoff Library.

233–234 The March 1936 decision from the U.S. Patent Office Board of Appeals is available at the Utah Library.

234–235 The best attempt to sort through and make sense of all of Vladimir Zworykin's patent cases can be found in *The Great Television Race: A History of the American Television Industry 1925–1941*, by Joseph H. Udelson (Tuscaloosa: Univ. of Alabama Press, 1982).

237 Sally Bedell Smith, *In All His Glory: The Life and Times of William S. Paley: The Legendary Tycoon and His Brilliant Circle* (New York: Simon and Schuster, 1990).

242 AT&T agreement with Farnsworth is available at the Utah Library.

247–250 The text of Sarnoff's RCA Family Dinner speech was obtained by the author, along with dozens of other speeches and RCA documents, in an eBay auction of bound papers from the estate of longtime RCA corporate attorney Robert D. O'Callaghan.

250–257 "Investigation of Concentration of Economic Power: Hearings Before the Temporary National Economic Committee," Congress of the United States, Seventy-sixth Congress, first session, January 16 though 20, 1939. Transcript available at Library of Congress; Quotes about the formation of the investigation are from the Congressional Record; "Gain in Television Laid to Patenting: Farnsworth Tells Monopoly Board [Patent] Protection Made His Work Possible," *New York Times*, 20 January 1939.

CHAPTER TWELVE: ALL'S FAIR, WORLD'S FAIR
Material was drawn from many of the same sources as the previous chapters.

259 Documents and clippings about the Farnsworth Television and Radio Corporation's initial public offering of stock available at the Utah Library.

261–267 David Gelernter, *1939: The Lost World of the Fair* (New York: Avon Books, 1995).

263–264 The *New York Times Sunday Magazine* edition devoted to the World's Fair published 5 March 1939.

266 "The Talk of the Town," *The New Yorker*, 13 May 1939, page 13.

CHAPTER THIRTEEN: BREAKDOWN, BREAKOUT
Same sources as previous chapter, as well as my October 2000 visit to the Farnsworth farm in Brownfield, Maine, the site of the family home that burned down in 1947.

272 RCA issued a one-page press release about its deal with Farnsworth. The document, available at the Sarnoff Library, is the only reference to

Farnsworth this author could find among the documents housed at that facility.

278–279 See Stanford University Web site for background information about David L. Webster.

CHAPTER FOURTEEN: POST WAR

Information was drawn from many of the previous sources, including *The Box: An Oral History of Television, 1920–1961*, by Jeff Kisseloff (New York: Viking, 1995) and *In All His Glory: The Life of William S. Paley: The Legendary Tycoon and His Brilliant Circle*, by Sally Bedell Smith (New York: Simon and Schuster, 1990).

282 Information on the 7 January 1949 anniversary show from the NBC Collection at the Library of Congress.

290–291 Quote about the Nixon-Kennedy debate, from *The Powers That Be*, by David Halberstam (New York: Alfred A. Knopf, 1979).

292 "What Does Farnsworth Think of 'Baby'? Inventor of TV Says 'Too Many Cowboy Movies," by Ernest E. Williams, Fort Wayne *News-Sentinel*, 21 March 1957.

292 Clip of Farnsworth's appearance on CBS's "I've Got a Secret" can be viewed at farnovision.com.

293 Edward R. Murrow's quote and related background information can be attributed to *Who Killed CBS? The Undoing of America's Number One News Network* by Peter J. Boyer (New York: Random House, 1988).

EPILOGUE

Information drawn from Pem Farnsworth's *Distant Vision: Romance and Discovery on an Invisible Frontier, The General: David Sarnoff and the Rise of the Communications Industry*, by Kenneth Bilby (New York: Harper & Row, 1986), several other previously mentioned sources, and finally, to my visit to U.S. Statuary Hall, U.S. Capitol, Washington, D.C.

295 "I.T.T. Hopeful on Experiments to Harness the H-Bomb's Power," by Gene Smith, *New York Times*, 4 January 1961, page 1.

298 See National Inventors Hall of Fame Web site, invent.org.

298 Extensive information about G.E.'s 1986 acquisition of RCA can be found in Ken Auletta, *Three Blind Mice: How the TV Networks Lost Their Way* (New York: Random House, 1991).

299 Donald Glenn Fink quote from *The Box: An Oral History of Television, 1920–1961*, by Jeff Kisseloff (New York: Viking, 1995).

INDEX

Entries in *italics* refer to illustrations.

Academy of Television Arts and Sciences, 150, 291

Advertising, 70, 98, 102, 282, 298–99

Aldrin, Buzz, 297

Alexanderson, Ernst, 55, 71, 131–32, 160

AM (amplitude modulation), 75

Amazing Stories, 146, 147

American Broadcasting Company (ABC), 281, 284, 298

American Marconi, 37, 39, 43, 44

American Science and Inventions (Wilson), 166

Antitrust, 69, 159–60
  suit against RCA, 194–96
  See also Monopoly
  Investigation

Armstrong, Edwin Howard, 45–46, 73–77, 165, 181, 238, 299

Armstrong, Marion M., 74, 76–77

Armstrong, Neil, 297

Astaire, Fred, 210

Astor, John Jacob, 103

Astor, William Waldorf, 103

Atomic Energy Commission (AEC), 295, 296

AT&T, 5, 45, 46, 68, 96–102, 130, 166, 242, 252, 256

Aylesworth, Merlin, 103

Baekeland, Leo, 165

Baird, John Logie, 55, 128–30, 223–27

Bastian, Jacob (grandfather), 13

BBC, 224, 226–27

Bell, Alexander G., 2, 14, 121, 165, 299

Bell Laboratories, 55, 130–31, 163, 166, 253

Berle, Milton, 282

Bilby, Kenneth, 108, 109, 160, 266

Binns, Jack, 42

Birdseye, Clarence, 166

Bishop, Roy, 88–89, 90, 116–17, 135–37

Braun, Karl, 20–21

Broglie, Louis de, 120

Brolly, Archie "Arch," 150, 162, 185, 197, 203–4, 240, 282

Bucky, Dr. Gustav, 212–13, 232

Bush, Vannevar, 252–53

Cantor, Eddie, 58

Carlyle, Thomas, 38

Carpentier, Georges, 30, 32, 33

Carrier, Willis Haviland, 165
Carver, George Washington, 165
Cathode rays, 121
Cathode ray tube, 21, 27, 116
Chamberlain, Neville, 246
Chaplin, Charlie, 152
Chevalier, Maurice, 153
Christensen, Carl, 126, 127
Churchill, Winston, 276
Clark, Ronald, 118, 212
Columbia Broadcasting System (CBS),
    193–94, 236–37, 274, 282,
    287–90, 298
Commerce Department, U.S., 47, 99
Commercial Cable Company, 37
Coolidge, Calvin, 99
Coolidge, William, 163, 253
Cox, James, 45
Crawford, Arthur, 124
Crocker, William H., 90, 135
Crocker, William W., 90, 135, 137
Crocker group, 111, 127, 135, 139,
    149–51, 154, 157, 162, 181, 190,
    240–41
Cummings, Bill, 115

Davis, John, 100–101
De Forest, Lee, 45, 151, 163, 165, 192,
    238
Dempsey, Jack, 30–34, 49, 114, 151
Disney, Walt, 151
Disney Company, 298
Dolores, Baby, 219
Downs, Hugh, 282
Dreher, Carl, 77
DuMont, Allen B., 273
DuPont, 5, 166

Eastman, George, 165
Eastman Kodak, 5, 166
Eddy, Bill, 71, 215, 220, 240, 282
Edison, Thomas A., 2, 5–6, 14, 105,
    132, 163, 165–66, 188, 299
Edward VIII, King of England, 224–25

Einstein, Albert, 23–26, 62, 117–18,
    174–75, 188, 196, 207, 211–13, 230,
    232–33, 267, 279, 285–86
photoelectric
theory, 3, 23, 120–21
Einstein, Elsa, 213
Eisenhower, Gen. Dwight D., 275–76,
    280, 288, 289
"Electric Oscillator System," 123
EMI, 224
Ennis, Earle, 137–38
Essig, Sanford, 186
Evans, Charles, 122–23
Everson, George, 50, 53–56, 61–63,
    81–91, 111, 115, 125, 127, 134–36,
    139–41, 149–50, 180–81, 197, 214,
    237, 240–42, 254, 272

Fagan, J. J., 87–88, 90, 135–36, 154
Fairbanks, Douglas, Sr., 152, 153
Farnsworth, Agnes (sister), 16, 53, 56,
    57, 62, 126
Farnsworth, Albert, 14–16
Farnsworth, Carl (brother), 16, 278,
    279
Farnsworth, Elma G. "Pem" (wife), 2,
    53, 56–63, 78, 79–80, 83–84,
    86–87, 111–14, 116, 124–27,
    137–41, 152–53, 155, 168, 183–85,
    189–91, 197, 214–16, 218, 223–26,
    228–32, 241, 243–44, 277–79,
    283–84, 287, 294, 296, 300
Farnsworth, Kenneth Gardner (son),
    183, 185, 190, 216
Farnsworth, Kent (cousin), 18
Farnsworth, Kent (son), 284, 291–92
Farnsworth, Laura (sister), 16
Farnsworth, Lewis (father), 9–10,
    13–16, 21–22, 51
Farnsworth, Lincoln (brother), 16, 279
Farnsworth, Philo Taylor, xiv, 198, 294
atom bomb project and, 279
awarded TV patent after Zworykin
    suit, 220–21, 234–35

Farnsworth, Philo Taylor (*cont.*)
award named after camera of, 291
belated recognition of, 299–300
birth and background of, 13–14
break with McCargar and
company reorganization, 238–44
CBS and, 237
changes name to Phil, 51–52
childhood and education of, 9–27,
52–53
corporate-controlled innovation vs., 77
courtship and marriage of, 56–61
Crocker group backs, 86–91
Crocker group pressures to sell,
149–51, 154
death of, 297
death of father, 51
death of son, 190–91
Depression and, 189–90
disillusionment of, with TV, 292–93
early dream of, 2–3
early financial backers, *50*, 53–57
early interest in invention, 14–19
Einstein inspires, 117–18, 121
Einstein meeting, 286–87
European trip of 1936, 223–32
first demonstrates TV, *110*, 135–38,
216–18
first explains TV idea, 26–27
first patent for "television system,"
121–24
first successful TV experiment,
127–28
FRC testimony, 168–74
fusion research, 284–87, 295–97
Green Street lab and, 91, 111–17,
124–27, 134–41
Green Street lab fire, 138–39
Green Street lab visitors, 151–53
ignition lock invention, 11–13,
18–19, 22
inventive brilliance of, 1–7
I've Got a Secret appearance, 292
as last lone inventor, 6

Maine property of, 243–44, *270*,
278–79
marriage problems, 190–91, 215–16
marriage to Pem and move to LA,
61–63, *78*, 79–85
Monopoly Investigation and, 252–57
musical gift of, 17–18, 52, 86–87
named "outstanding young man of
1939," 276–77
in Navy, 52
nervous breakdown of, 277–79
patent attorney hired by, 84–86
patents and company sold by, 284
patents awarded to, 161–62
patents expire, 279
patents licensed to RCA, 271–73
Philco and, 182–86, 196–97, 222
post-war TV expansion and, 283–85
RCA fights, for patents, 161–62, 171,
192
RCA sued by, 200–209, 212, 214–15,
219–21
Sarnoff and, 6–7, 143
Sarnoff meeting, final, 291
Sarnoff visits and makes offer to, 177,
179–82
stock market crash and, 148–49
Television Laboratories and, 139–41
TV standards and, 274
World's Fair TV demonstration and,
267–69
Zworykin steals work of, 154–57
Farnsworth, Philo Taylor (grandfa-
ther), 13
Farnsworth, Philo Taylor, III (son),
141, 191, 268, 279
Farnsworth, Russell Seymour (Skeezix)
(son), 216
Farnsworth, Serena Bastian (mother),
13, 14, 17, 51, 140
Farnsworth Papers, 214
Farnsworth Television, 197, 214, 219,
241–43, 259–60, 267–68, *270*,
272, 277, 283–84

Federal Communications Commission
    (FCC), 210, 244, 254–55, 266, 268,
    273–74, 277, 287–88
Federal Radio Commission (FRC), 99,
    168–74, 197, 210
Federal Trade Commission (FTC),
    67–68, 94, 158
Fermi, Enrico, 279
Fernseh company, 227–28, 241–42
Fessenden, Reginald A., 162–64
Fink, Donald Glenn, 274, 299
Fitzgerald, F. Scott, 94
Fleischmann, Max, 87
FM (frequency modulation), 75–76
Ford, Henry, 165
"Forging an Electric Eye to Scan the
    World" (Sarnoff), 4
Franck, Richard, 162
Frankfurter, Felix, 246
Franklin, Benjamin, 164
Franklin Institute, 217–18, 224

Garden, Mary, 104
Gardner, Cliff, 53, 57, 59–60, 62,
    111–17, 125–27, 137–38, 150, 153,
    155, 179, 185–86, 197, 216, 240,
    243–44, 278
Gardner, Elma (Pem). See Farnsworth,
    Elma G.
Gardner, Lola, 185, 243
Gardner, Ruth, 126
Gardner, Verona, 57, 58
Gehrig, Lou, 277
Gelernter, David, 263
General Electric (GE), 5, 31, 44, 46, 55,
    68, 71, 96, 102, 131, 156, 158, 166,
    194, 252–53, 284, 298
General Motors, 166, 261
    Radio Corporation, 105
George VI, King of England, 225
Gernsback, Hugo, 8, 11, 19–20, 44–45,
    47, 70, 129, 133, 145–47, 172–73,
    176, 209–10, 249–50, 291
Gifford, Walter, 96–102, 131

Gillett, King Camp, 165
Goebbels, Joseph, 230
Goerz, Paul, 227–31
Goldmark, Peter, 237
Goodyear, Charles, 165
Gorrell, Leslie, 50, 53–55, 61, 81,
    83–84, 86–87, 125–27, 139–40
Gray, Elisha, 121
Green Street laboratory, 113–14, 124,
    149–55, 177, 299
Grigsby–Grunow, 159
Grimditch, Mr., 185–86

Haley, George, 243
Hancock, Clarence, 251
Harbord, Gen. James G., 67–69,
    99–100, 104, 157, 160, 236, 275–76
Harding, Warren, 45
Hertz, Heinrich, 119
Hindenburg dirigible, 241
Hitler, Adolf, 174, 195, 227, 229–31,
    243, 246, 249, 259
Holland, Walter, 184
Honn, Harlan, 89
Hoover, Herbert, 3, 98–99, 102,
    104–5, 130, 160, 169, 194
Hoover, Herbert, Jr., 151
Hopp, Julius, 32–33
Howe, Elias, 165
Howes, Durward, 277
Hughes, J. H., 42
Humphries, Bob, 126, 127

I Love Lucy (TV show), 289
Image Dissector (television camera),
    83–84, 176, 179–80, 206
Image Orthicon camera, 291
International Telephone and Telegraph
    (ITT), 284, 295
Invention
    demand and, 162–64
    lone inventor
        vs. corporations and, 77, 162–67,
        172–73

Invention (*cont.*)
  research laboratories and, 5–6, 72
Ives, Herbert, 54–55, 130

Jazz Singer, The (film), 80
Jefferson, Thomas, 164
Jenkins, Charles F., 55, 132–34, 192
Jewett, Frank B., 253
Johnson, James P., 58
Jolliffe, Charles, 172
Jolson, Al, 58–59, 66, 79–80
Justice Department, U.S., 4, 177, 194, 196, 288, 289

Karloff, Boris, 83
Kennedy, John F. "Jack," 108, 245, 290–91, 295–96
Kennedy, Joseph, Jr., 108, 245
Kennedy, Joseph P., 92, 106–9, 148, 177, 213–14, 239, 245–46, 291
Kennedy, Rose, 107–8, 245
Kennedy, Rosemary, 108
Khrushchev, Nikita, 290
Kinescope, 132, 142, 154, 176, 235
King Kong (film), 210
Kraft Television Theater (TV show), 282
Kukla, Fran & Ollie (TV show), 282

Land, Edwin H., 166
Lawrence, Ernest, 152, 276
Lewis, Tom, 76
Light, science of, 118–20
Lightbulb, 163
"Light Valve" patent, 123
Lincoln, Abraham, 38, 201
Lippincott, Donald, 122–23, 168–69, 173–74, 181, 200–203, 205–9, 215, 220, 260, 278, 285
Lippincott, Ruth, 215
Loew, Marcus, 31
Lopez, Vincent, 104
Lubcke, Harry, 150, 162, 291
Lyon & Lyon, 85–86, 121–22

McCargar, Jesse, 87, 89, 135–36, 149–50, 151, 162, 182–84, 197, 214, 237–40, 260
McCarthy, Joseph, 289–90
McDonald, Eugene, 49
Magnetism, 15–16
Manhattan Project, 279, 285
Marconi, Guglielmo, 37–38, 42–44, 64, 70, 119, 151, 165, 237–38, 299
Maxwell, James Clerk, 118–20
Meadows, Jayne, 292
Minow, Newton, 293
Monopoly Investigation (1939), 250–57
Moore, Gary, 292
Morgan, Ann, 31, 33, 245
Morgan, Henry, 292
Morgan, J. P., 31, 32, 148
Morse, Samuel F. B., 2, 14, 165, 299
Mullen, Mr., 200
Multipactor patent, 152, 155
Murray, Albert, 155–57
Murrow, Edward R., 290, 293
Mussolini, Benito, 237–38

Nally, Edward, 32, 44, 67
National Broadcasting Company (NBC), 3, 101–4, 158, 193–95, 211, 248–49
  Blue, vs. Red, 102, 104, 281
  TV network, 266, 281, 298
National Inventors Hall of Fame, 299
National Statuary Hall, 300
National Television Standards Committee (NTSC), 274, 299
Nazi Party (German), 174, 195, 227–32, 241–42
Newton, Sir Isaac, 23–24, 118
New York Herald, 36–37, 43
New York Times, 4, 34, 49, 101, 129, 158, 173–74, 295
Nicholas, Edwin A. "Nick," 250, 260–61, 271–72, 283–84
Nipkow, Paul, 20

Nipkow Disk, 20, 128, 130
Nixon, Richard, 290–91

Olympic Games (1936), 227
O'Mahoney, Joseph, 251–57
Otis, Elisha, 165
Owens, Jesse, 227

Paley, Sam, 193
Paley, William S. "Bill," 192–94,
    236–37, 276, 289, 293
Patent(s)
  engineers at RCA and, 71–72, 192
  Farnsworth files for, 121–24, 196–97
  Farnsworth licenses, 242
  Farnsworth vs. RCA and, 199–221
  laws, history of, 163–65
  licensing, 69–70, 72
  Monopoly Investigation and, 252–57
  RCA and, 44–49
  secrecy and, 22
Perkins, Marlin, 282
Philadelphia Ledger, 218
Philco, 47, 69, 159, 183–87, 196–97,
    236, 266, 273
Photoelectric effect, 118–21
Pickford, Mary, 137, 152–53, 216–17
Planck, Max, 119–20
Popular Mechanics, 147
"Porter, Mr.," 155–56
Purdy, Edna, 12

Radio, 4–5
  De Forest and, 45
  first fight broadcast, 30–34
  first regular station, 45
  licensing and, 69–70, 72
  Marconi and, 37–38
  as public service, 98–99
  Sarnoff transforms, 30, 44–45
  stations, 47, 65–66, 193–94
  vacuum tube sets, 46–47
  waves, 119, 120
Radio City, 195

Radio combine, 46, 68–69, 159, 194
Radio Corporation of America (RCA),
    3–4, 284
  antitrust charges vs., 67–69, 74–75,
    158–60, 194–95
  AT&T vs., and NBC, 98–102
  buys Armstrong patent, 73–75
  buys mechanical TV patents, 192
  color TV and, 287–89, 293
  Dempsey fight and, 31–32
  Depression and, 148, 149, 177, 191–92
  dismembered by GE, 298
  experimental TV station in Camden,
    187
  "Family Dinner," 247–50, 252
  Farnsworth offer, 180–82
  Farnsworth patents and licensing
    and, 260–61, 271–73
  Farnsworth sues,
  for patent interference, 156–57,
    199–209, 214–15, 219–21, 233–35
  GM, Victor and RKO deals, 104–9
  investment in TV increased, 182
  Laboratories, 160, 162, 172, 186,
    188–89, 196, 275, 287
  Monopoly Investigation and, 252–56
  New Deal and, 210–11
  patent policies attacked, 159
  patents of, 44–49, 64, 69–72, 167
  Philco vs., 184, 186–89
  post–war TV expansion, 281–83
  radio leadership and, 66–67
  stock, 94–95
  TV lab set up, 145
  World's Fair and, 263–69
Radio Craft, 210
Radio Manufacturers Association
    (RMA), 273
Radio Music Box, 44–45
Radio News, 19, 47, 70, 129, 133, 147,
    163
RCA/EMI system, 226–27
RCA Victor, 106, 158
Rickard, Tex, 30, 33

Rieber, Frank, 285–86
Rigby Star (newspaper), 18
RKO Pictures, *92*, 106–9, 177, 210
Rockefeller, John D., Jr., 195
Rockefeller, Nelson, 298
Rockefeller Center, 195
Rockefeller family, 46, 177
Rogers, Ginger, 210
Rogers, Will, 104
Roosevelt, Franklin D., 31–33, 45, 194,
   210–11, 213–14, 245–47, 250–51,
   257, 267–68, 275–76
Ruffo, Titta, 103
Rutherford, Tobe, 197, 216, 240

Sammis, T. W., 43
San Francisco Chronicle, 1, 137–38
Sarnoff, David, *28, 64, 178, 280*
  antitrust suit and consent decree,
   157–60, 194–95
  Armstrong vs., 73–77
  AT&T fight and, 96–102
  becomes RCA general manager,
   29–32
  becomes RCA president, 157–60
  CBS and Paley vs., 193–94
  childhood of, 34–37
  death of, 297–98
  death of Edison and, 188–89
  death of Marconi and, 238
  Dempsey-Carpentier radio broadcast
   and, 30–34
  Depression and, 148, 191–92
  education of, 39
  Einstein and, 211–13, 232–33
  in Europe before WW II, 244–49
  Farnsworth and, 6–7, 143–45, 154,
   156–58, 160–61, 176–77, 186–89
  Farnsworth at Green Street lab visit,
   177, 179–82
  Farnsworth licensing negotiations,
   271–73
  Farnsworth tribute by, 272–73
  finances of, 93–94
  first interest in TV, 131
  FRC hearings and, 169–70, 172–73,
   175
  Harbord and, 68–69
  Kennedy and, *92*, 107–9
  Marconi and, 37–38
  marriage of, 48
  Monopoly Investigation and, 252, 254
  NBC created by, 101–4
  Philco vs., 196
  post–war expansion of TV by,
   281–83, 287–91, 293
  radio programming and, 44–45,
   65–67, 95–96
  radio vs. TV and, 4–5
  RCA patents and, 44–49, 69–70
  RCA research begun by, 70–72
  reads about Farnsworth, 3–4
  sense of destiny of, 38–39
  telecast of 1936 by, 235–37
  Titanic and, 39–44, 49
  Victor Company and, 105–6
  work routine of, 95
  World's Fair of 1939 and, *258*,
   261–69
  WW II and, 275–77
  Zworykin and, 235, 282–83
Sarnoff, Edward (son), 108
Sarnoff, Lizette Hermant (wife), 48,
  68, 103, 108–9
Sarnoff, Robert (son), 108, *280*, 298
Sarnoff, Thomas (son), 108
Saturday Evening Post, 40–41
"Scanning Images with an Electronic
  Pencil" (Farnsworth), 176
Schairer, Otto, 156, 192, 201, 254–55,
  261, 271–72
Schenck, Joseph, 152
Science and Invention (later *Popular
  Mechanics*), *8*, 10–12, 18–19, 23,
  53, 147
Science Wonder Stories, 147
Securities and Exchange Commission
  (SEC), 213–14, 242–43, 259

See It Now (TV show), 290
Sheik, The (film), 83
Simpson, Wallis, 225
Singer, Isaac, 165
Smith, Samuel B., 201–4, 208–9
Stanford, Leland, 90
Steamboat Willie (cartoon), 151
Steinmetz, Charles, 212
Stevenson, Adlai, 289
Sullivan, Ed, 282
Swanson, Gloria, 108

Taft, President, 42
Tall, William, 15, 16
Taming of the Shrew, The (film), 137, 216
Television
  birth of, at World's Fair, 266–69
  bandwidth problem, 171, 173
  channels assigned, 274
  color, 274, 287–88, 293
  Einstein's photoelectric effect and, 121
  electromagnets and, 82–83
  expansion of, after WW II, 282–83
  Farnsworth becomes interested in, 19–22
  Farnsworth determined to invent, 3, 52, 54–56, 60–61, 63
  Farnsworth first explains idea, 26–27
  Farnsworth raises money to complete, 85–88
  first live image televised, 151
  first model blows up, 84–85
  first tube built, 115–16, 126–28, 134–35
  first patents filed, 121–24, 197
  FRC hearings of 1930 on, 168–74
  high–definition, 274
  movies and, 80–81
  Nielsen ratings and, 289, 299
  rival inventors of, 128–34 (*see also* Zworykin, Vladimir)
  Sarnoff and, 160–61

  standards set, 273–75
  as teaching tool, 112
Television Laboratories, 139–40, 149, 179, 182, 184
Television News, 147, 172, 176, 209–10
"Television's Twenty Fifth Anniversary Special," 282
Temporary National Economic Committee, 251–52
Tesla, Nikola, 165, 238, 299
Texaco Star Theater (TV show), 282
Titanic, *28*, 39–44, 49
Tolman, Justin, 22–24, 26–27, 84, 205–6, 219
Tolstoy, Lev, 38
Toscanini, Arturo, 245–46
Tracy, Spencer, 276
Tunney, Gene, 114, 151
Turner, Seymour "Skee," 214–15, 217–18
Tykociner, Joseph, 204, 220

U.S. Congress, 4, 44, 68, 94, 158–59, 162, 164, 250–51
U.S. Constitution, 164
U.S. Navy, 44
U.S. Patent Office, 161–62, 164–65, 199–201, 214, 260–61, 299
  Farnsworth v. Zworykin, 219–21, 233–35
U.S. Postal Service, 299
U.S. Senate, 272–73
  Interstate Commerce Committee, 159
U.S. Supreme Court, 99, 238, 287
UHF (ultrahigh frequency), 274
United Artists, 152
United Fruit, 68

Vacuum tubes, 20–21, 83, 163
Valentino, Rudolf, 83
Varian, Russell, 150, 162, 185, 197, 278
Verne, Jules, 146
VHF (very high frequency), 274
Viacom, 298

Victor Talking Machines Company,
    105–9

Wallace, Mike, 282
Warner, Harry, 97
Warner Brothers, 80
Washington, George, 164
Washington Evening Star, 169
Weber and Fields (comedy team), 104
Webster, Daniel, 243–44
Webster, David L., 278–79
Wells, H. G., 146
Westinghouse, 45–46, 68, 73, 96, 102,
    145, 154–56, 158, 166, 194, 298
Westinghouse, George, 165
White, J. Andrew, 31–33
Whitney, Eli, 164
Wild, Rudolph, 229, 232
Wilson, Dr., 208–9
Wilson, Mitchell, 166–67
Wilson, Woodrow, 30

Wireless Age, 31, 33
Wireless telegraph, 37–38, 119
World's Fair of 1939, 261–69,
    299–300
World War II, 259–60, *270, 272,*
    274–75
Wright Brothers, 2, 165, 299
Wrigley, Phil, 282

Young, Brigham, 13
Young, Owen, 44, 45, 67, 69, 99–100,
    157, 160

Zenith, 47, 49, 69, 75, 159, 236, 266,
    273–74, 284
Zworykin, Vladimir, *142,* 144–45,
    154–57, 160–61, 171, 176, 180, 182,
    186, 192, 196, 199–203, 205,
    207–9, 211, 219–20, 233–35,
    254–55, 266, 282–83, 288, 293,
    299